D0415761

Introduction to
Language Pathology
Fourth Edition

Introduction to Language Pathology

Fourth Edition

David Crystal
*Honorary Professorial Fellow, University College
of North Wales, Bangor*

Rosemary Varley
University of Sheffield

Whurr Publishers Ltd
London

© 1998 Whurr Publishers Ltd
First edition published 1980 by Edward Arnold
(Publishers) Ltd
Second edition published 1998 by Cole and Whurr
Limited
Reprinted 1990 by Whurr Publishers Limited
Third edition published 1993 by Whurr Publishers Ltd
Fourth edition published 1998 by Whurr Publishers Ltd
19b Compton Terrace, London N1 2UN, England

Reprinted 1999, 2001 and 2002

All rights reserved. No part of this publication may be
reproduced, stored in a retrieval system, or transmitted
in any form or by any means, electronic, mechanical,
photocopying, recording or otherwise, without the
prior permission of Whurr Publishers Limited.

This publication is sold subject to the conditions that it
shall not, by way of trade or otherwise, be lent, resold,
hired out, or otherwise circulated without the
publisher's prior consent in any form of binding or
cover other than that in which it is published and
without a similar condition including this condition
being imposed upon any subsequent purchaser.

British Library Cataloguing in Publication Data
A catalogue record for this book is available from the
British Library.

ISBN 186156 071 0

Printed and bound in Great Britain by Athenæum Press Ltd,
Gateshead, Tyne & Wear

Contents

Chapter 6   226

Preface to the Fourth Edition

Introduction to Language Pathology was first published in 1980, and eighteen years on we have had the opportunity to prepare the fourth edition. The first two editions were authored solely by David Crystal, and the book represented an innovative way of introducing the subject matter of language pathology. In contrast to other introductory texts, *Introduction to Language Pathology* presented a model of the processes involved in communication which allowed the reader to understand not only something of individual pathologies, but also of how such pathologies were linked to the processes involved in normal communication. I was delighted when the publisher asked me to collaborate on the third edition of the book. My background was different to that of David Crystal: he approached the subject from within linguistics, whilst my background is in clinical language pathology and psychology. As a result, the third edition showed a greater therapeutic dimension, with the appearance of sections on the holistic approach to patient management and a new chapter on the assessment and treatment of communication disorders.

In this new edition, all chapters reflect the increasing influence of information-processing psychology on language pathology. Such a perspective combines well with the model of the communication chain that has been a feature of previous editions of the book, and produces a more balanced treatment of all the academic disciplines that contribute to language pathology. In view of the increasing sophistication of applications of both linguistics and psychology to language pathology, the section on the influences of medical and behavioural approaches to disorders (Chapter 2) has been radically revised. New themes in language pathology have been introduced, such as the ability of individuals with communication disorders to participate in conversations (Chapter 5), and the distinctions developed by the World Health Organisation to enable understanding of how a disorder may affect an individual's life in many different ways (Chapter 6). A new feature is the introduction of revision questions at the end of each chapter: these aim to assist the reader in identifying the key themes which the chapters introduce.

The revision of a book is a time-consuming task, and I would like to thank Richard Mark and Richard William Parry, and Constance and Raymond Varley for creating the time and opportunity to carry out the work needed for this new edition.

Rosemary Varley
Sheffield, June 1998

Preface to the Third Edition

Five years on, and the publisher has provided an opportunity for a radical revision of the text. It is timely. So much has happened in the 15 years since this book first appeared that it would no longer have been acceptable to reprint it and leave the earlier chapters largely unchanged. It is not simply a matter of new research findings and investigative techniques becoming available in such domains as medical science, psychology and linguistics; new attitudes have emerged in the subject which need to be taken into account. There is a concern nowadays to see patients in a more 'holistic' frame of reference than was the case a decade ago (see Chapter 1). Changes in terminology need to be dealt with. The task of therapy itself has come to be taken much more seriously, as an object of research in its own right, and the theoretical issues there need to be systematically addressed (see Chapter 6). Methods of teaching the subject, too, have changed, and new demands are made of introductory texts (see the tutorial activities after each chapter).

Given the need for a fundamental revision, I was faced with something of a problem. I ceased being director of the course in Linguistics and Language Pathology at Reading University in 1984. This was the course for which this book was originally written and it gained from my being closely in touch with the needs of my students and with the concerns of my colleagues in all the contributing disciplines and professions. As I no longer teach courses in the subject, how was I to be sure that any revision was up-to-date, and a fair reflection of the current needs of those encountering the subject for the first time in the mid-1990s?

It was time to call in the cavalry, and I am most indebted to my co-author, Rosemary Varley, who teaches on the speech therapy course at the University of Sheffield, for her readiness to collaborate on the work of revision. She has had the unenviable task of working through the whole book and proposing alterations, expansions and additions – and then, as if that were not task enough, writing the new material to suit.

She has performed her task with great thoroughness and insight, and given the book a therapeutic dimension which it previously lacked, and which I, coming from a different professional background, would never have been able to provide.

David Crystal
Holyhead, May 1993

Preface to the Second Edition

I began the first edition of this book by commenting on the irony that the name of the subject of language disorders, and the associated profession, should be a matter of such dispute at the time of writing. Nearly a decade has passed, a new edition is being prepared, and the matter, it seems, continues to rouse just as much emotion. Recent issues of the monthly bulletin of the American Speech-Language-Hearing Association, *ASHA*, have carried a series of letters representing the whole spectrum of opinion. In August 1987, for example, we find a writer condemning 'pathologist' and 'language' and opting for 'speech therapist'; in January 1988 another writer considers such a change to be retrograde; but in February 1988 there is support expressed for the anti-pathologist position, the writer sharing the view that the term is a source of confusion in the minds of the public. Further contributions are to be expected. In Britain, too, the matter has been regularly raised in the 1980s, and has come to the fore again in the month I began to prepare this new edition. In the College of Speech Therapists Bulletin for April 1988, following another chain of correspondence on the topic, it was proposed that the whole matter should be referred for judgement to the new President of the College, Professor Sir Randolph Quirk who, as an expert in the English language, might be able to devise a suitable name. It would be nice if this particular issue could be solved *excathedra*; but the history of language planning suggests otherwise. My feeling is that the debate over the name of the profession will be with us for a while yet, and I have therefore not rewritten my opening chapter, which seems as relevant today as it was a decade ago. *Plus ça change, plus c'est la même chose.*

And yet, things *have* changed. The 1980s has been a time of great movement in the field of language pathology, and in the lives of those professionals who work with it. When the time came for this book to be reprinted, therefore, it seemed essential to make a new edition, so that information about current issues could be introduced, and the facts updated about the many new books, tests and journals which have developed from a trickle into a flood during the decade. In this second edition, therefore, an extra chapter on 'current trends' has been written, the footnote references in all parts of the book have been radically revised, and the appendix on tests and assessments has nearly doubled in size, as has the section on further reading. I have also corrected a scattering of typographical errors and unclarities of exposition which found their way into the first edition. In this way, I hope that the book will maintain its relevance for those who will embark on their study of language pathology as we approach the new millennium.

David Crystal
June 1988

Preface to the First Edition

The 1970s have seen the study of communication disorders at an important transitional stage in its development. In Great Britain, a series of government reports has initiated entirely new attitudes towards several of the professions involved – to speech therapy (the Quirk Report, 1972), remedial language teaching in schools (the Bullock Report, 1975), and to the education of the handicapped (the Warnock Report, 1978). New degree courses at undergraduate and postgraduate levels have broadened the academic basis of training in the subject, and several new journals have appeared, reflecting these interdisciplinary connections. There have been considerable advances in investigative techniques, both in special instrumentation and in analytic procedures, which have produced enormous amounts of fresh data. But most of all, there has developed a new critical awareness of the limitations of the traditional categories, nomenclature and practices involved in the study of handicap in general, and of speech disorders in particular. The influence of such developments is undoubtedly fundamental, though it is by no means clear what shape will finally be given to the academic and clinical discipline currently being formed. Meanwhile, new terminology exists alongside the old; newly trained therapists and teachers have to work alongside older-trained but more experienced colleagues; there is a persistent demand for collaboration between specialisms (in both clinical and teaching practice and in research). It is an intellectually stimulating and clinically rewarding time. But for new students of the subject, or for lay persons wishing to develop an awareness of the subject, the excitement and stimulation are often somewhat diminished, as they struggle to master the competing traditions, techniques and terminologies.

My aim in writing this book has been to reduce the confusion regularly admitted by people who encounter the field of communication disorders for the first time. The lack of orientating textbooks at first-year level is only too apparent. I have therefore tried to do two things: to provide a general view of the field which will enable the student to interrelate the main components of study; and to provide enough of an introductory account of each of these components to enable students to see their role in clinical investigation. It has been an exercise in the old manner of trying to see both the wood and the trees simultaneously. But in a short book, something must give; and my hope is that the brevity with which many areas have been covered will be justified by the overall perspective which I have tried to achieve. The book has another deliberate bias. Several years of running a first-degree course in this field has brought home to me the unique problems posed by its multidisciplinary character. At Reading, we have a weekly 'bridging seminar' in which the aim is to juxtapose the contributory lecture courses and associated reading, and to focus on differences in theory, method and above all terminology which identify the various subjects. I have been repeatedly struck by the way in which apparently innocuous terms give rise to major problems of interpretation and attitude. I have therefore tried to anticipate terminological problems throughout this book, and explained all technical notions as they have arisen. While this procedure does not slow the pace of the book in places, I am sure it is a desirable emphasis, in the present state of the field.

The other characteristic of this book is that I have adopted a relatively conservative approach to the subject. I have for the most part incorporated the traditional categories of classification in speech disorders, and contented myself with pointing out the main difficulties to which several of these categories give rise. Only in a very few cases have I gone so far as to recommend a usage, or the avoidance of a usage. Nor have I introduced as much of an orientation from clinical linguistics as I know will one day be needed. This would be premature, given the limited application of that subject to date; in view of its relatively undeveloped form, such an approach is best handled at monograph level (see my *Clinical linguistics* (1981/7)). The point is worth stressing, for I am anxious that readers who have encountered my previous work in linguistics will not expect from the present book too radical an orientation arising out of my background in that subject. The underlying philosophy of the book does reflect very largely what I have learned from linguistics, as will be apparent in several places. But many of the descriptive sections reflect no more than what I have learned from those disciplines with which I have found myself collaborating increasingly in recent years. In general, I have tried to strike a balance between these influences – especially, between the classical medical concepts and the newer behavioural ones, as discussed in Chapter 2. I am in no doubt that, in the long term, it is the latter emphasis which will promote the development of the explicitly principled intervention procedures which language pathology so badly needs. For the present, I leave it to more advanced courses and textbooks to take further the implications of the linguistic orientation, when this becomes apparent throughout the book.

David Crystal
August 1979

Acknowledgements

A book of this kind betrays innumerable influences, all of which I would acknowledge if only I could remember them. I know I gained a great deal from my membership of the Academic Board of the College of Speech Therapists over several years: colleagues there taught me a healthy respect for each of the contributing disciplines to this complex field. Successive generations of my language pathology students have, perhaps unwittingly, been an invaluable source of information about the problems that need to be tackled in writing about the field at an introductory level. There is no space to acknowledge the help I have had from my many academic, medical and therapist colleagues who have discussed their approaches with me; but I am specifically grateful to those who read through various drafts of this book and commented most helpfully on its content – John Bamford, David Chapman, Margaret Davison, Paul Fletcher, Mike Garman, Graham Ratcliffe, Marion Trim, Renata Whurr. For the second edition, I have benefited from further comments received from Pamela Grunwell and John Connolly. And as always, the general support, advice and practical help I have found from my wife, Hilary, has been a major factor enabling the book to progress. It is my sincere hope that what I have learned from all these people is enough to ensure that the outcome will do no disservice to the patients and pupils whom they serve.

David Crystal
(From the First Edition)

Chapter 1
The Scope of the Subject

What's in a name? That which we call a rose
By any other name would smell as sweet
(Romeo and Juliet, II.ii)

A Question of Terminology

It is an unfortunate irony that the subject which professes to deal with the difficulties and disorders of language should itself be in difficulties over its name. But such is the case, even though there is little real dispute as to what this subject of study actually consists of. The kinds of things that go on in speech clinics in Canada and the United States of America, under the supervision of people called 'speech and language pathologists', are very much the same as those that go on in the United Kingdom under the supervision of people called 'speech and language therapists', or in Australia under the supervision of people called 'speech pathologists'. Likewise, in continental Europe, labels vary, but the job remains largely the same: in France one is an 'orthophonist'; in Belgium and Germany, a 'logopaedist'; in the Czech Republic, a 'phoniatrist' . . . What, then, is the job that all these people do?

All these people are professionals, trained to investigate and treat abnormal manifestations of communication, from whatever cause, in children and adults. The skills involved are many, and take three or four years of training to acquire. A rather fuller description is provided by the American Speech-Language-Hearing Association (the body that, in the USA, issues certificates of clinical competence to those who graduate from training programmes). They state that clinicians:

> work to prevent speech, voice, language, communication, swallowing and related disabilities. They screen, identify, assess, diagnose, refer, and provide treatment and intervention . . . to persons of all ages with, or at risk for speech, voice, language, communication, swallowing and related disabilities. They counsel individuals with these disorders, as well as their families, caregivers, and other service providers. (1996 formulation)

1

In a similar vein, *Communicating Quality* (1996), a document produced by the Royal College of Speech and Language Therapists in Britain, identifies key areas of the clinician's responsibility. These include specific statements of the speech and language therapist's role in the prevention of speech and language difficulties and in the assessment and treatment of communication disorders when they occur.

There is, it would seem, considerable agreement about what these professionals are doing – enough, at least, to suggest that a single name for the subject would not be a problem. Why is this not so?

Speech, Language and Communication

There are (in 1998) 17 universities across Britain and Ireland, offering a total of 21 undergraduate and master's-level training courses in speech and language therapy. These 21 courses offer a bewildering array of course titles and, even ignoring minor differences between titles, there are 11 different titles on offer. This is particularly remarkable when one considers that most academic disciplines show agreement on their name: one goes to a university to read psychology; French; linguistics; philosophy – so why the extraordinary proliferation of discipline labels within speech and language therapy? The situation would be remarkable indeed if there was no overlap between the 11 variants of course title. Fortunately the situation is not quite so confusing. Of the 21 courses, 13 include 'speech' within the title, eight include 'language' and four include 'communication'. A further variation on course name concerns how speech/language/communication are suffixed: 'therapy' appears in seven course labels, 'pathology' in a further 10, and 'clinical sciences' or 'studies' in eight. The first task in understanding the debate regarding the name of the subject is, accordingly, to differentiate between the terms 'speech', 'language' and 'communication'.

There is, to some degree, a hierarchical relation between the three terms: speech is a manifestation of language, and, in turn, language is a component – and a very important component – of human communication. 'Communication disorder' is often used as a superordinate term, encompassing both speech and language disabilities, and other disabilities too. There are difficulties, however, in the use of superordinate terms in that their meanings are inevitably rather broad. Those courses whose titles include 'communication' prefix the term with 'human' or 'clinical'. This is because 'communication' has a breadth of meaning that allows it to apply to non-human systems of communication, including animal signalling systems, but also to human artefacts such as computer and telephone systems.

The term 'speech' is one that is included within the job title of the North American, Australian and British professions. Speech is an acoustic or sound signal, produced by the combined action of various components of the vocal apparatus: the lungs, the larynx (or voice box), and various structures within the mouth (such as the tongue and lips). The movements of these structures result in vibration of air, and so an acoustic signal. However, speech is more than just a vibration in the air. After all, the lungs, larynx and oral structures perform other movements which result in an acoustic output – for example, yawning, sneezing or coughing – but these would not be regarded as speech. Speech has the characteristic that it encodes a linguistic message. It has a complex structure: the sounds of speech combine to form words, words combine to form sentences, and both words and sentences carry meaning.

We are already into the territory of the next term – 'language'. Speech is the realization of language via an acoustic modality or channel, but other modalities are available through which we can send or receive linguistic messages. Instead of sending a message via speech, we can choose to write something down. The choice of whether to use speech or writing in sending messages depends on which is likely to be the more appropriate in a particular situation. Where the recipient of the message is remote in space or time, writing may be the more effective. When we need a permanent record of the message, it is again best to 'have it in writing'. Where constraints of this kind do not operate, we will use speech. In addition to sending messages, we receive messages. Acoustic-speech messages are heard and then understood (*auditory* or *speech comprehension*). Written messages are read and then understood (*reading comprehension*).

Table 1.1. Modalities of language use

	Auditory/Vocal	Visual/Graphic
Message receiving	Listening	Reading
Message sending	Speaking	Writing

We have now identified four modalities through which linguistic messages can be sent or received and these are summarized in Table 1.1. The speech/auditory channel is often referred to as the 'primary' channel. This is because it is the language channel we acquire first, and often with no explicit instruction. In contrast, reading and writing are learned later and through formal instruction at school. The 'secondary' status of the reading/writing channel is also indicated by the observation that, while all human cultures have spoken languages, many languages have never been written down, and even within supposedly literate cultures there are many adults who are unable to read. Recent estimates within the UK, for example, suggest that levels of illiteracy are increasing, with 5 to 10% of school-leavers failing to attain functional or useful levels of reading ability.

In addition to the 'usual' auditory/vocal and visual channels for sending and receiving linguistic messages, other compensatory channels are available in the event of damage to the above modes. Braille reading, for example, allows the blind to 'read' via a tactile route instead of the usual visual route. Sign language permits the deaf to send and receive messages via a visual/gestural route, so by-passing problematic auditory/vocal processing.

Messages carried by all these modalities, whether primary or secondary or special modalities, have certain common characteristics. In particular, they have a complex hierarchical structure: units combine to form a unit at a higher level (e.g. sounds/letters form words, words form phrases and sentences). Also, the units and their combinations carry meaning. Language in all its modalities is a symbolic system: words represent or 'stand for' other entities. These can be concrete entities such as 'dogs', 'daffodils' or 'dictionaries', or abstract constructs such as 'honesty' or 'intelligence'.

The final term we need to define is 'communication'. This is a super-ordinate term which can encompass both speech and language. Communication is the sending and receiving of messages. It refers to any message, not just the highly structured symbolic messages of language. A sneeze might tell you that I had a cold or maybe suffered from hayfever, but it is not a hierarchically structured or symbolic linguistic message. The study of patterned human communication, in all its modes, is known as *semiotics*. The ways in which humans communicate outside language are many and various. Patterns of eye contact, the posture adopted, and the amount of space or touching which takes place between individuals will send different messages. The facial expression and eye contact accompanying a linguistic message may entirely alter the message that is conveyed . The term 'non-verbal communication' (NVC) subsumes all these visual and tactile features of interaction.

We often see popular expressions such as 'the language of gesture', the 'language of the face', or 'body language'. However, in the light of the distinctions we have made between the terms 'language' and 'communication', these must be seen as metaphorical extensions of the term 'language'. They are not literally 'language', it is argued, because there are crucial qualitative differences between what goes on in speech/writing and what goes on in facial expressions/gestures, etc.[1]

---

[1]A similar, extended sense characterizes certain behavioural processes and activities studied by psychologists, sociologists and others. In relation to child learning, for example, we often encounter the phrase 'the language of play'. In relation to social anthropological studies of culture, we encounter 'the language of ritual'. Sometimes, other terms from linguistic analysis are used in such fields ('the grammar of dance', 'the syntax of sex'). Such phrases are often simply figures of speech coined to make a particular rhetorical effect; occasionally they are a serious attempt to use linguistic models in order to guide scientific investigation of a previously unstudied topic. But in either case, they are far removed from the strict sense of language found in the present book.

Two criteria have been proposed as critical. The first is to point to the major difference in *productivity* between spoken language and gestural communication. Productivity refers to the creative capacity of language users to produce and understand an indefinitely large number of words and sentences. Words in spoken language are continually being invented and dying out. Fresh combinations of words are continually being produced and understood. It is probable that most, perhaps all, of the sentences in this book are new sentences to you, i.e. sentences that you have not read or heard before; and yet, because you have learnt the rules of the English 'language', you are able to decode these fresh combinations and arrive at their meaning. By contrast, gestural communication lacks productivity. Gestures are not continually being invented and dying out. Fresh combinations of gestures are not continually being produced. There is in fact a very limited range of gestures you can make using your hands, posture, face and so on; and similarly, a very limited set of meanings that can be communicated in this way. *Webster's Third New International Dictionary* contains over half a million words. A 'dictionary' of body language would find it difficult to accumulate more than several hundred contrasts.

The second main difference between spoken language and gestural communication is in their internal organizations, or structures. The former displays what has been called *duality of structure*; the latter does not. Duality of structure refers to the way language is organized in terms of two abstract levels. At one level, as has already been suggested, language can be seen as a sequence of units, or segments, which lack meaning. Segments such as *p, t, e,* etc. do not have any meaning in themselves. However, when they are put together into certain sequences, and we look at the larger units so formed, then suddenly meaning is found: *pet*. At this second, higher level of analysis, language has meaning. It is this capacity, to produce meaningful units out of meaningless segments, which identifies a behaviour as being a language. By contrast, normal gestural communication lacks duality of structure. In addition, the minimal units of body 'language' are meaningful: the closing of one eye, the raising of one eyebrow, the clenching of a fist.[2] Moreover, if a sequence of gestures is used – say, a wink followed by a shrug of the shoulders – there is a clear and direct relationship between the units in sequence and the units in isolation: the 'meaning' of the wink, and of the shrug, is preserved, which again suggests the lack of any real duality of structure.

Distinctions between speech, language and communication, as we shall see later, are useful in differentiating between different types of

---

[2]It might be possible to break some of these units down into combinations of (meaningless) features, and thus to demonstrate a limited kind of duality of structure, but attempts to do this for normal gesture systems (as opposed to the complex systems of deaf sign language) have not so far been very plausible.

communicative handicap. We have already said that 'communication' can be used as a superordinate term, which can encompass both speech and language disabilities, and we shall be using the term in this way later in this chapter. Patients with a hoarse and croaky voice will have particular difficulties making themselves audible in a noisy environment, and so their difficulty in speaking will result in reduced communicative efficiency. In the same way, individuals who have a language disability – for instance, difficulty in finding an appropriate word and placing that word within a sentence – will be less effective communicators, as they are likely to experience considerable difficulty in conveying their thoughts, ideas and feelings. 'Communication disorder' then can subsume speech and language handicap, but it can also include a disability that is distinct from speech or language. A young adult with Down's syndrome, who exuberantly greets total strangers with a hug, might be viewed as exhibiting inappropriate non-verbal behaviour. In this instance, we have a communicative/interactional problem that is independent of speech or language.

The Name of a Profession

Now that we have made these distinctions between the terms 'speech', 'language' and 'communication', we can examine the debate that has taken place in the British profession regarding its name. The debate, which began in 1973, was finally resolved in 1991 when the profession changed its name from 'speech therapy' to 'speech and language therapy'. Therapists in some districts have carried the change further and labelled themselves 'communication therapists'. A wholesale change of name of a profession inevitably causes a degree of confusion, but when, in addition to change at a national level, there are regional variants of name, the potential for confusing the patients who receive the therapy service and the professionals who work alongside the speech and language/communication therapist is immense.

Prior to 1991, the British profession was named simply 'speech therapy'. What are the implications of this term, and the associated term 'speech therapist', which have caused so much controversy over the last 30 years? There were two main objections to these labels. First, the profession does a great deal more than deal solely with speech. When there is a breakdown in a person's communicative abilities, it is often the case that much more than speech is affected. Other modes of communication can be involved, such as listening, reading, writing or signing. And even within speech, as we have seen, there is far more involved than the surface sounds. Beneath the surface lies a world of grammar and meaning, and this may also contribute to someone's problems in communication. Accordingly, therapists who were working with children with poor understanding of language, or who were introducing a gestural communication system to patients who had difficulties in controlling the movements of their tongue, or who were working with patients who had suffered a stroke to regain their writing abilities, found it incongruous to be called 'speech' therapists. 'Speech' was viewed as too restricting. Such people preferred instead to talk about 'speech and language' therapy or 'communication' therapy.

But if 'speech' caused problems, the term 'therapy' caused even more difficulty. This term is used in relation to a broad spectrum of activities, such as in 'beauty therapy' and 'aromatherapy', which are unrelated to its original sense of medical treatment. Many of these skills do not involve professional training of any kind, and those that do are often not comparable to the specialized academic training which speech and language therapists receive. As a consequence, many speech and language therapists feared that, if they continued to be referred to as 'therapists', their status would be misunderstood, or would be diminished in the eyes of the other professionals with whom they work. A particularly misleading implication, in their view, was that the term suggested that their only function was treatment, neglecting their role in assessment and prevention of disabilities. These fears were not entirely well-founded, as the medical notion of *therapeutics* is an extremely broad one, subsuming all aspects of patient management (including surgical, pharmacological and psychotherapeutic). If this notion was felt to summarize well what physicians did, the analogous use of the term in the context of language disability might not be as misleading as was feared.

As an alternative to 'therapist', consideration was given to the term 'pathologist', which is used throughout North America and Australia. 'Pathology' is a medical term, falling within a tradition where it is rigorously defined. One medical dictionary (Blakiston's) defines it as 'a branch of biological science which deals with the nature of disease, through study of its causes, its process, and its effects, together with the associated alterations of structure and function'. There are two central features of this definition for our purposes: it refers to 'disease', and this in turn refers to a disturbance of normal structure and function. In view of the fact that many of the conditions which speech-language clinicians treat are medical in origin, the result of disease, this alignment of their profession with the clinical word seems eminently sensible. On the other hand, by no means all of the conditions which are treated in a speech and language clinic are medical in origin, in any clear sense. Patients may have an apparently normal physical structure and function. Voice disorders may occur despite normal vocal apparatus (see further p.199). The ENT (ear, nose and throat) department of the hospital to which a patient is referred may not be able to find anything physically wrong – no detectable pathology, in other words. Does it then make sense for this patient to be sent to the speech and language clinic and immediately have the disability placed under the heading of speech or language 'pathology'? Thanks to an extension of the meaning of the term 'pathology' in the past 100 years, this should no longer be a problem. The word has been extended to the study not only of disease but also of abnormal mental and moral conditions, according to the *Oxford English Dictionary*, since at least the 1840s. More recently, its sense of 'deviation from any assumed normal state' has become increasingly current, and the term 'speech-language pathology' falls within this development. Certainly in the USA, where there are more practitioners of this subject than in any other country, the designation 'speech-language pathologist' is the accepted norm.

With objections from within the profession to both components of the label 'speech therapist', in 1973 the British College of Speech Therapists held a poll of its membership to determine whether an alternative name might be found. The membership was asked to choose between 21 alternative names that had been proposed, the majority of which (13) were variants on the terms speech/language/communication and therapist/pathologist/specialist/practitioner. Not surprisingly, faced with so many alternatives, the results were inconclusive. No one label received an overwhelming majority. In fact, none of the alternatives received as many votes as 'speech therapist'! Accordingly, a further vote took place (in 1974), the seven names receiving the largest number of votes in the earlier ballot being short-listed. But again, no decision was reached – indeed, only a small proportion of the membership voted the second time. The College concluded at the time that the name should be unchanged. But the matter was not dropped. Five years later, the question was raised again, further votes were taken, and the issue was finally reduced to a single choice: 'speech pathologist' versus 'speech therapist'. The vote produced a two-to-one majority in favour of 'speech therapist'. But the issue still did not rest. In 1983, a further ballot was held and the profession continued to vote to retain the name 'speech therapist'. Finally, in 1990, the fifth ballot on the issue, two-thirds of the profession voted to change the name of the profession to 'speech and language therapy'. Whether the issue is finally resolved is open to question in the face of regional variants of name such as 'communication therapy'.

Lest this should be thought to be a peculiarly British obsession, it should be pointed out that a similar concern has often been expressed in other countries where this profession is practised. At present there is also a need to consider the merits of consistency throughout Europe – particularly in these days of the European Union – and throughout the English-speaking world. Nor is the terminological question trivial. The issues involved are those of professional identity and status, academic orientation, and intellectual, clinical and financial rewards.

The terminological issues which have caused such difficulties for clinicians in selecting a label that adequately names their profession also dogged the choice of the title for this book. It is called 'Introduction to Language Pathology' for a number of reasons. 'Language' is included within the title as it is a major facet of human communication and also because the concept of 'speech' is encompassed within it. The broader term 'communication' does not appear within the title because with its breadth comes ambiguity – there is confusion with non-human communicative systems. An attempt by one of the authors to telephone the 'communication department' of a hospital in which 'communication therapists' worked, resulted in the call being put through to a group of telephone engineers. In addition, there are many reasons why communication may fail between two human beings, which are outside the concerns of this book. Two individuals with opposing views which cannot be reconciled may experience a breakdown in communication, and we often hear the phrase 'communication broke down between A and B' with reference to talks between trade unions and employers, or warring factions within and between nations. We also hear of 'communication problems' in marriages and between generations of a family. We have selected 'pathology' as the second element of our title, as opposed to 'therapy', because the greater part of this book describes a model of the normal communicative process and the possible deviations from it. We make no claim to provide systematic guidelines for therapy.

What Counts as Language Pathology

When would you say that someone was communicatively 'disabled'? Sometimes the disability is fairly obvious; but by no means is it always so. Let us begin with the most obvious case. Everyone would agree that there will be problems if a person lacks ability in one or more of the main modes of language use (speaking, listening, reading, writing) and in the various components of non-verbal communication; and such disabilities are common. There are many who totally lack the ability to communicate in speech, or who have severe hearing impairments, or who cannot read and write. But these disabilities, it should be noted, are not equal in importance. We have already noted that the speech–hearing route is the primary modality in language. Disabilities in speech–hearing have more fundamental effects than problems with reading and writing. Within the primary modality, it is speech that generally attracts the most attention, because it is so much more obvious a facility to develop and use than is hearing and understanding. Consider the relative ease with which you are able to disguise lack of understanding of another's talk, for instance, in a lecture, with the embarrassing experience of having to speak upon a subject or answer a question on which you know very little.

Could there be anything more serious than the complete absence of ability to speak and to understand speech? That there are indeed such possibilities becomes clear when we put the study of language into the broader context of communication as a whole. At least if you are hearing-impaired and without speech, and so denied easy use of the auditory-vocal channel of communication, you can communicate via visual channels through reading and writing or by gesture and signing. Given this perspective, the possibility of more serious breakdowns in communication than in speech–hearing alone is perhaps now obvious. A combination of vocal–auditory and visual disability, for example, will pose special problems. Such problems would identify the population of 'deaf-blind' children and adults. It is a disability that was first widely publicized when the story of Helen Keller was told. In such cases, tactile bases of communication have to be developed.

But language pathology is concerned with disorders beyond failures of sensory systems (hearing and vision) and movement systems (speaking and writing). Sensory systems are routes along which information travels to the brain; they allow the brain to monitor both the internal bodily environment and the external world for salient information. Movement systems permit action, or the modification of our environment in ways consistent with our needs; our visual receptors may inform us that a good friend is approaching, so we act by turning and producing a greeting. The brain lies at the centre of this information-processing system, and damage to the brain results in communicative disorders that cannot be resolved simply by changing the route of information input (for example, from hearing to vision or to tactile information) or the kind of output (for example, from speech to writing or to signing). Individuals with damaged brains present language pathologists with some of their most challenging problems.

Inability to communicate at a fundamental level presents a vivid picture whenever it is encountered. But it has always been disability in speech – the primary index of language ability – that has attracted most attention since the earliest times. One of the earliest references is in an Egyptian papyrus of around 3000 BC, which refers to the speechlessness that can come following head injuries. Many Greek and Roman scholars referred to speech problems. Aristotle, for example, in the *Problemata*, reflects: 'Why is it that of all animals, man alone is apt to become hesitating in speech?' Complete loss of speech and stuttering are the two types of disability which are repeatedly referred to by writers of the classical and medieval world. The themes emerge strongly after the Renaissance. Sir Francis Bacon, for example, wrote about stuttering (referred to as 'stut') in his *Natural History (Sylva Sylvarum*, 1627, Cent. IV, Sec. 386) (the spelling has been modernized):

The cause may be, in most, the refrigeration of the tongue, whereby it is less apt to move. And therefore we see that naturals [i.e. idiots] do generally stut less because it heateth; and so we see that they that stut, do stut more in the first offer to speak than in continuance; because the tongue is by motion somewhat heated. In some also it may be (though rarely) the dryness of the

tongue, which likewise makes it less apt to move, as well as cold; for it is an
affect that it comes to some wise and great men, as it did unto Moses . . .

An interesting early account of the results of a stroke (see further, p.114)
was that of Dr Samuel Johnson. He suffered a stroke in June 1783, when
he was 73, which robbed him of his speech, but left him able to write.
From many letters describing his feelings, here is an extract of one
written three days after the stroke.[3]

> On Monday the 16th I sat for my picture, and walked a considerable way with
> little inconvenience. In the afternoon and evening I felt myself light and easy,
> and began to plan schemes of life. Thus I went to bed, and in a short time
> waked and sat up as has long been my custom, when I felt a confusion and
> indistinctness in my head which lasted, I supposed about a half a minute: I
> was alarmed and prayed God, that however he might afflict my body he
> would spare my understanding. This prayer, that I might try the integrity of
> my faculties I made in Latin verse. The lines were not very good, but I know
> them not to be very good. I made them easily, and concluded myself to be
> unimpaired in my faculties.
>
> Soon after I perceived that I had suffered a paralytic stroke, and that my
> Speech was taken from me. I had no pain and so little dejection in that
> dreadful state that I wondered at my own apathy, and considered that
> perhaps death itself when it should come, would excite less horror than
> seems now to attend it.
>
> In order to rouse the vocal organs I took two drams. Wine has been
> celebrated for the production of eloquence; I put myself into violent motion,
> and, I think, repeated it. But all was vain; I then went to bed, and strange as it
> may seem, I think, slept. When I saw light, it was time to contrive what I
> should do. Though God stopped my speech he left my hand, I enjoyed a
> mercy which was not granted to my Dear Friend Laurence, who now perhaps
> overlooks me as I am writing and rejoices that I have what he wanted. My first
> note was necessarily to my servant, who came in talking, and could not
> immediately comprehend why he should read what I put into his hands.

Such an account may be compared with the more recent stories about
the effects of strokes, illustrated below (p.15).

Problems such as speechlessness and stuttering are obvious enough,
but they by no means exhaust the range of topics which would have to
be included under the heading of 'language pathology'. These will be
discussed in Chapter 5, where each specific disability will be described
in a separate section. Is it possible, in the meantime, to characterize
language pathology in very general terms? Two criteria have been
suggested. First, communication becomes a matter for concern when it
impedes rather than facilitates interaction. When it draws too much
attention to itself, then the listener or reader is distracted from the

[3]Letter to Mrs Thrale, 19 June 1783, No. 850 in the Chapman collection. It is
reprinted in Macdonald Critchley's collected papers, *Aphasiology and Other Aspects
of Language* (London, Edward Arnold, 1970), p.78

meaning that the speaker or writer is attempting to convey. Such a situation arises when speech becomes very weak or inaudible, or handwriting becomes too faint to read. It happens when speech, even though audible, is unintelligible, or when writing, even though visible, is illegible. It happens again when the speech or writing, although intelligible, is unpleasant – an abnormally harsh tone of voice, for instance, or an erratic layout or line direction. If speech is non-fluent – full of hesitations and laboured pronunciation – there is cause for concern; or when it makes use of sounds, grammar or vocabulary which are outside the normal range of the language that the speaker uses. The opposite of this is also a cause for concern: when speakers fail, to some degree, to make use of the sounds, grammar or vocabulary of the language used around them, or use these features in ways considered by the community to be inappropriate to their age, sex, occupation, or the like. Similarly, just as difficulties in sending messages, through either speech or writing, will impair communication, so also difficulties in receiving messages will impair the communicative process. Failures to understand speech, inability to read, and incorrect interpretation of non-verbal signals will result in communicative failure, and so will be classed as language or communicative pathology.

There is, however, one problem against which the student of language pathology must always guard. This is the danger of confusing a *genuine* difficulty of communication, for any of the above reasons, with an *apparent* difficulty, due to the prejudice or intolerance of the listener and the society of which the listener is a member. It is often the case with regional accents, for example, that strong feelings are evoked: some accents are said to be 'nice' or 'musical', whereas others are said to be 'ugly' or 'harsh'. Most people have feelings of this kind, and their study is interesting in its own right.[4] The trouble comes when people attempt to impose their own standards of speech upon others, insisting, for instance, that a certain pronunciation is 'wrong' or 'slovenly', when in reality it may be the normal way of speaking for some social group. Such criticisms may take the form of a defence of imagined standards of excellence in a language – as one newspaper put it, 'let us preserve the tongue that Shakespeare spoke!' At other times these criticisms constitute a linguistic mask which hides an underlying distrust of the social values of the group involved. Either way, from the viewpoint of the language pathologist, such criticisms are beside the point. To attempt to change someone's accent or dialect when there is strictly no need to do so – or, putting this another way, when the only motivation to do so comes from an attitude of superiority – involves considerations of a quite different order from anything discussed in this book. In some ways, the different attitudes involved can be summarized by drawing a contrast between

---

[4]See, for example, J. Holmes, *An Introduction to Sociolinguistics* (London, Longman, 1992).

speech and language therapy and elocution. Elocution is the art of clear speaking in public, as judged by the cultural standards of the time; it aims to develop the speaking voice to its aesthetic and rhetorical peak, well beyond that which is necessary for the continuance of everyday communication. Unfortunately, as a profession, elocution has often been associated with the instilling of attitudes of inferiority about one's natural accent or voice (as satirized, for example, in the figure of Henry Higgins and his attitude to Eliza Doolittle, in *Pygmalion/My Fair Lady*). It should be plain, however, that the concern of the elocutionist is very different from that of speech pathology. A speech–language clinician is concerned to develop or restore language to an everyday norm, and would resist pressure to make this language conform to any real or imagined higher standards of aesthetic, rhetorical or social excellence.

So far the discussion of communicative disability has dealt with individuals who differ in their communicative abilities in significant ways from other members of their community. But there is a second criterion in the identification of communicative abnormality which, although less obvious than the first, is just as important. This refers to cases where people are concerned about their speech without there being any real cause for them to be so. From the point of view of the listener, the speakers are communicating adequately – in terms of all the criteria mentioned above (audibility, intelligibility etc.) – but they none the less think that all is not well. They may feel that their voice is too high or too harsh, or they may feel that their speech is unduly hesitant. This sometimes happens after people have undergone surgery which has altered the structure or function of their vocal tract: the new voice may be much more efficient than the old, to anyone who listens, but because individuals were used to their 'old voice', the new voice may sound quite wrong in their ears. Alternatively, parents might believe that their child has difficulty in talking, when in fact objective assessment reveals no such difficulties. Such unrealistic perceptions might have a negative effect on the subsequent communicative development of the child. And in other areas too, such as during the recovery of communication following a stroke, or in stuttering therapy, such pessimistic attitudes are not uncommon. These attitudes are often the target of treatment from the speech and language therapist, as without confidence in communicative ability the individual might withdraw from interactions.

The Effects of Communicative Disability

What is linguistic disability like? How does the patient feel? Such questions occur to anyone encountering this subject for the first time, and it makes sense to get as much insight as possible into the nature of these difficulties at the very outset of our study. But where can we get the information? Unlike other forms of disability, patients cannot tell us much, by definition! If they could, they would not be linguistically

disabled. But, in fact, it is possible to break out of this circle to some
degree, as the quotation from Dr Johnson will have shown. And there
are now many books and articles written by the parents, relatives,
friends and professional advisers of the linguistically disabled, as well as
by the patients themselves, attempting to convey some insight into the
nature of the various handicaps, and the acute effect they can have on
family and social life. Take, for example, the opening lines of *The Siege*,
by Clara Claiborne Park, which is subtitled 'The battle for communication with an autistic child' (Penguin, 1972); here, the linguistic problem
is only a part of a more pervasive social and emotional impairment, but
its importance to the author is evident throughout the book:

> We start with an image – a tiny, golden child on hands and knees, circling
> round and round a spot on the floor in mysterious self-absorbed delight. She
> does not look up, though she is smiling and laughing; she does not call our
> attention to the mysterious object of her pleasure. She does not see us at all.
> She and the spot are all there is, and though she is eighteen months old, an
> age for touching, tasting, pointing, pushing, exploring, she is doing none of
> these. She does not walk, or crawl upstairs, or pull herself to her feet to reach
> for objects. She doesn't *want* any objects. Instead, she circles her spot. Or she
> sits, a long chain in her hand, snaking it up and down, up and down,
> watching it coil and uncoil, for twenty minutes, half an hour – until someone
> comes, moves her or feeds her or gives her another toy, or perhaps a book.
>   We are a bookish family. She too likes books. Rapidly, expertly, decisively,
> she flips the pages, one by one by one. Bright pictures or text are the same to
> her; one could not say she doesn't see them, or that she does. Rapidly, with
> uninterrupted rhythm, the pages turn.
>   One speaks to her, loudly or softly. There is no response. She is deaf,
> perhaps. That would explain a lot of things – her total inattention to simple
> commands and requests, which we thought stubbornness; the fact that as
> month follows month she speaks no more than a word or two, and these only
> once or twice a week; even, perhaps, her self-absorption. But we do not really
> think she is deaf. She turns, when you least expect it, at a sudden noise. The
> soft whirr as the water enters the washing machine, makes her wheel round.
> And there are the words. If she were deaf there would be no words. But out
> of nowhere they appear. And into nowhere they disappear; each new word
> displaces its predecessor. At any given time she has a word, not a vocabulary.
> (pp. 9–10)

Here is another example, well into the story this time. It is an extract
from Elizabeth Browning's story of her severely handicapped child,
partially deaf and with a severe language disorder: *I can't see what
you're saying* (London, Elek, 1972):

> One day at tea-time Freddy was in his high chair when he suddenly saw
> something which reminded him of something else. The crying out began, and
> he had taken to making 'asking' noises. Jean said she had seen him with a
> match-box in the bathroom and rushed upstairs and returned with it,
> triumphant. She was met by a face with eyebrows raised in hope and a smile

hovering. The ensuing disappointment resulted in a howl of rage and frustration and a hand and arm hit the matchbox away. Heather remembered something in the garden and rushed out for that but with the same result. We then all left the table and searched the house until, at last added to the pile of objects like so much Kim's Game, the cherished thing was found. By this time Freddy was banging his head on the high chair tray in agonies of frustration and crying and throwing himself about, and the rest of us were soon reduced to pieces of chewed string with our nerve-ends jangling and our patience extended to breaking-point. When the treasured object was finally found, the ensuing peace and calm was very alarming and much too un-nerving to be enjoyed. We all knew it would only last until the next time he lost something. (p. 18)

Stroke: A Dairy of Recovery was written by Douglas Ritchie in 1960 (London, Faber & Faber). One year after the stroke, he felt like this:

My speech? I might have had two or three stray words but I could not tell. In the Centre I rarely spoke to anyone. I had nothing to say and I was embarrassed because I could not say anything. I read all the spare time I had. In the ambulance, where I used to spend upwards of two hours daily with four and five people week after week and where I was less embarrassed, I used sometimes to try different words. One week I was optimistic and the next there was nothing. But I had no doubts about speaking as normally as I did before I had the stroke: it was a question of time and of finding the man or woman who could find me the switch.

My writing was more depressing. I had only written 'Good luck, Clif' or a message like 'cigarretes' (spelt wrong – this might have roused my suspicions, but it did not), and for the rest made the excuse that I did not write with my left hand. But it was my mother's birthday in May and I felt that I should write her a letter. I no sooner had the paper in front of me when every single word galloped out of sight. I was left staring at the blank sheet. Nearly half an hour passed, panic grew; this was nothing to do with my left hand. At length my wife came in and she dictated slowly, letter by letter, 'many happy returns . . . '. I managed to forget my panic for a time. (pp. 96–7)

These, and other accounts of different types of disability,[5] testify to the all-encompassing, profound effect of language disability on all who become personally involved with it. Students commencing their studies of this field cannot fail to be affected by it. And yet, as with all the caring professions, they must learn to distance themselves from it, otherwise their professional judgement and objectivity will be impaired. This is perhaps the central difficulty, as well as the attraction, of working in this field – whether as researcher or as professional: one needs to develop and combine the human qualities of mature and sympathetic caring with the academic skills of methodical analysis and interpretation. Both are needed for real insights into the nature of language disability. It is for this reason that this opening chapter has focused on both modes of

[5]A number of accounts are listed in the first section of Further Reading (p. 251).

knowing, juxtaposing ideas about terminology and theoretical frame-works, on the one hand, with personal anecdote and history on the other. It is a pattern that will recur throughout this book.

A Holistic Approach

It is very easy in a book concerned with any disability to become enmeshed in the disorders, finding theories that provide satisfactory accounts of disorders both in the surface or behavioural signs and in the underlying mechanisms that produce the abnormal behaviours. It is possible to marshal our facts, provide a convincing account, and in the midst of all this academic rigour lose sight of the fact that communication disorders are part of a person, and that such disabilities have very serious implications for an individual's ability to function successfully within human society.

To understand an ability such as language and communication, and the consequences of its disruption, it is often productive to ask 'Why is this behaviour here?', 'What advantages accrue to the possessor of this faculty?' This in turn involves considering the speculative accounts of how and why language evolved in the human species. Humans are unique in their possession of sophisticated communicative systems. Other species have been shown to have rudimentary communicative systems; for example, bees and vervet monkeys.[6] Non-human primates – chimpanzees and gorillas in particular – have been taught to use sign or visual symbols. But such communicative systems are primitive in comparison to the flexibility and creativity of human language. The origins of language are unknown, but one influential hypothesis suggests that the evolution of language was linked to early man beginning to live in larger and increasingly complex social groups. Language allows group members to sustain social bonds and deal with disputes. In other primate species, the grooming of other group members' fur is an important mechanism in maintaining group cohesion. But increasing group size means that physical grooming is no longer possible in sustaining bonds between group members. Talking allows an individual to address a number of listeners at the same time and also frees the hands to continue with other activities, such as foraging for food.[7]

The origins of language may be social, but once it has been mastered it endows its possessor with a powerful resource. Language permits the exchange of information – for example, not only about the location of food sources but also about how a new task could be performed, such as hunting and capturing an animal larger and more powerful than the

---

[6]For a review, see J. Aitchison, *The Articulate Mammal* (London, Unwin Hyman, 3rd edn, 1992).

[7]See R. Dunbar, *Grooming, Gossip and the Evolution of Language* (London, Faber & Faber, 1996).

hunter. Language allows the expert to instruct the novice and the transfer of knowledge across generations. Cultural innovations and knowledge, such as the manufacture and use of certain tools, can be accumulated.

Human communication and, in particular, facility with language, brings social and informational advantages, and this is true of contemporary human culture just as much as its evolutionary history. Human beings who lack this facility may face very severe disadvantage in these areas. Social relationships may be difficult to form and sustain; learning may be difficult, particularly where learning is from oral or written instruction such as in a classroom. Because language is the medium of so much of human learning (imagine a classroom or lecture theatre where there was no spoken or written language!) there will be intellectual consequences of a language disorder simply because the knowledge that impaired individuals have about their culture is reduced. The consequences of a language impairment suffered later in life – for example, following a stroke – may be less severe, but there are still likely to be difficulties in embarking on new learning. How do you learn to use a new kitchen gadget? Either through reading the instruction book or through somebody explaining its operation to you. Inability to read or to understand another's speech will make acquisition of a new skill difficult.

Beyond building up their store of knowledge, language endows its possessors with a powerful intellectual resource. Language permits planning and talking through solutions to problems in ways other than 'trial-and-error' problem-solving, or learning from mistakes not to attempt the failed solution again. Trial-and-error learning has a place in skill and knowledge acquisition, but it suffers from the limitation that there are some errors which may not allow the problem-solver a further attempt at the problem – for example, learning to land an aircraft. Language is important for intellectual activities in other ways. When you are puzzling over a difficult problem and trying out solutions 'in your head', you will be aware that you are talking silently to yourself. This internal dialogue with yourself is called 'inner speech'. You become aware of it in problem-solving situations where a solution to a problem is not immediately obvious. It appears in memory tasks, such as when you have been given complex verbal instructions to remember. Language therefore acts as scaffolding to other intellectual activities, such as memory and the reasoning out of solutions to problems; and individuals with language impairments may have to find other ways to support their thinking at times of high intellectual demand.

In any concern to analyse the intricacies of a behaviour, it is therefore important not to lose sight of the broader perspective. This is necessary not only to understand the patient's predicament, but also to understand the nature of the disorder. A fundamental principle within all the caring professions, which include speech and language therapy, is a concern for the whole person and hence an emphasis on *holism* or the *holistic approach*. Holism demands that the patient is not viewed as just an instance of a particular communicative problem – for example, a difficulty in producing fluent speech; rather, the frame is set much wider. First, the focus is not solely on the patient's most obvious communicative difficulty; therapists view patients in relation to the whole of their communicative abilities and evaluate their effectiveness both as senders and receivers of messages of all types (spoken, written, signed, nonverbal). Second, holism involves addressing the consequences of an impairment particularly on social and intellectual domains. We shall now look briefly at each of these issues.

Holism in communication

Patients are referred to a speech and language therapist often with some preliminary diagnosis of the communication difficulty – for example, delayed language development, stuttering, or abnormal tone of the voice. The clinician must consider the whole of the individual's communicative system – that is, linguistic functioning together with non-verbal behaviour. The client must be assessed as both a sender and receiver of messages, and areas of strength and deficit identified. An anecdote may make the point most effectively here. One of the authors was working in a large general hospital. A patient, who was one of the porters from the hospital, was referred with the symptom of an abnormally high-pitched voice for an adult male. The patient was anxious about his voice, and reported that he was often mistaken for a woman on the telephone. He was particularly concerned at his inability to find a girlfriend, which he attributed to his high-pitched voice. Therapy began and was successful in lowering the pitch of the voice to some degree; however, the anxieties about the voice and the difficulty in recruiting girlfriends remained. Then, one day, the clinician, while out of the therapy treatment rooms, met the porter in the hospital corridor. Previously all conversations had been held in a treatment room, where the patient entered the room and sat down. The conversation in the hospital corridor revealed that the patient was an 'invader of personal space'. One area of non-verbal communication deals with the physical distance between participants in conversation (*proxemics*). The amount of space between individuals varies between cultures, and is dependent on factors such as the intimacy of relationship of the participants. Within British culture and for a non-intimate relationship, the usual distance between participants is approximately an arm-length. The patient in this case habitually strayed within this area, making the other participant feel threatened and anxious. Treatment at this point moved to work on non-verbal communicative behaviours – in particular, work on maintaining a comfortable interpersonal distance. In this case, a narrow focus solely on speech missed crucial factors which affected the patient's efficiency as a communicator.

In addition to integrating observations regarding language with non-linguistic components of communication, it is necessary for the language pathologist to view the language system in its entirety. Language is made up of sounds, vocabulary and grammar. In assessing the effectiveness of the individual's language system, we need to consider this total system, rather than isolated components of it.

Communication and cognition

We have already suggested that language has an important role in supporting other areas of human intellectual activity, such as learning and memory. But the nature of the relationship is not unilateral: as well as language providing the scaffolding for other intellectual activities, other intellectual or cognitive functions support communicative abilities. Cognition is a very broad term, encompassing processes such as memory, attention, perception, learning and reasoning. Language is classified as a cognitive function, and it is closely integrated with many of the above processes – for example, incoming acoustic information has to be attended to and perceived, and in order to be understood has to be related to some stored memory trace. Patients who have very poor memory abilities – for example, people suffering from dementia – are likely to have communicative problems: they may have difficulties retrieving the words they need; they might forget what has just been said to them; they might forget what they are in the process of saying. To examine the communicative deficits without taking into account the broader cognitive picture will result in an incomplete description of problems, which is then only of partial value, particularly in the planning of intervention.

Whole person

The third aspect of holism is to remember the whole person – the person's reactions to the disability, the response of the family and friends, the environment in which the individual lives and works, and the social and economic consequences of any handicap. The extract below was written by a young man who had suffered a stroke. Before his illness he had worked as a journalist; however, the stroke had profound effects on his ability to speak and to read and write, in addition to causing a paralysis on the right side of his body:

> I had a stroke. And it's painful (psychological, mental). My leg, arm, fingers, brain, it's gone. I can't read. I can't write. What's wrong. It's very confusing. God, don't take my freedom, please. I can't take anymore.

It takes little imagination to understand the emotional, economic and social consequences of this man's handicap. Helping patients come to terms with their difficulties is a major challenge for the speech and language therapist. With adults it may involve counselling patients and their spouses, and such work is also important with the parents of handicapped children. Working with those around the patient, and assisting them in dealing with the difficulties associated with the disability, can result in creating a more supportive environment in which the disabled person will live.

Consideration of the environment within which the communicatively disabled person operates is also a factor of concern. Opportunities have to be created within that environment to facilitate communication. For example, background noise needs to be controlled in the hearing-impaired person's environment, and opportunities to develop lip-reading should be encouraged, by speakers allowing their lips to be seen as they talk. This approach – considering the carers' behaviour and the physical environment of the communicatively-impaired individual – is an important factor in the treatment of communicative disability and will be discussed further in Chapter 6.

We have set a broad frame in which to study language disability: the wider aspects of communicative disability; communication in relation to cognition; and the social and emotional consequences of disability. The focus in this introductory book is inevitably on the first component – the nature of communicative disability. At all points, however, we hope that the reader will place these disabilities into the broader frame, and there will be illustrations throughout the following chapters which we hope will assist the reader to achieve this end.

Revision Questions

1. Write down definitions of the terms 'speech', 'language' and 'communication'.
2. Produce a diagram which captures the relationship between the three terms.
3. Outline the elements of a holistic approach.

Tutorial Activities

1. A child is referred to a speech and language therapist from a community where adults, without any speech difficulties, use an accent that has the following differences from Received or Standard Pronunciation: *th* →*f, h* → Ø. The first rule means that the first sound, *th*, is replaced by an *f* sound (see p. 44 for phonetic description). The second rule means that *h* is omitted. Practice saying the following words, using the above rules: *thumb, thorough, thought, thirty, house, hill, home, happy.* The adults who use this accent are generally characterized as being of low socio-economic status. The child referred to the speech–language pathologist has the above sound changes from

Received Pronunciation, in addition to a number of other sound changes, which although common in children's speech are not usual among the adult speakers of this community (e.g. $s \rightarrow t$, $k \rightarrow t$, and so *soap* is pronounced as 'toap' and *coat* as 'toat').

Should the speech and language pathologist seek to change all these sound changes from the standard accent?

In considering your answer, consider the following factor: In some parts of the UK socio-economic and educational advantages may accrue to individuals who use the standard accent. For example, a speaker with a standard accent may be more likely to be successful at a job interview, and teachers may have more positive attributions and higher expectations of pupils who speak with the standard accent.

(a) Should the clinician attempt to alter the *th* and *h* substitutions?
(b) If the attempts to alter the *th* and *h* sounds were successful, what would be the child's position within the speech community?
(c) How is the family of the patient going to perceive speech and language therapy?

2. Communication impairments have profound educational, social and economic consequences for sufferers.

(a) Identify possible educational consequences of a serious language disorder in a 7-year-old child. This child's speech is very difficult to understand: vocabulary is limited for his or her age, and sentences are short and contain many grammatical errors. The child also has difficulty in understanding long and complex questions and commands. Consider how the child will cope both within the classroom (for example, what other areas of attainment might be affected and how might the child relate to teachers and classmates?) and in the playground.

(b) In the section on the holistic approach, we saw an extract written by a young man who, prior to a stroke, was a journalist. He had a high level of educational attainment, and was a university graduate. His stroke left him with paralysis of the right side of his body, difficulty in talking but reasonable understanding of spoken language, and difficulties in reading and writing (the paragraph on p. 19 took about 30 minutes to write). Imagine that you are an occupational counsellor who advises handicapped individuals on employment opportunities. What employment, or employment training, would you recommend for this man?

Chapter 2
Approaches to Language Disability

Communicative disorders occur in many different forms, and range from conditions such as autism and cleft palate to the apparently inexplicable failure of some children to learn their native language at a normal rate and in a normal way. A similar range of conditions can be observed in communicative disorders which appear in adulthood. Disorders may follow major medical events, such as surgery to the speech production mechanism to remove a tumour, but they can also occur in the absence of such serious illness. For example, a novice teacher might report a hoarse voice at the end of a day spent in a noisy classroom.

In some of these disorders a medical condition is involved, but not in all. What is common to all conditions is that there is a disruption of communicative *behaviour*. Language pathologists are trained to assess communicative behaviour and, where communicative disorders are identified, to plan and implement intervention programmes. These interventions are again *behavioural*: the language pathologist attempts to alter communicative behaviour by enabling an individual to learn new skills and competencies. Language pathologists are not directly engaged in the administration of surgical or pharmacological treatments for communication disorders, although they may be a part of a professional team that does administer such medical interventions. But given that the language pathologist's role is directly one of assessment and modification of behaviour, it will be of no surprise that the theories and procedures of the behavioural sciences (linguistics and psychology, in particular) form a major part of the education of speech and language clinicians, and also of their interventions with patients. The behavioural sciences, however, cannot be the only influence on the field of language pathology. Clinicians have to be thoroughly conversant with a medical frame of reference for the simple reason that in a large proportion of cases some medical condition *is* involved, and while they are professionally concerned only with the communicative problems the patient has to face, they must see these in the context of the well-being of the person as a whole.

In this chapter we will examine the influence which the behavioural and medical sciences have exercised over language pathology. These influences are profound and are sometimes referred to as the behavioural and medical 'models', although we prefer the term 'approach' to 'model'. In Chapter 3 we present a model of the communication process. This model is presented primarily in terms of behaviour – what people do when they communicate – rather than what anatomical or physiological basis underlies the communicative process. The physical basis of the model of the communication chain can be found in Chapter 4. In these two chapters we will see the influence of these two fundamental perspectives on language pathology. In Chapter 5, we will discuss a range of communication disorders, and show how medical and behavioural influences are integrated when considering instances of communicative pathology. Both behavioural and medical approaches share the term 'science' in their labels, and thus we can expect to find evidence of a scientific philosophy and methodology in approaches to communication disorders. We will begin by discussing the hallmarks of a 'scientific' approach.

A Scientific Approach

Early in the sixteenth century, Nicolaus Copernicus carefully observed the movements of the planets and stars and formulated the belief that, contrary to the established view that the Earth was the centre of the universe and that the Sun, Moon and planets circled around it, the Earth was revolving and that the planets moved around the Sun. Galileo Galilei supported and extended this explanation (or *theory*) some half a century later. These early astronomers observed and described a phenomenon (the movements of planets) and then sought an explanation as to why the phenomenon occurred. Their curiosity extended to questioning the underlying reasons for the phenomenon, and to providing an explanation which linked observations to the underlying causes.

The hallmark of scientific reasoning is that phenomena and events are understood in terms of their causes. A scientific experiment attempts to manipulate the postulated causes of a phenomenon (called the *independent variables*), and then to see if the phenomenon (called the *dependent variable*) responds to the manipulation. We conduct many mini-experiments in the course of our everyday lives. For example, we notice that the tomato plants at the back of the greenhouse are not as tall as those at the front. We make a guess (a *hypothesis*), based on our knowledge that light is essential for plant growth (gained from earlier experiments), that the tomatoes at the back are deprived of light when compared to those at the front. To test our hypothesis, we move the smaller plants to the front and then wait to observe the effect on the dependent variable, height. If growth rates improve, we might feel our initial hypothesis is confirmed. If there is no change in relative height, we would be forced to review the initial hypothesis. Was it lack of water that caused the stunted growth? Were the tomatoes at the back a dwarf variety? Further experiments are thus suggested by the initial results, with *control* of these new factors or *variables*. This everyday experiment is not a true scientific experiment as it lacks the rigour necessary in a scientific methodology; for example, height would have to be measured very precisely both before and during the experimental manipulation of the factors (or *conditions*). But it *is* an experiment in that an idea or hypothesis is first developed and then tested by seeking objective evidence to determine its truth or falsehood.

A scientific ethos, with its emphasis on seeking the underlying reasons for events, suggests a powerful approach to combating forms of pathology. In intervening to reduce or eliminate deviation from a normal state, the identification of the causes of the pathology, and then the elimination of those causes, suggests a highly effective way to reduce abnormality. This is the approach adopted by the medical sciences in tackling disease. The medical sciences seek to restore the individual to a state of health by eliminating the source, or the *aetiology*,[1] or cause, of disease. This may involve the study both of the direct cause of disease (such as a particular virus), as well as the predisposing factors which lead to the disease (i.e. those factors in the body or the environment which make the body susceptible to a disease, such as a particular lifestyle or diet). The value of this strategy is indicated by the degree to which it has been extended to deal with other types of pathology – and here we use 'pathology' in the extended sense defined in Chapter 1 as 'deviation from any assumed normal state'. Attempts to reduce problems such as crime or truancy may often involve identifying the source of the behaviour, such as unemployment, poor housing, or youth boredom.

Let us take an example from the medical world of how the approach of eliminating causes operates. The patient is a 3-year-old boy who complains of earache. His parents also report that they have noticed a degree of hearing difficulty over the previous few days. The doctor, in taking a medical history, discovers that the child has recently had a severe head cold. At this point the physician might already form a hypothesis of what might be wrong with the patient. Often during a cold, a tube running between the back of the nose and the ear (the Eustachian tube – details of the anatomy of the ear can be found in Chapter 4) can become blocked with mucus. Subsequently the mucus can become infected by bacteria. This causes an expansion of the mucus and pressure on the eardrum. Eventually the pressure may cause the eardrum to burst. The doctor could seek evidence to confirm or reject the hypothesis by a physical examination of the patient, focusing

---

[1]This is the older spelling. American texts and some British texts use *etiology*.

especially on the state of the eardrum. If the doctor observes that the eardrum is red and inflamed, or perhaps already perforated and with discharge leaking from it, the diagnosis would be of 'middle ear infection'. The cause of the abnormality is bacterial infection, and in order to attack that cause, the physician might prescribe an appropriate antibiotic.

Let us now take an example of the language pathologist using a similar approach – of seeking the cause of the disorder – in order to determine the best line of treatment. Peter, aged 3, is saying little more than a few words and phrases. He is referred by his family doctor to a local speech and hearing clinic. The language pathologist makes an initial assessment of Peter's language ability and concludes that there is indeed an abnormal development of language, compared with other children of Peter's age and background, and so there is a diagnosis of 'language delay' (see p. 151). The cause of the disorder will be investigated through taking a case history from the parents. Factors of interest would include the history of the pregnancy and the birth. Here the clinician is attempting to identify if the mother suffered any illnesses during the pregnancy which might have affected the normal development of the embryo. The birth history could provide information on whether there was any possibility of damage to the child at birth, for example, through oxygen deprivation (or anoxia). The case history might also reveal if there is a family history of language disorder, illuminating genetic or environmental factors in the disorder. Other possible medical bases for the problem might also be considered: Peter's hearing might be tested; he might be referred to a paediatrician for a thorough medical examination. These investigations may indicate a clear medical cause, such as a hearing impairment. But what if everything is normal in medical terms? The search for a cause of the disorder might switch to the investigation of aspects of Peter's behaviour. He might be found to be a distractible, hyperactive child, who is unable to pay enough systematic attention to his linguistic environment to be able to learn from it. A psychologist's opinion might be sought here. Or perhaps Peter comes from a home background where he has been given little chance to learn from his environment – a social explanation for the problem.

A case such as this illustrates how a language pathologist uses the approach of seeking the causes of a disorder in order to understand the problem and to suggest ways of tackling the disorder. The search for cause is likely to encompass medical, behavioural and social–environmental considerations and, where a plausible source of the disorder is identified, the first strategy is to eliminate or ameliorate the causes. Hearing loss can be treated through elimination of ear infections and surgical procedures, and residual hearing impairment might be ameliorated by the provision of appropriate hearing aids. Attention problems can be tackled through behavioural programmes that assist the child to learn how to pay sustained attention. Such problems can also be treated with pharmacological intervention, although such an approach is sometimes controversial. If an environmental cause is suspected, the parents might be the target of intervention; they could be taught how to structure the child's physical environment and their own behaviour in ways that would maximize the opportunities for language learning – an approach which is sometimes described as 'parent skilling'.

This example illustrates how the language pathologist's concerns in using a medical approach may extend to both medical and behavioural components of a disorder. We shall now consider how the medical and behavioural sciences have contributed to the theory and practice of language pathology.

Aspects of the Medical Approach

Let us look in a little more detail at the medical approach, which is the older and more revered of the two. The example of the child with a language delay reveals the extent of the influence of medical practice on both the vocabulary and the procedures or process of language pathology. This process operates as follows. We have a difficulty which is noticed either by ourselves or others. We go to a *clinic* and we become *patients*. We tell the clinician about the difficulty, thus providing the doctor (or language pathologist) with subjective evidence about the nature of our condition. Those aspects of the difficulty which lead to our complaints are known as our *symptoms*. The clinician takes a *case history* in which an attempt is made to extract from us everything that could have a direct or remote bearing on the *presenting condition*. There is then an examination, where the clinician aims to provide objective evidence (or *signs*) about the nature of the condition. Taken together, the signs and symptoms of the problem enable the clinician to arrive at a judgement concerning the nature of the difficulty. This judgement, and the process that led to it, are known as *diagnosis*. To be more specific, the clinician makes a selection from a set of possible hypotheses about the disease; by comparing one set of signs and symptoms with another, the aim is to reach a hypothesis which would explain most satisfactorily the present condition of the patient. A more precise name for this technique is *differential diagnosis*.

Once a diagnosis has been made, a course of *treatment* may be begun. Alternatively, the patient might be *referred* on to a specialist clinic either for further assessment or for a course of specialized treatment. At the end of the treatment, the patient's progress is reviewed and, if the condition has been resolved satisfactorily, the patient will be *discharged*. Some disorders can be resolved (they have a good *prognosis*), leaving the patient with no residual deficits, as in the example of the child with a hearing loss due to a middle ear infection; but this is not always the case. Other disorders have profound and long-term effects on an individual's functioning. One such example would be the genetic disorder, Down's syndrome.[2] The individual is born with an extra copy of chromosome 21 (hence the disorder is also known as trisomy 21). Although medical intervention to correct genetic abnormalities (often called gene therapy) has now begun, this work is in its infancy and offers treatment for conditions in which there are faulty genes, rather than extra chromosomes as in the case of Down's syndrome. This genetic disorder cannot be remedied: we cannot 'cure' it. Knowledge of Down's syndrome tells us that we can expect a level of intellectual or cognitive functioning which is below the usual level. This is important in planning any treatment. In setting targets for treatment, we cannot demand that the child suffering from Down's syndrome should perform at the same level as a normal child; rather we have to adjust targets, with the aim of maximizing the child's learning potential. Identifying a likely prognosis is important, therefore, in deciding on the goals of the treatment programme. It is also important that patients and their families are aware of the prognosis – is a 'cure' being offered, or is the clinician hoping to maximize abilities but within clearly defined limits?

Although there are many conditions for which the medical strategy of 'eliminating causes' is not a practical basis for intervention, the medical sciences have contributed a body of knowledge which provides an important frame of reference for analysing communicative disability. There are a number of branches of medicine which are of particular relevance to the language pathologist. The foundation subjects of the medical sciences – anatomy and physiology – are a necessary part of the curriculum in the education of language pathologists (see Chapter 4). Certain conditions – for example, disorders of the voice – can be properly understood only if grounded in knowledge of the structure (anatomy) and function (physiology) of the respiratory and voicing systems.

A number of medical specialisms are of particular relevance to language pathology, and clinicians may often work alongside medical practitioners from these fields. The specialisms of particular importance are paediatrics, neurology, and ear, nose and throat (ENT) medicine (the latter sometimes called otorhinolaryngology). *Paediatrics* is concerned with diseases and conditions of childhood. A considerable number of children who are referred to language pathologists will at the same time be seen by a paediatrician. They will include children with overt conditions such as Down's syndrome or cerebral palsy, but also children who for no apparent reason are failing to thrive and to reach the milestones of normal development within a normal time-band. *Neurology* is the branch of medicine which deals with diseases and conditions of the brain

---

[2]The term 'mongolism' was once used to refer to this disorder (characterized by learning difficulties; broad flat face; slanting eyes; enlarged tongue and lips; small nose; heart/kidney abnormalities; hand and foot abnormalities; slow reflexes), but now the appropriate medical label is 'Down's syndrome', after the English physician, J. L. H. Down (1828–1896); 'Down Syndrome' is also used, especially in the USA.

and the system of nerves which links the brain to all parts of the body. Like most fields of medicine, it can be subdivided into further specialisms, such as paediatric neurology and neurosurgery. Individuals who have experienced conditions such as a stroke, Parkinson's disease, or cerebral palsy may often be referred to language pathologists from neurology clinics. *ENT medicine* addresses diseases and conditions of the bodily structures involved in the production and hearing of speech. For example, conditions which affect the normal functioning of the 'voice box', or larynx, will result in the involvement of clinicians from both ENT medicine and speech and language pathology in the management of the disorder.

Language pathology has inherited an important body of knowledge and sets of procedures from medicine. With this inheritance has come traditional ways of approaching patients and their impairments. But there now exist many challenges to these conventional ideas about tackling disease and the nature and process of the doctor–patient interaction. Medical science, given its focus on causes of disease, might define 'health' as 'the absence of disease'. But is this an acceptable definition? Let us imagine a speaker with a stammer or a fluency disorder which results in disruptions to the flow of speech by repetition or prolongation of sounds (see p. 188). After a programme of intervention, this individual learns strategies to control the stammer to such an extent that most of the people with whom he or she subsequently interacts would not characterize the speaker as showing any form of communicative impairment. Similarly, objective assessments made in the clinic show levels of speech dysfluency indistinguishable from those of normal, or non-impaired, speakers. This evidence might suggest that the dysfluent speaker is 'cured'. There is now an absence of communicative impairment and so the speaker can be regarded as being in a state of 'communicative health'. But what if this individual does not believe himself or herself to be cured, and that at any moment the stammer will return and cause embarrassment and communicative failure? As a result, the 'cured' stammerer avoids as many communicative exchanges as possible and life becomes organized around the avoidance of situations which involve talking, influencing employment choices, social contacts and such everyday activities as the place to shop (for example, the supermarket is to be preferred to the local delicatessen if one wishes to avoid speech). Although this speaker might show communicative 'health', in that there is an absence of evident impairment, the degree of control of lifestyle in order to avoid speaking would suggest that he or she lacks communicative 'well-being'. A definition of health in terms of presence of well-being is probably more important than the negative definition of health as the absence of disease or impairment.

The medical approach is also challenged by the increase in long-term (or chronic) disorders in modern societies. Paradoxically, this increase is partly due to the success of the medical sciences in tackling many conditions which previously would have been fatal. Advances in intensive-care medicine have permitted individuals with severe head injuries to survive, albeit with serious disabilities. Progress in neonatal intensive care means that very premature babies can survive, although again a proportion of these babies may go on to experience a range of cognitive and other physical problems. The control of several diseases through the development of effective antibiotics, or through early detection programmes such as breast or cervical cancer screening, means that more people survive into old age. Although old age is not inevitably accompanied by physical decline, there are chronic conditions linked to ageing which have a substantial impact on the quality of life. Medical science has met the challenge of chronic illness through the development of palliative medicine – that is, intervention which focuses on alleviation of symptoms, and particularly on pain relief, without the elimination of the underlying cause. In instances of chronic communicative disability, such as the linguistic problems that might follow a severe stroke, there is now recognition that the management of the condition cannot be motivated only by the single strategy of eliminating impairments. Proper and total management would also include the consideration of ways of maintaining quality of life, for example through the maintenance of social contacts via support groups, both for the disabled persons and those who care for them.

Chronic disease has presented the medical sciences with new challenges. In addition, the nature of the relationship between the doctor and the patient (or therapist and patient) is also facing changes. In the past, a consultation between a professional and patient was one between an expert and a supposed novice, which led to inequalities of power and authority within the relationship. Increasingly, however, patients are no longer novices, and in some situations may know more about their condition than their medical practitioners. This is particularly the case in many chronic conditions where there now exists large amounts of information in various published media – books, health magazines and patient information groups on the Internet, together with self-help groups and charities, all of which act to make patients more knowledgeable about their illness. There is a trend in many areas of health planning to involve the users of a service in its development and management. The patient is likely to be involved to a greater degree in decisions regarding the treatment of a disorder, with '*informed* consent' being a prerequisite of any medical intervention. This trend of patient involvement is sometimes termed *empowerment*, to reflect the shift from traditional patterns of power and authority within clinician–patient interactions.[3]

---

[3]See M. Bury, *Health and Illness in a Changing Society* (London, Routledge, 1997), for an overview of these issues.

There are other limitations of the medical approach. Often it provides only the beginnings of an explanation of a communicative disability, and often no explanation at all. For those communicative disabilities where there is no evident medical condition involved, such as disorders of speech fluency or stuttering, the medical sciences may contribute little to the understanding of the disorder. And even where a medical condition is apparent, it is important to remember that the language pathologist deals with disruptions of behaviour. The assessments and treatments which the language pathologist administers are directed at behaviour. Radiological imaging of body structures, tissue biopsy, and laboratory analysis of body fluids such as blood or urine are not part of the language pathologist's assessment armoury. Treatments are also behavioural – for example, when assisting the patient to learn new vocabulary or sentence structures. The language pathologist is not directly involved in drug or surgical interventions. The medical approach gives an indication of the individual's probable limitations in responding to treatment (part of medical prognosis) when the individual is suffering from some identifiable medical condition, but it does not give any positive guidelines as to how the treatment should be carried out. For example, if John has been diagnosed as suffering from a hearing impairment, the process of medical diagnosis will indicate the limitations of John's hearing, and the possibilities of recovery, and these facts will be important to the clinician who must collaborate in a remedial programme; but the medical information by itself does not tell the clinician or teacher what language structure to teach first, or how to move from one type of linguistic structure to another. Likewise, we may know which area of a person's brain has been damaged following a stroke, and having this knowledge may give us an idea as to how far the patient will respond, and how far we may expect treatment to be successful; but this knowledge does not necessarily tell us which linguistic structures to rebuild first. To obtain help on such matters, we need an alternative way of describing linguistic disability, and one which addresses the issues of behaviour in a more direct way.

Aspects of the Behavioural Approach

The medical approach is in principle a familiar one. Several of its terms (such as 'symptom' and 'diagnose') have come into popular use. The other main approach used in language pathology is by no means so familiar. It is a more recent development, deriving from the progress made in such twentieth-century subjects as psychology, sociology and linguistics. These subjects can be gathered together under the umbrella of the 'behavioural sciences', as they share the characteristic that they study the behaviour of humans and other animals. It is this general sense which is intended when we talk of the 'behavioural approach' in language pathology.

The main problem with this label is that it might trigger off the wrong associations in the mind of a reader who knows about certain important themes in psychology; so perhaps we should begin by commenting on what the label does *not* refer to. In particular, it does not refer to the specific school of thought in psychology (and also in philosophy) known as 'behaviourism'. This school, associated in America with the names of J. B. Watson, Clark Hull, and B. F. Skinner, and in Russia with Ivan Pavlov, restricts the study of humans and animals to their observable patterns of behaviour, ignoring any mental processes which are not directly observable and measurable, e.g. such notions as consciousness and introspection.

Students of language pathology share the behaviourist psychologist's concern to describe accurately the observed linguistic patterns in communicative behaviour, and the analytic techniques of linguistic science assist in this. But language pathologists do not restrict their study to these patterns; they frequently draw upon theories of the types of mechanisms within the human mind which are responsible for generating both normal and aberrant language behaviour. These invisible mental systems might include constructs such as a 'mental dictionary' or 'lexicon', which is a store of the words that a particular speaker has learned. Alternatively, there may be reference to operations performed by a 'parser' – a hypothesized process which 'chunks up' heard sentences into small constituents for subsequent analysis. The operation of the parser is thought to be seen in some 'garden-path' sentences, where the language decoder is led up the garden path and makes errors in the chunking of a sentence. For example, the sentence, *The hungry dog the conscience of the rich*, may require you to read it twice before you decode it accurately. (Your 'parser' might have mistakenly categorized *dog* as a noun, and as part of a noun phrase *the hungry dog*, instead of its actual verb status in this sentence.) These hypothesized mental processes and stores – lexicons and parsers – are not directly observable. Their existence can be inferred only from observable behaviours, and errors such as the garden-path sentence are often informative in developing theories of the mental mechanisms which underpin language behaviour. Errors occur relatively infrequently in normal language, but with great regularity in disordered language, and hence there has been considerable interest in pathologies of language from scientists concerned with developing theories of the mental processes which underpin language behaviour.

The 'behavioural sciences' are therefore distinct from 'behaviourism', which is a specific school of thought within psychology. In this book there will be two main sources of information within the behavioural approach. First, as the book is about (abnormal) language behaviour, linguistics will be one main source. Psychology will provide the second, and in particular the subfields of psycholinguistics (which, as its name suggests, provides a bridge between linguistics and psychology) and cognitive psychology. Other specialisms within psychology are also important, including developmental psychology and neuropsychology (see further p. 56).

In what way can linguistics and branches of psychology contribute to the study of communication disorders? What is a behavioural approach? At the core of this approach, not surprisingly, is a focus on the patient's behaviour. Detailed descriptions and analyses of the patient's behaviour are produced and the profile of behaviours is then compared to what is identified as normal. Behaviours of the patient which are markedly discrepant from normal are then targeted for treatment, which consists of moving abnormal behaviours, in gradual steps, towards more normal patterns. Let us return to our example of Peter (p. 25), the 3-year-old with abnormal language development. Despite extensive investigations, we may have failed to identify any obvious cause for this problem. Peter appears to be a child of normal intelligence, with no behavioural problems other than his language development. Medical investigations have revealed no physical abnormalities, thus excluding problems such as a hearing impairment or brain damage. His home environment is all that we would hope for in terms of the quality of his relationship with his parents and the opportunities for learning. At this point we have to accept that Peter's difficulties have no obvious cause, and concentrate our efforts on doing something that will assist him in learning language. In order to plan treatment, a detailed analysis of his behaviour is needed. We need to identify what Peter can and cannot do, and what he does incorrectly. Linguistic science provides us with a variety of models for analysing communicative behaviour, and the speech and language therapist will need to be familiar with these in order to produce a description of Peter's language. Armed with this analysis we can then compare Peter's behaviour to that of other 3-year-olds and so identify his areas of strength and deficit. This may sound an easy procedure, but the identification of what is normal in any human behaviour, and in particular in the behaviour of young children, is difficult because of wide variability in the pattern of even normal development. However, if we are reasonably confident of our normative data, we can then begin treatment by gradually moving Peter's abnormal behaviour towards what has been identified as normal.

This example shows that a behavioural approach is essential to treatment planning for the speech and language therapist. It is not an alternative to the medical approach, as each approach focuses on different aspects of the diagnostic–treatment process of language pathology, and so both are essential influences.

An issue which is fundamental to the illustrative case of Peter is that a behavioural approach rests upon the elicitation of a sample of communicative behaviour and subsequently its description. How easy is it to carry out this process of investigation? In fact, it turns out to be extraordinarily difficult, for a mixture of practical and theoretical reasons. Let us look, first of all, at the basic task of describing the patient's linguistic behaviour. Put yourself in the position of the clinician. The first thing you must do is obtain a sample of the patient's linguistic behaviour which is typical – a 'representative sample'. The patient has come to the clinic in the local hospital, perhaps for the first time, and meets you for the first time. How typical will the patient's language be? How typical would *your* language be – faced with unfamiliar faces and surroundings? There is obviously a difficulty here, in that it is essential to develop a rapport with patients before you can feel confident that the kind of language they use to you is similar to that which they use at home and with friends. Indeed, in very problematic cases, it may even be that patients choose to use no language to you at all, to begin with. This is often the case with young children, who may take a long time to get used to you – several weeks if you are seeing the child only once or twice a week, for half an hour at a time. And even when children do begin to show an interest in communicating with you, it make take even longer before you feel sure that you have a clear sense of the strengths and limitations of their linguistic system. One therapist, after spending a great deal of time in an initial session trying to elicit simple one-word, 'naming' sentences from a child by showing him a picture book, and asking him to say what the objects were in the pictures, was somewhat startled to hear him outside the waiting-room informing his big brother 'me can do them word in there'! He had shown no sign in her presence of any ability to use such a lengthy sentence, nor had his mother given any hint that he sometimes at home came out with such things.

This issue – of the 'ecological validity' of the data sample collected – is one which is common to many branches of the behavioural sciences. Human behaviour will alter with the context or environment in which it occurs (consider, for example, if a sample of your language behaviour collected when talking with friends in a pub would be representative of your communicative behaviour in a tutorial). If an individual's behaviour is recorded in a laboratory or a clinic it may well be behaviour representative of performances within this highly constrained context. But if the behavioural scientist is interested in making generalizations from the laboratory behavioural sample to behaviour in other contexts, there is a major question of the validity of such generalizations. This issue is a particularly acute one for the speech–language clinician. Communicative behaviour changes very markedly across contexts (see p. 18), and the clinician is interested to generalize from clinic-based language behaviour to the communicative behaviour typical of everyday interactions with family, friends, teachers and work-mates.

But let us assume that you have solved this initial problem, and are faced with a patient whom you have come to know, and who is at ease in your clinic – or perhaps you are at ease in the patient's own home (i.e. you have made a 'domiciliary visit'). What are you going to talk about?

Or, putting this another way, does it matter what you talk about? It does indeed. Some patients, for instance, find it particularly difficult to talk about certain areas of vocabulary (such as parts of the body, or colours). Others find it possible to talk only about what is going on in the room around them; they are unable to discuss 'absent' topics, such as what happened the day before, or what will be on television this evening. Some patients find it difficult or impossible to answer very general, 'open' questions such as 'What's happening in the picture?', but are able to answer a question where certain alternatives have been presented clearly before them (e.g. 'Is the man running or jumping?'). It is not usual to think of your conversation with someone as being a 'task' to be handled, but that is exactly what you are doing with linguistically disabled patients. And part of the clinical skill will be to make the patients' task of understanding your language as easy as possible, by trying to get your language at exactly the right level so that they will understand and respond. It is not an easy level to find. If you do not simplify enough, your patients may get disheartened. If you simplify too much, they may think you are talking down to them. 'Why does everyone talk to me as if I were stupid?' one stroke patient once complained. 'Why does everyone talk to me as if I were deaf?' complained another, deaf, patient, with equal feeling!

But let us assume that you have sorted out this problem, and have decided what kind of conversation you want to elicit from your patients – whether a carefully pre-planned dialogue, or spontaneous chat, or whatever. How are you going to record your conversation? Remember that you want to analyse this recording later, so a great deal of thought must be given to technical and practical matters. Where are you going to put the tape-recorder? Will patients be upset if they see it? Will they want to destroy it (usually only a problem with children)? And again: Where will you put the microphone? If you want to hear not only what the patient says, but also what *you* say, how are you going to position the microphone so that you pick up both voices well – and at the same time exclude as many background noises as possible, such as passing traffic, children in the room next door, and the like? While the recording is in progress, how will you make notes so that the events in the room, invisible to the audio tape, will be remembered afterwards? So often, one listens to a tape several hours later, and encounters a particularly puzzling piece of language – or an even more puzzling silence – and cannot recall what the patient was doing at the time. One way around this problem would, of course, be to video-record the conversation. This is sometimes done, but what is the effect on *your* behaviour when someone points a video camera at *you*? Are you at your most spontaneous and natural? If our aim is to record behaviour which is typical, the use of video may sabotage this goal. Despite these difficulties, video-recording has its place – particularly in recording the non-linguistic components of an interaction.

But let us assume that you have solved the problem of keeping an accurate record of the conversation, and of the context in which it took place. Your patient has gone home, and you now have all the time in the world to listen again to the tape and analyse what is there. Unfortunately, this ideal world rarely exists. When one patient leaves, the next may be waiting outside. And yet others waiting behind. It is a problem which many clinicians solve by reorganizing their case load so that, at least for the more problematic cases, they give themselves some opportunity to carry out the careful description of their patients' behaviour that is a prerequisite of systematic treatment. But for many others, either for lack of training or of opportunity, they must be satisfied with much less.

But let us assume that this problem has been solved, and that somehow time has been made available for you to analyse the patient's language. How will you set about doing this? The right technical equipment, if this is available, will facilitate matters. When you consider the many tiny details that distinguish the various sounds of speech from each other, or the speed at which sentences are often spoken, with words being run together in various ways, it will be evident that making a description of what is on the tape will not be a straightforward matter. One device which helps is known as a 'tape-repeater'. This is a loop of tape attached to a tape-recorder. When the appropriate switch is pressed, it repeats indefinitely the last five seconds or so of tape, thus allowing you an opportunity to hear a problem utterance over and over. Only by dint of such repeated listenings can you sometimes be sure that you have written down *exactly* what was being said – and in fact in no conversation is it ever possible to get everything right. The tape-repeater, at least, ensures that whatever *can* be transcribed, will be, with maximum saving of time. But in addition to such technical assistance, you will need to have had considerable training in the skills of transcribing and describing speech.

Note, first of all, this distinction between 'transcription' and 'description'. A transcription, in its commonest use, is a precise notation of all the sounds used in speech. It is technically known as 'phonetic transcription' (see p. 44), and it has to be able to cope with all the possible sounds that the human vocal apparatus can produce. It is obvious, therefore, that our everyday alphabet will not have sufficient letters in it to enable you to write down all these possibilities. Special symbols and accents have to be used, and the sounds they reflect have to be recognized, so that the whole of a patient's speech can be written down precisely and consistently. This process can be illustrated by comparing the way in which two patients said the sentence: 'The three little kittens jumped into the basket'. Without knowing what the symbols mean, it will none the less be obvious that two very different types of pronunciation are involved, neither of which would it be possible to distinguish using the standard alphabet.

[ðə ˈfriː ˈlɪkəl ˈkɪtənz ˈdʒʌmp ɪnuː ðə bàːskɪt]
[də ˈfwiː ˈlɪkl kìtənz ˈdʌmpt ɪntʊ də ˈbæskɪt]

Each symbol, of course, is only a shorthand way of referring to the way a sound is made. If we were to write out in full everything we did with our vocal organs when we uttered the sound *b*, it would take up a great deal of space. The symbol [b] is simply a convenient way of summarizing all this information.[4]

It is often the case, however, that if we compare the transcription made by even very experienced transcribers of speech there can be considerable differences in what they record. This is known as low *inter-rater reliability*. This is particularly the case if it is severely disordered speech that is the object of the transcription. It is also possible to find low *intra-rater reliability* in transcriptions (i.e. given the same speech sample, there are considerable discrepancies in the transcriptions produced by the same individual on two occasions). Low intra-rater reliability is often an indication of insufficient training or perhaps lack of practice of transcription skills. Because of the difficulties with the reliability of transcriptions of speech, such transcriptions can be supplemented with objective instrumental means of recording speech activity. Equipment such as a nasometer (which measures the amount of air flowing through the nose), electropalatograph (which records contacts between the tongue and the roof of the mouth), and spectrograph (which captures the acoustic characteristics of the speech sound wave) are available in some speech clinics. These devices are not an alternative to transcription; rather, the findings of instrumental investigations need to be integrated with the auditory analysis. The equipment is expensive and its use demands considerable expertise on the part of the clinician. Inevitably, both factors combine to limit the routine clinical use of such instrumentation.

The term 'transcription' is also used in a more general sense, referring to the writing down of what is heard on a tape, but without giving phonetic details – an *orthographic* transcription. This is in fact the most convenient form of transcription when doing an analysis of grammar, vocabulary, or conversational interaction, where phonetic details would be obscuring or irrelevant. An example of an orthographic transcription, giving no phonetic information, is shown on p. 45. There are also 'mixed' transcriptions, in which a limited amount of phonetic detail is included: an example is given on p. 183. There is no one 'perfect' transcription. When working clinically you need to choose a transcription which suits your purpose.

---

[4]Phonetic symbols are usually put in square brackets, to distinguish them from the letters used in the everyday alphabet, and also from certain other types of transcription used in linguistics, see further (p. 44).

All transcriptions are a form of description – in the sense that what they do is make a permanent record of the sounds of speech. But when we talk about description in relation to grammar and other areas of language, rather different considerations apply. In particular, a grammatical description will require the mastery of a terminology which allows you to identify the way in which patients build up their words, phrases and sentences. In grammar, you need to be able to notate the various patterns of construction that patients use, and sometimes quite a complex-looking apparatus for labelling sentences is involved. Learning to recognize parts of sentences as clauses, phrases, subjects, verbs and objects, and such like, is as much an aspect of linguistic description as is the phonetic description summarized in the notations above (see further p. 44).

We have only just begun the task of carrying out a description of our patient's linguistic behaviour, but already it will be apparent that the operation is an exceedingly complex one, which requires considerable professional skill if it is to succeed. Obviously, too, we must know a great deal about the nature of language before we even begin – for otherwise how should we know what to look out for, in making our description? It is not enough simply to observe patients in order to describe their behaviour. In fact, observation without information is valueless. Imagine your reaction if asked to go into a room and 'observe' someone, and to report back in five minutes. You would be confused, because you would not know what it was that we wanted you to look out for. The way people scratch their chin, or sniff, may be a noticeable feature of their behaviour – but are such points the ones that need to be noted? Presumably we do not want a detailed account of *everything* the person is doing, so your problem will be to decide which particular points are the important, or salient ones, for our purpose. So what is our purpose? What do we want to know? If we provide you with some information about this in advance – perhaps give you a set of guidelines to follow while carrying out your observation – you will feel much happier. At least then you will know what you are supposed to be doing, and be able to concentrate your skill in doing it. What, then, do you need to know in advance about language, that will enable you to see a pattern in the linguistic behaviour of the patient?

Linguistics

The first thing to be clear about is what is involved under the heading of 'language'. What counts as language? We have already seen (Chapter 1) that language is not to be identified with the notion of communication. There are many forms of communication and only one of these is linguistic. Language is in the first instance auditory – vocal communication, i.e. listening/speech; in the second instance, it is the encoding of speech in the visual or tactile medium (as with reading/writing and some forms of signing). Language does not include non-verbal communication or extra-linguistic features such as voice quality.

This does not mean that the non-linguistic aspects of communication can be ignored. On the contrary, holism (p. 16) requires the clinician to understand the whole of the patient's communicative system. Individuals with a severe disorder in understanding spoken language, which renders much of what they hear as incomprehensible, may still retain non-verbal 'listening behaviours'. For example, they may orientate their body towards the speaker, watch the speaker's face (sometimes called making 'eye contact'), and give little nods and vocalizations such as 'mhm', which give the speaker the impression that the listener is engaged with and comprehending the conversation. These non-linguistic signals of active listening are of great communicative importance. Such individuals are likely to have greater opportunities for social engagement than equally linguistically impaired people who are unable to signal active listening. But such behaviours are no substitute for language. Because such people are unable to decode the sounds, structures and vocabulary of the linguistic message, it will not be possible for them to contribute to the topic, to give their own opinion, or to introduce a new topic. To develop a full potential for communication it is necessary to come to grips with language sooner or later. Because of the great differences between language and other forms of communication in terms of productivity and duality of structure (p. 5), there is very little that can be carried over from knowledge of non-verbal communication into the learning of language.

Language is complex, and in order to understand its complexity, we need now to examine in more depth the question 'what is language?' and to look at the models of language that are used within the academic discipline of linguistics. In order for us to communicate, we must agree to use a particular means – a particular code, or language. And that means agreeing to a particular set of rules that govern the way in which the code, or language, is to be used. If we agree to use two flags in various positions around the body to signal letters, as in semaphore, then we cannot suddenly in the middle of a message start using three flags. The message would become uninterpretable, because we would no longer share the same system. And it is the same with language, though here the rules are more extensive and more complex. Unless we follow the same set of rules, linguistic communication is impossible. As a result of the process of learning our mother-tongue, each of us has developed an internal sense of what are the regular patterns of our language. It has largely been an unconscious process – though sometimes it becomes an explicit one, as when in school we are taught to use certain constructions and avoid others. And it remains largely an unconscious ability. Without formal training, people do not have the ability to *define* the rules governing the ways utterances may be constructed in their language. And yet everyone *knows* the patterns which lie behind these rules, for they are able to recognize acceptable utterances in their language, can correct unacceptable ones, and even pass judgement on their typicality or appropriateness. For example, here is a list of six nonsense words, three of which have been constructed according to the rules of English pronunciation, and three of which have not. It is not difficult to distinguish the two types:

bov   vbo   vob   ovb   blov   lbov

Working out *why* some of these sequences might turn up in English, and why some do not, however, is not a simple task – especially when you consider the whole range of the pronunciation system. Similarly, we can look at a set of sentences and decide which are acceptable and which are not. Here are some cases:

> The cat sat on the mat.
> Cat the sat on mat the.
> On the mat sat the cat.
> Sat on the mat the cat.

The job of attempting to define explicitly the rules which describe the construction of acceptable utterances in language is carried on as a part of linguistics, and we shall have to look more closely at what is involved in carrying out this task in due course (see p. 44, ff.). For the present, it is important simply to note that to learn a language is to learn the system of patterns and rules governing the way utterances are constructed, and it is our implicit knowledge of these patterns and rules which constitutes the real measure of our language ability.[5] We should also note that it is of course possible for us to make mistakes and break these rules. The likelihood of violating language rules increases if we talk when extremely tired, or stressed, or inebriated. We will notice an increase in false starts and hesitations; we may begin a sentence but not complete it. We may have difficulties finding words and maybe make more 'slips of the tongue' (for example, 'cup of tea' emerges as 'tup of tea'). At times then, our actual linguistic performance may not match up to our knowledge of our language.

We use our *intuitions* as evidence for the psychological reality of the rules we postulate for our language. For example, if in a grammar book you are told that there is an active voice and a passive voice for sentences

---

[5]This distinction between our unconscious knowledge of the language's rules and our actual use of these rules when we choose to speak or listen has been formulated by Noam Chomsky as the distinction between *competence* and *performance*. See the exposition in J. Lyons, *Chomsky* (London, Fontana, 3rd edn, 1991).

in English, as illustrated by such sentences as *The cat bit the dog* and *The dog was bitten by the cat*, you might well ask, 'How do we know that this is so?' The answer is: if you reflect upon the meaning of these two sentences, your intuition tells you that they mean the same, and that moreover there are lots of other sentences linked just as these are (*The man saw the car* and *The car was seen by the man*, etc.). If you feel that these sentences are closely linked, then this is one of the things that grammar-book writers should tell the non-English-speaking world about – and they do so using the labels 'active' and 'passive' as ways of summarizing all the sentences that share the characteristics of each of the two types above. A grammar, in this way, is seen as a formulation of the agreed intuitions of the native speakers of a language. One reason that would lead you to conclude that a grammar book was unsatisfactory would be if the book told you that it was all right to say such sentences as *Cat mat the on sat the*. It is, of course, unlikely that any grammar of English would do such a thing, but there are many less ridiculous cases over which there has been considerable controversy, e.g. should a grammar 'prescribe' that you should use such constructions as *the man whom I saw . . .*, or refuse to allow you to end a sentence with a preposition?[6]

For clinicians this distinction between rules and usage, and the fundamental role of intuition in finding out about language, is of central significance. They too need to be able to distinguish what is idiosyncratic and casual from the underlying linguistic system in their patients. Their main concern is to ensure that patients learn rules for the language as a whole, and are not satisfied with using single sentences. It may not be too difficult a matter to teach patients to say *The cat sat on the mat* (e.g. the therapist might just get the patient to repeat the sentence, a word at a time); but what have patients learned about the abstract structure of that sentence? Do they realize that there are three main parts to that sentence (*The cat/sat/on the mat*), and that they could replace each of these parts with corresponding parts, to produce an inexhaustible supply of such sentences – *the cat/dog/man/ . . . sat/walked/ran . . . on the mat/in the road . . .?* This is a much more difficult task for therapists. But without access to these abstract rules of a language, patients are also denied access to the infinite creativity of language.

Once there is some agreement about the patterns and rules of a language, this body of knowledge can be used to evaluate the linguistic performance of the individual with disordered language. Clinicians work by eliciting and monitoring the patient's linguistic behaviour and looking within this for the patterns of usage that might provide clues as to the nature of the underlying linguistic system. There are a number of broad possibilities regarding the relation of a disordered system to that

---

[6]For a discussion of prescriptivism, see F. R. Palmer, *Grammar* (Harmondsworth, Penguin, 2nd edn, 1984), Chapter 1.

which is present in the community to which the patient belongs. Sometimes it is evident that individuals are using a reduced version of the language heard around them. In other cases, individuals may have idiosyncratic systems: 'they are doing their own thing'. This might occur if a language-disordered child is raised in a bilingual environment, and works out a language system which is based on an idiosyncratic blending of patterns from different languages. But children raised in a monolingual environment might also develop an idiosyncratic system because the hypotheses they form about patterns in the language that surrounds them are either incorrect or provide only a partial account of their native language.

A further possibility, and one quite common after brain damage in a previously normal adult speaker, is that there is considerable variability in the pattern of language behaviour. Sometimes the individual gains access to a relatively normal set of language units and the rules for their combination, and at another time this access is blocked. This results in large degrees of variability in the performance of the brain-damaged patient: at one moment a correct sentence is produced, and at the next speech output degenerates into fragments of sentences, containing many errors. In all these instances there is a need to obtain and then analyse a sample of the patient's language and to identify the patterns that occur within the data. From the analysis, a hypothesis is formed, and treatment is a process of testing out the hypothesis. Again we see the influence of a scientific approach – rigorous methodologies for analysing data and a process of hypothesis formulation and testing. If the hypothesis is correct, then the patient will progress. If not, it is back to the drawing-board: more meticulous analysis, more formulation of hypotheses, more testing. It can be a long-term, laborious and altogether engrossing exercise, but its challenge is rewarded by progress in both human and intellectual terms.

Models of Language Structure

Let us assume that we have before us a sample of language ready for description and analysis. How should we organize our description of this linguistic material? A balanced and properly technical discussion of the kinds of model available would come from the field of linguistics. For present purposes, all we need to do is provide an outline of the main characteristics of a linguistic model relevant for clinical purposes, and as a perspective for the detailed discussion of pathologies in Chapter 5.[7]

---

[7]For a more detailed exposition of linguistic models, see J. Lyons, *Chomsky*, op. cit., Chapters 5–7. For further reading on linguistics, see J. Lyons, *Language and Linguistics* (Cambridge, Cambridge University Press, 1981), D. Crystal, *The Cambridge Encyclopedia of Language* (Cambridge, Cambridge University Press, 2nd edn. 1997).

In this model, an initial distinction is made between the notions of *language structure* and *language use*. Under the first heading is subsumed all the formal features of language, as directly observed in a spoken utterance (or its equivalent in writing). Most views of language classify these formal features into three main types, which for speech are usually referred to as *phonology, grammar* and *semantics*. These are said to be the three main 'levels' or 'components' of language. They may be studied in various orders: some linguistic theories begin with grammar, some with semantics or phonology. Basically, what is involved in each level is the following.

Phonology

At this level, we study the way the 'sound-system' of a language (or a group of languages) is organized. The human vocal apparatus can produce a very wide range of sounds, but only a relatively small number of these are used in a language to express meanings. The sounds do this through being organized into a system of contrasts, the various words of the language being distinguished from each other by substituting one type of sound for another. For instance, *pot* is distinguished from *got* by the contrast between /p/ and /g/ at the beginning of these words. How many contrastive units of this kind are there in English? The answer depends a little on how you analyse what you hear, and what dialect of English you are studying; but in one influential account of southern British English, there are 44.[8] We have listed these contrastive units, or *phonemes*, in Table 2.1, along with some examples, because it will be useful for illustrating disorders of phonology in Chapter 5. It should be noted that it is usual practice to transcribe phonemes in slant brackets (see further below). There are, of course, many variations in the contrasts listed in Table 2.1 which we have not referred to. For instance, when the contrast between /t/ and /d/ is made at the beginning of a word, it is generally more forceful than if it is made at the end of a word (compare *tin/din* and *bit/bid*). Moreover, the list gives information only about the way in which a word can be split up into a single sequence of phonemic units, or *segments*: *big* has three phonemic segments, for example, /b/ + /ɪ/ + /g/. It does not give information about the constraints on the sequence and position in which phonemes may occur in a language. It was this knowledge which enabled you to decide that whereas *vob* is a possible word in English, *vbo* is not (p. 39). These restrictions on the sequence and position of sounds are called *phonotactic constraints*.

Also within phonology is the study of the way in which words (and of course phrases and sentences) can be said in different tones of voice, by

---

[8]See A. C. Gimson revised by A. Cruttenden, *Gimson's Pronunciation of English* (London, Edward Arnold, 5th edn. 1994).

varying the pitch, loudness, speed and timbre. These tones of voice cannot readily be analysed into segments, and they thus constitute a different field of phonology – *non-segmental phonology* (as opposed to the *segmental phonology* illustrated in Table 2.1). Non-segmental contrasts also need to be transcribed, and usually a system of accents or numbers is devised to indicate what is going on in the speech. For example, *yès*, with a grave accent, might be used to mark that the pitch of the voice is falling from high to low; *yés*, with an acute accent, might be used to mark a voice pitch rising from low to high. The contrast in meaning would be evident enough: *yés* is the tone you might use if you were puzzled; *yès* if you were giving a definite answer. There are, as we shall see, disorders of language which affect segmental phonology alone, non-segmental phonology alone, or both together.

Table 2.1. The phonemes of southern British English

/iː/	as in	seat	/t/	as in	tin
/ɪ/		sit	/d/		din
/e/		set	/k/		cap
/æ/		sat	/g/		gap
/ʌ/		cut	/tʃ/		chop
/ɑː/		cart	/dʒ/		job
/ɒ/		cot	/f/		fat
/ɔː/		caught	/v/		vat
/ʊ/		put	/θ/		think
/uː/		shoe	/ð/		this
/ɜː/		bird	/s/		sin
/ə/		swimmer	/z/		zoo
/eɪ/		say	/ʃ/		shoe
/aɪ/		sigh	/ʒ/		vision
/ɔɪ/		boy	/h/		hat
/əʊ/		know	/m/		mat
/aʊ/		how	/n/		not
/ɪə/		here	/ŋ/		sing
/ɛə/		fair	/l/		live
/ʊə/		sure	/r/		road
/p/		pig	/w/		wet
/b/		big	/j/		yes

Phonology is the study of the pronunciation system of a language. It is therefore very reliant on the associated subject of *phonetics*, with which it is sometimes confused. But there is a crucial difference. Phonetics studies the characteristics of human sound-making, especially of those sounds used in speech, and provides methods for their description, classification and transcription. It studies sounds in three main ways. First, it studies the way they are made by the vocal organs (this branch of the subject is known as *articulatory phonetics*). Second, it studies the physical properties of speech sound, as transmitted between mouth and ear (*acoustic phonetics*). And third, it studies the perceptual response to speech sounds, as mediated by ear and brain (*auditory phonetics*). It is thus grounded in the anatomy and physiology of the human being, and in the physics of sound waves, and can proceed regardless of the language or speaker. The methods of analysis used in phonetics are valid no matter what language the speaker happens to be using. The subject is sometimes called 'general phonetics' for this reason, and it is this which is the essential difference between this subject and phonology. Phonetics studies all human sounds, regardless of the language they happen to turn up in; phonology studies only the way in which a selection of these sounds are organized within a partic-ular language. The distinction is reflected in transcription: phonetic transcription is identified by the use of square brackets; a phonological transcription, as we have seen, by slant brackets.

From the clinical point of view, the distinction between phonology and phonetics is an important one. It is possible to have disorders which affect only the phonological system of a person's speech, the phonetic abilities of that person remaining intact. In such a case, the patient would be able to make all the sounds required in English, but would have diffi-culties in organizing these sounds into a system for making contrasts in meaning (see further, p. 201). Conversely, it is possible to have disorders which are purely phonetic in origin, and where the phonological system remains unimpaired. For example, someone whose tongue is slightly paralysed would sound phonetically deviant, but such speakers might none the less be able to use their tongue enough to be able to make all the contrasts they need to in English. They could make all the contrasts listed in Table 2.1, for instance, but several of them would sound 'odd'. But probably the majority of 'pronunciation problems' in patients' speech result from a combination of both phonological and phonetic factors, and these prove the most difficult to analyse.[9]

Grammar

As we have seen, the phonemes of a language combine to produce higher order units that have meaning. The most widely used term to identify these larger units is *word* – a notion which is relatively easy to identify in the written language (it is the unit surrounded by spaces), and somewhat more difficult to identify in speech (where there are few equivalent pauses). One way of defining grammar is to say it is the subject which studies the internal structure of words, and the way in which words combine to form larger units, such as phrases, clauses, sentences

---

[9]For further reading on phonetics and phonology, see P. Roach, *English Phonetics and Phonology* (Cambridge, Cambridge University Press, 2nd edn, 1991); J. Clarke and C. Yallop, *An Introduction to Phonetics and Phonology* (Oxford, Blackwell, 2nd edn, 1995).

and sentence sequences. The two parts of this definition are sometimes summarized under separate headings. The study of word structure is called *morphology*. The study of word sequence (or, putting this the other way round, sentence structure) is called *syntax*. Many books see the field of grammar as divided up in this way – into the subfields of morphology and syntax – but not all theories of grammar make such a clear division between the two. In fact, there are more different models of grammatical analysis than of any other aspect of linguistic structure, and accordingly it is often this field which poses the greatest problems for clinicians who need to appreciate the strengths and weaknesses of the grammatical model they propose to use. A patient analysed using, say, the generative grammatical theory of Chomsky, will look very different from one analysed using the method of grammatical description proposed by the British linguist, Randolph Quirk, and his colleagues.[10] But of course it is the same patient.

It will be useful to outline a few of the grammatical distinctions that will be required later in this book, and for this we propose to use terms relatable to the Quirk model, as this approach is very widely used clinically. There are, however, major parallels between this approach and that used by several other linguists. Five basic notions are involved: sentence, clause, phrase, word and morpheme. The relationship between these can be illustrated from a single sentence:

The cat bit the dog and the dog bit the cat.

This sentence would be said to contain two *clauses*, linked by a *connector*:

The cat bit the dog   and   the dog bit the cat

Each clause can then be analysed into a series of *elements* of structure, labelled Subject (S), Verb (V), Object (O), Complement, Adverbial. In the present sentence, the Subject-Verb-Object structure is used (twice):

The cat	bit	the dog	the dog	bit	the cat
S	V	O	S	V	O

An element of clause structure may be just a single word (as in *bit*), or may constitute a *phrase*:

the cat	the dog	the dog	the cat

---

[10]For an introduction to generative grammar, see A. Radford, *Transformational Grammar* (Cambridge, Cambridge University Press, 1988). For the latter approach, see R. Quirk and S. Greenbaum, *A University Grammar of English* (London, Longman, 1973).

Phrases might become extremely complex:

The big fat ginger-haired cat bit *the dog from down the street*

Phrases may then be analysed into their constituent *words*, and the words, in turn, may be analysed into their component parts, if any, as in:

dis- abiliti -es

The various prefixes and suffixes, along with the roots of words, are referred to as *morphemes*; these constitute the minimal units of grammar.

From a clinical point of view, each of these notions has considerable relevance. It is possible to differentiate the grammatical ability of patients in terms of whether their problems are located primarily at the level of the word, the phrase, the clause or the sentence. Within one of these levels, moreover, it is possible to determine patterns of preference, as when a patient consistently omits verbs from clause structure (thus producing such sentences as *daddy ball*, for 'daddy kicked the ball', or *daddy garden*, for 'daddy is in the garden'). Two emphases in particular identify this approach in contrast to the traditional ways of analysing grammar sometimes taught in school. First, there is little attention paid to the *length* of a sentence; rather, all the effort is put into determining the *structure* of the sentence, and evaluating its complexity. Two sentences might be equally long, after all, but be very different in terms of their internal complexity. Compare:

The man and the dog and the cat and the mouse are in the picture.
The man who has been standing in the corner has just bought a new car.

Both sentences are 15 words long, but the second is plainly more complex than the first. Second, the notion of 'parts of speech' is not so important in this approach. Often, people have been taught that there is a fixed number of parts of speech – noun, verb, adjective, preposition etc. The problem with this old notion is that it is impossible to work with it without knowing something about the structure of sentences. If we ask you, 'What part of speech is *round*?', it is not possible to provide an answer, without first putting the word into a sentence. Compare the following uses of *round*; it is:

a verb in *we must round the buoy*;
a preposition in *it's round the corner*;
an adjective in *I see a round table*;
a noun in *it's your round*;
an adverb in *he turned round*.

In other words, in order to decide what part of speech a word belongs to, you must look at the sentence structure in which it appears – and that is why the approach outlined above spends so much time on matters of sentence structure rather than parts of speech. Sentence structure is the logical place to start; the parts of speech (or 'word classes') are brought in in passing, as the analysis proceeds.[11]

Semantics

Semantics is the study of the way meaning is organized in language. From one point of view, it involves studying the various grammatical structures outlined above to establish the range of meanings they express. We have already seen that the sentence *the cat bit the dog* can be analysed grammatically as having three parts, which are labelled Subject–Verb–Object. But we could attempt to define the meaning that these parts convey, in which case we might conclude that the 'meaning' of the Subject in this sentence is 'the doer of the action', the 'meaning' of the Verb is 'the act itself', and the 'meaning' of the Object is 'the receiver of the action'. This would be the beginnings of a semantic analysis of grammatical structure. Likewise, we can take the notion of the *word*, and ask not 'how does it combine with other words?' but 'what does it mean?' This is a quite familiar notion, in fact, for we are all used to seeing the meanings of words listed – in dictionaries. But a dictionary is only a starting-point for a semantic analysis of vocabulary; its alphabetical organization is a convenience when we want to look things up, but it is an irrelevance when it comes to studying the ways that words relate in meaning to each other. *Aunt* is at one end of the dictionary; *uncle* is at the other. But it is obvious that these words have a very close relationship in meaning, and any useful semantic analysis ought to be able to show this. There are indeed many types of meaning relationship between the words of a language – antonyms, such as *good* and *bad*; synonyms, such as *punctuality* and *promptness*; hyponyms, such as *cat* and *animal*;[12] and so on. The main business of semantic analysis is to establish the structure of the vocabulary, or lexicon, of a language – a task that has so far been carried out for only small areas of vocabulary.

But in a broader sense there is far more involved in semantics than the study of the meaning of items of vocabulary and grammatical structures. The concept of 'meaning' is so wide ranging. It can include the whole question of how meaning is expressed throughout a

[11]For an introduction to grammatical analysis, see F. R. Palmer, *Grammar* (Harmondsworth, Penguin, 2nd edn, 1984). For the application of this model clinically, see D. Crystal, P. Fletcher and M. Garman, *The Grammatical Analysis of Language Disability* (London, Whurr, 2nd edn, 1989).

[12]Hyponymy expresses the relationship of inclusion – an X is a kind of Y. Thus, a cat is a kind of animal – but an animal is not a kind of cat.

text – notions such as plot, subplot and character. It can include the
question of what has *not* been said, as well as what has been said, as
when one sentence presupposes another (e.g. if someone asks you, out
of the blue, 'When did you stop eating radishes?', the question presupposes that there was a time when you ate radishes – even though no
actual statement is made to that effect). Again, it can include the inten-
tion in the mind of the speaker, as when someone says 'I feel cold' when
what is *really* meant is 'I want you to shut the window'. And then there
are such little-understood areas of meaning as the expression of the
emotions using tone of voice (compare p. 42), or the expression of
'social meaning' – as when one's language gives away one's class, or job.

Given that we are in the job of helping patients to express and understand linguistic meaning, it is perhaps ironic that semantics, the branch
of linguistics which might most be of assistance, is the least-developed
branch of that discipline. But it should not be surprising when we
consider how intangible is the notion of 'meaning' – and how much of it
there is to subject to analysis. The points of contact between semantics
and clinical linguistic analysis are pitifully few, but this will undoubtedly
be a major growth area in the next decades.

Pragmatics

If we examine the history of modern linguistics, we find that grammar
and phonology have the longest history of study. Semantics was a
neglected area for many years, and the domain of pragmatics came to
prominence only in the 1980s. This topic covers a wide area and is difficult to define briefly: essentially it is the study of the factors that govern
our choice of language (the sounds, constructions, words) in social
interaction, and the effects of our choice upon others. The subject
includes the analysis of what it means to be appropriate and co-
operative in our speaking behaviour, and it thus begins to explain what
is involved when we use language to convey politeness, intimacy,
playfulness, rudeness, awkwardness, and a range of other 'social'
attitudes. For example, we change our language structure and content in
relation to the formality of a situation – we might greet an older stranger
with a formal 'Good morning', 'Pleased to meet you', but a familiar
contemporary with 'Hi', 'What's new?' We can see in Figure 2.1 (p. 50)
that pragmatics is located between language structure and language use.
This reflects the fact that our choice of language structures is mediated
by the context and use we wish to put them to.

Another component of pragmatics, of considerable relevance to
language pathology, is how we use language to achieve certain social
goals. We can use language to seek information, make promises, issue
threats, and for many other purposes. These uses of language are
termed *speech acts*. Speech acts often have rules (or *felicity conditions*)
for their appropriate use attached to them. For example, if someone

utters the words 'I now pronounce you man and wife', for this to be an appropriate speech act it requires that the person has the authority to marry people. The speech act of enquiry or questioning has the felicity condition attached to it that, normally, we do not have the information already available to us. This is what makes the question 'Connie, what is your name?' sound inappropriate, as it appears that we already have the information. The listener may try to make sense of the utterance by interpreting it as a request for a surname. It is worth noting, however, that it is quite usual in educational contexts for students to be asked questions to which the questioner already knows the answer. The same applies also to patients. It would seem that in this situation we suspend the usual felicity conditions on an act of questioning.

Conversational analysis is a further approach within pragmatics that has made a considerable impact on the applied field of language pathology in recent years. This approach focuses on conversation, and looks at how the participants in a conversation work together to sustain a successful interaction. An example of the collaboration between participants includes the split-second negotiation of turns in conversation. Although instances of two speakers talking at the same time do occur, there is usually a remarkable synchrony between participants. As one speaker finishes talking, another begins to speak, often with an infinitesimal pause between the turns. Where overlapping talk does occur, the problem is soon resolved with one of the speakers quickly dropping out of the exchange. The negotiation of turns is achieved through the exchange of a variety of non-verbal, vocal and linguistic signals. For example, the contour of intonation may fall towards the end of a turn; the speaker may make a prolonged eye contact with another participant to signal that the speaking turn is coming to an end; and other postural and gestural cues may signal the end of a contribution. It is often the case that individuals with very serious disorders of language are able to send and receive turn-taking cues and thus are able to maintain some degree of conversational interaction.

Pragmatics has had a very great impact on language pathology in a very short time. This impact has been not only in identifying instances of pragmatic abnormality in patients (see p. 177), but also in the areas of assessment and treatment of communication disorders, forcing clinicians to reconsider many of their activities in speech and language clinics (see Chapter 6). There has been more focus on communication as interaction – that communication involves speakers, listeners and a physical context to the interaction. In treatment, this leads to the awareness that not only can we remediate communication disorders by developing the behaviours of the patient as either a sender or receiver of messages, but we can intervene to change the physical context of the communication or change the behaviours of the individuals (or *interlocutors*) with whom the patient normally interacts. A second influence of pragmatics on the assessment and treatment process is the recognition that language and other forms of communication are used to achieve social goals – that they have a very definite function. We do not talk for the enjoyment of hearing our own voices; we talk in order to influence the behaviour of others – to inform them, to entertain them, to seek information. Many therapists have become aware that the language of the speech clinic lacks this range of uses. The interaction can be very constrained, and is not typical of communication in the world outside the clinic. This clearly is a very dangerous situation if we hope that the behaviours learned and practised in the clinic are to be taken and used elsewhere.[13]

We can summarize in the form of a diagram (Figure 2.1) what has been said so far about the structure of language. This model can of course be extended to cope with the analysis of written language. Writing has both a grammar and a semantics, so there is no need to modify the diagram in those respects; but instead of phonology it contains a writing system, i.e. a set of spelling and punctuation rules. The study of the writing systems of languages is known as *graphology*. Written language also varies in relation to context (compare a legal document with a note to the milkman), and so pragmatics is also of relevance.

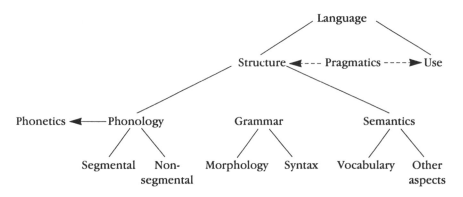

Figure 2.1 The main branches of linguistic analysis

We will make use of this model of language again in Chapter 5. When we come to analyse instances of linguistic disability, we find that some patients have particular difficulties with a single aspect of language struc-

[13]For an introduction to pragmatics, see G. Yule, *Pragmatics* (Oxford, Oxford University Press, 1996), R. Lesser and L. Milroy, *Linguistics and Aphasia* (London, Longman, 1993). For the clinical application of ideas from all levels of language structure, see K. Grundy, *Linguistics in Clinical Practice* (London, Whurr, 1989), M. Perkins and S. Howard, *Case Studies in Clinical Linguistics* (London, Whurr, 1996). S. Chiat, J. Law and J. Marshall, *Language Disorders in Children and Adults* (London, Whurr, 1997).

ture, and so we can identify 'phonological deficits', 'syntactic deficits' and the like. Some patients will have complex problems where we can identify difficulties at a number of levels of language structure. There may also be disabilities under the heading of pragmatics. It is worthwhile emphasizing that disruptions may occur in encoding and/or decoding at any level. For example, a patient may have problems encoding the sentence *the boy chased the dog* or in decoding (understanding) it. Thus just as some patients may have difficulty in constructing the sentence, others may struggle to understand whether *the boy* in the above sentence is the Subject – the 'doer' of the action – or the Object – the 'recipient' of the action. We will return to these concerns in later sections.

Psychology

The second strand of a behavioural approach to language pathology is to examine communicative disabilities from the perspective of psychology. Psychology involves the scientific study of human behaviour (and also other animals – though this will not be part of this book). Just as linguistics does not confine itself to the study of observable linguistic behaviour, hence allowing speakers' intuitions about their language as a valid object for study, so psychology studies invisible mental events as well as overt behaviours. The importance of linguistics to the study of disordered communication is perhaps more obvious than the role of psychology. Language is fundamental in human communication; linguistics is the scientific study of language; and so disruptions of language require insights from linguistics for their description. But how does psychology contribute to the understanding of communicative disorders?

The concerns of the psychologist interested in language are different from those of the linguist. Whereas the linguist is interested in identifying the components of a language and producing a set of rules that describe the patterns in which these components occur (see p. 39), the psychologist addresses the mental systems which are responsible for the understanding and production of linguistic messages. A simple way of differentiating these concerns would be that the linguist is interested in the 'what' of language ('What are the units and patterns of combination of units within a language?'), whilst the psychologist is concerned with the 'how' ('How are the units and combinations within a language comprehended and produced?'). Let us address the concerns of the psychologist first through consideration of behaviour more generally.

Any relatively complex organism has to survive and prosper in a constantly changing environment. In order to be able to do this it needs to be able to take in information about its environment. This enables the organism to identify food sources and other attractions such as potential mates, but also to track predators and other dangers. An ability to monitor the internal bodily environment is also necessary, so that the organism can detect states such as hunger, pain or abnormal temperature. The ability to monitor the environment therefore requires sensory processing, or systems that relay information from the external environment, or the internal environment of the body, to a central system which is capable of recognizing the inputs (perception) and then acting by avoiding threats and approaching attractions. The central system is a brain which is capable of linking incoming information to stored knowledge (memory) gained from previous encounters and experience of things in the world, and then organizing actions. A particularly complex organism like a human being does not solely react to events in the external or bodily environment. We are capable of thinking about things which are not present; for example, we can imagine being hungry, or think about a doughnut even when one is not immediately available to view. Our attitudes and emotions to objects and events can also influence our perceptions and actions. On viewing a snake in a zoo, some individuals will experience extreme anxiety and will act to escape from the vicinity of the snake as quickly as possible. Others can view the snake with a degree of composure, whilst still others will want to handle and touch the snake.

The psychologist is interested in the mental processes involved in receiving information, how incoming information is stored and subsequently retrieved from memory, and how actions are determined and performed. A psychologist interested in the process of language would address the mechanisms by which linguistic information, both spoken and written, is received and recognized, and subsequently its meaning understood. Speaking and writing are forms of action, and so the psychologist might be interested in the processes involved in retrieving words from memory or generating a sentence. A theory of the mental mechanisms involved in the processing of language is important in language pathology because many disorders of language result from failures of these mechanisms. The child who has failed to learn language at a normal rate, with no obvious reason for this delay in development (such as a hearing loss or a home environment which provides inadequate opportunities for language), is likely to have maturational delays or dysfunctions of the mechanisms responsible for the processing of language. Hence, the child is unable to extract salient information from incoming language input, or recognize recurring patterns, perhaps because of failure to store previous instances of the patterns in memory. We see here again the influence of the medical approach and an interest in the causes which underlie disorders, but this time in a behavioural guise.

In addition to providing fundamental insights into disorders of language processing, psychology is important in providing a broader perspective on behaviour. The relation between language and many other components of human behaviour is close and interdependent. Any number of examples may demonstrate this point. A psychologist colleague was conducting a series of experiments on spatial memory – the experiment required subjects to memorize the position of a set of toys on a grid. The task was supposedly non-linguistic. Subjects, however, employed a linguistic strategy in completing the task by creating stories about the figures, which then assisted their recall of their location. In this example, a non-language behaviour – spatial memory – is supported by language. But it is possible to identify interrelations which operate in the opposite direction, where language is supported by other behaviours. The importance of attention in language is an example of this. Paying attention requires selecting one facet of the complex sensory world around us and being able to bring to the foreground that component and place other possible distracting inputs in the background. This is what we are required to do in lectures. Ideally we are able to attend selectively to what the lecturer is saying and are able to ignore the noisy air-conditioning, the traffic noise from outside, or the sound of the overhead projector. The ability to pay selective attention is vital for language. Before understanding other speakers' messages we have to attend to what they are saying and sustain that attention. As a speaker, particularly if we are producing long strings of utterances, we have to hold on to our topic and not allow other thoughts to intrude into the message. It seems that many of the difficulties that schizophrenics have when speaking result from the inability to prevent irrelevant thoughts from intruding into their consciousness (see p. 158).

Psychology, like linguistics, can be subdivided into a number of fields, some of which have a great deal of relevance for language pathology. Those with obvious applications to communication disorders are cognitive psychology, developmental psychology, neuropsychology, social psychology and abnormal psychology. The training of a language pathologist will, typically, cover all of these aspects.[14]

Cognitive psychology

Cognitive abilities, cognitive deficits and *cognition* are terms that are regularly used in the discussion of individuals with communication disorders, though they are often not defined. Cognition concerns all the skills involved in the processing of information – in receiving and registering information, storing it, manipulating and transforming it, and retrieving and using it. The range of mental functions covered here includes perception, attention, memory, learning, concept formation, and thinking and problem-solving. To some extent these abilities are studied by all branches of psychology, but cognitive psychology is a distinctive approach with its own methodologies.[15]

---

[14]For an overview of psychology, see H. Gleitman, *Psychology* (New York, W. W. Norton, 4th edn, 1995).

[15]For an introduction, see M. W. Eysenck and M. T. Keane, *Cognitive Psychology* (Hove, Erlbaum, 3rd edn, 1995); also S. Pinker, *How the Mind Works* (Harmondsworth, Allen Lane, 1997).

Ideas from cognitive psychology have had a very great impact on language pathology, particularly in the last decade. This influence was first seen in investigations of the language disorders that followed brain damage, or aphasia (see p. 165), but is now extending to investigations of disorders of language learning. Cognitive psychology was strongly influenced by an analogy with the computer processing of information. Processing a piece of information, such as understanding a word, was conceptualized as being broken down into a series of sub-component processes, each of which operates in sequence or series; that is, only when one process is complete can the product of that processing be fed on to the next stage of the analysis. This approach is known as *sequential* or *serial* processing. An alternative view is that information can be processed in *parallel* – that a number of sub-component processes can be operating at the same time.

Information-processing psychology has had such a profound influence on language pathology because complex behavioural problems, such as word comprehension difficulties, can be broken down into sub-component stages, which in itself renders a complex problem more tractable. If a model of word comprehension suggests that a series of processing stages operates before the meaning of the word can be successfully decoded, it may then be possible to assess the integrity of each stage. For example, a simple model of word comprehension might suggest that the identity of the phonemes in an input have to be established (e.g. is the input 'foad' or 'foal'?). A second stage of processing would involve recognizing whether the input is one that has been encountered before (e.g. is 'foad' a word which has been previously encountered or is this a novel input?). A final stage of processing of words which have been previously encountered would be that the meaning of the word, and other information such as its grammatical class, would be accessed (e.g. 'foal' is a noun meaning 'juvenile horse'). Cognitive psychology makes issues of language processing more manageable in much the same way as linguistics renders the issue of language more tractable by breaking it down into sub-components such as phonology, grammar, semantics and pragmatics. Once a complex thing is reduced to its component parts, we can ask focused questions, such as 'What are the phonemes of English?' (versus 'What is English?'), or, in an instance of word comprehension difficulties, 'Can the listener decode the phonological structure of words?' (versus 'Why does the listener not understand what he or she is hearing?'). In Chapter 4 we present a simple information-processing model in our discussion of the communication chain.

Cognitive psychology gives us a framework for discussing the processing of language information in a listener's or speaker's mind. It also provides models of other cognitive processes (such as attention and memory) which are linked to language functioning. Many of the people with whom a language pathologist works have multiple cognitive impairments which can affect both their language processing and other aspects of behaviour. Brain damage, mental handicap (or *learning disability*) and profound developmental delay are all likely to impair a range of cognitive abilities. Speech and language therapists, often working with clinical and educational psychologists, need to be aware of the cognitive underpinnings of language, and the interactions between language and other cognitive functions.

Developmental psychology

This branch of psychology deals with changes in behaviour throughout the lifespan. The bulk of work has focused on the acquisition of knowledge and skills in infancy and childhood, but there is also a concern with changes in adulthood. We can see overlap between developmental psychology and many other branches of psychology. For example, the developmental psychologist might be interested in the development of memory (linking to cognitive psychology), or the development of social behaviour (linking to social psychology). But the characteristic feature of developmental psychology is a *diachronic* perspective on behaviour (looking at changes across time), as opposed to a *synchronic* perspective (behaviour at a particular point in time). The object of study might be overt behaviours such as motor skills – for example, the child's ability to stand, walk, run – or less accessible mental events such as memory or conceptual development. Another thrust of research is to identify those environments and adult behaviours which facilitate development and those that inhibit it.[16]

The applications of developmental psychology to language pathology are many. It informs the clinician about what can be regarded as a normal pattern of behaviour at any particular age – for example, what do we expect a normal 3-year-old to do? What is normal memory functioning in an 80-year-old? This information is often referred to as 'developmental milestones', particularly in the context of child development. Such information is vital when faced with a child referred to the clinic for investigation of language delay. One of the first goals of the clinician's investigation, once the language delay has been confirmed via analysis of the child's communicative behaviour, is to establish whether this child's problems are restricted to language ('a specific language

---

[16]For an introduction to developmental psychology, see L. E. Berk, *Child Development* (Boston, Allyn & Bacon, 4th edn, 1997). For texts that deal specifically with the acquisition of language, see D. Crystal, *Child Language, Learning and Linguistics* (London, Edward Arnold, 2nd edn, 1987); D. Crystal, *Listen to Your Child* (Harmondsworth, Penguin, 1986); P. Fletcher and M. Garman (eds), *Language Acquisition* (Cambridge, Cambridge University Press, 2nd edn, 1986); P. Fletcher and B. MacWhinney (eds) *The Handbook of Child Language* (Oxford, Blackwell, 1995).

deficit') or whether there are more global delays in development. The type of treatment required by the child and decisions on future educational provision will vary greatly, depending on whether we are dealing with a specific or a general developmental deficit.

There are difficulties in developing and using norms of development. Children (and adults) do not develop in unison and without divergence from some preordained blueprint. There is huge individual variability within normal development. Norms represent an idealized pattern of development, and few or no children will conform exactly to that pattern. They may show strengths in one area of development, such as language, and lag behind in others, such as motor skills. There is also the difficulty of identifying the point at which a difference from norms is considered a delay. If a 6-month delay in development is labelled as a cause for concern, but a 5-month delay is classified as slow but normal, are we justified in recognizing a qualitative difference between two individuals distinguished in this way?

The supply of developmental milestones to the clinician is of great value, but this is not the only contribution that developmental psychology makes to language pathology. Besides the identification of the sequence in which behaviours develop and the factors which might facilitate a child's learning, it enables the clinician to create a well-structured learning situation for children, which will maximize their learning potential. We also begin to understand, from studying the acquisition of skills and knowledge, how children go about the learning process. In learning language, are children passive, simply repeating the language that they hear around them, or are they active, forming hypotheses about language and then seeking data from the language they hear around them to confirm or reject these hypotheses? The evidence supports the active role played by children in language learning, and the clinician's task is therefore to provide a language environment which first encourages hypothesis formation, and then supplies sufficient data for children to confirm or reject their ideas about language.

Neuropsychology

This area of psychology deals with relationships between behaviour and the brain – for example, those areas of the brain involved in language function, memory or emotion. Such information is useful in dealing with patients with identified brain damage. From a knowledge of normal brain–behaviour relations, it is possible for the clinician to make predictions about what areas of behaviour might be impaired by a brain lesion in a certain location.

The degree to which direct correlations can be made between brain structure and mental functions is much debated. Certain functions – for example, movement and sensation – are capable of quite precise brain localization. The extent to which it is possible to localize complex functions such as language – often termed a 'higher cognitive function' – is less clear. A characteristic feature of a higher cognitive function is that it is underpinned by a number of component processes. We have already discussed how mental abilities such as perception and memory underlie language function. It is thus possible to destroy or impair the complex function by removal of one of the component processes. This notion was clearly stated in a famous maxim over a century ago by the British neurologist John Hughlings Jackson: 'To locate the damage which destroys speech and to locate speech are two different things' (1866).[17]

Within neuropsychology, it is possible to see differences between researchers in the extent to which they are prepared to localize behaviours to brain areas. But a common feature of neuropsychological investigations is the use of lesion studies to investigate brain–behaviour correlations. A *lesion* (an area of anatomical structural damage) may be naturally occurring (e.g. as a result of a stroke), or experimentally induced (as has often happened in animal studies). In investigations of the neuropsychology of language, lesion studies are restricted only to the 'experiments of nature' – naturally occurring accidents that damage the brain. As language is specific to the human species, animal studies are of little value. In the past, human lesion studies were conducted by investigating the pattern of behavioural abnormality that the lesion had created, and then, after the death of the subject, sometimes years later, a post-mortem examination would establish the site of the neurological damage. Advances in brain-scanning or brain-imaging techniques now allow the site and extent of a lesion to be established soon after it has occurred. Techniques other than lesion studies are also used in neuropsychology – particularly in the study of which half of the brain is used in the processing of different types of information – for example, pictures as opposed to words. The section on laterality (p. 100) gives examples of such procedures.

Although neuropsychologists differ in the extent to which they believe higher cognitive functions can be localized within the brain, the field is united by common methodologies. Recent years have seen the development of an especially productive sub-branch of neuropsychology – *cognitive neuropsychology*. As this title suggests, cognitive neuropsychology draws its inspiration from cognitive psychology, and uses lesion studies to test the validity of information-processing models developed by cognitive psychologists. The approach has done much to elucidate the nature of many language disorders which follow brain damage. The processes involved in the understanding and production of single words are now better understood. More complex sentence formulation models are in the process of being developed and tested. In addition, there is now more understanding of the difficulties in reading

---

[17]J. Hughlings Jackson, 'Notes of the Physiology and Pathology of Language'. In *Selected Writings of John Hughlings Jackson* (London, Staples Press, 1958).

and writing that can follow brain damage ('acquired dyslexia and dysgraphia').[18]

Social pyschology

Much of the work in describing non-verbal communication (eye contact, facial expression, posture, etc.) is undertaken by social psychologists. Their descriptive frameworks have come to be used in analysing non-verbal communicative disturbances in language pathology clinics. But beyond this, there has been only limited application of social psychology to language pathology. However, with the growth of interest in pragmatics, within both linguistics and language pathology, this is potentially an area of considerable importance. Pragmatics deals with the use of language within different social contexts, and speakers respond to factors such as the formality of a situation and the status of the participants to make their language appropriate to the situation (p. 48). Social psychology, which deals with how the individual perceives the behaviour of others and is influenced by others, would seem to be valuable in furthering our understanding of pragmatic abilities. Additional areas of relevance include the analysis of the factors in a social situation which might induce or ameliorate a voice disorder (p. 194) or which might influence the way stutterers view themselves and their stutter in relation to the social pressures placed upon them (p. 191).

Abnormal psychology

This branch of psychology deals with the study of behaviour that falls outside what is defined as normal. There are again difficulties, as there were in the discussion of normal development, in defining what is normal. The types of abnormal behaviours which a psychologist might address range from anxiety and depression to severe psychotic illnesses such as schizophrenia. From our discussion in Chapter 1 of the social and emotional consequences of a communication handicap, understanding of the causes of anxiety and depression and ways of dealing with them is essential for the speech and language pathologist. Individuals who suffer from a communication disorder and who then develop abnormal behaviours such as severe depression would be regarded as suffering from an emotional disorder which is secondary to the communication handicap. But the clinician will also come across individuals who have a primary psychiatric disorder which has, as a consequence, an associated communication disorder. Schizophrenia is one such example (p. 158).[19]

---

[18]For an introduction to neuropsychology, see B. Kolb and I. Whishaw, *Fundamentals of Human Neuropsychology* (New York, Freeman, 1996), A. Ellis and A. Young, *Human Cognitive Neuropsychology* (Hove, Psychology Press, 1996).
[19]On abnormal psychology, see G. C. Davidson and J. M. Neale, *Abnormal Psychology* (Chichester, Wiley, 6th edn, 1994).

Correlating Medical and Behavioural Data

It should now be clear that the two approaches to investigation – the medical and the behavioural – provide very different kinds of information about a patient, and that both are necessary if we are to get anywhere near a full understanding of the patient's abilities and limitations, and a positive rationale for treatment and rehabilitation. One question remains to be answered: is there a one-to-one correlation between the findings of a medical approach and those of a behavioural approach? Does a given category of disease always produce the same kind of abnormal linguistic behaviour? If, for example, we brought together a matched group of children who had had a certain kind of cleft palate condition, or who were deaf to a certain degree, or who had a certain level of subnormal intelligence – to what extent would we be able to show the existence of 'linguistic syndromes'? Would all the deaf children speak in identical ways? Or the cleft palate children?

Perhaps running contrary to popular expectations, the answer is no. No identity, certainly – and sometimes quite major differences emerge. The problem, of course, is the difficulty we have in matching the patients in the first place. Even if we match the group of cleft-palate children closely for age, sex, social class, severity of the cleft, and all the other factors that we know about, we are still left with several factors that we do *not* know about (see further, p. 207). Has there been any associated brain damage? How serious have been the ear, nose and throat infections the various children incurred? What kind of language has the parent been using to the children? Have the children been taught language in a more formal way? What about the varying emotional needs of the children? The questions could go on and on. What they amount to is an explanation as to why it is unlikely that there will be a very close correlation between a medically defined group of patients and a behaviourally defined group. And when the basis of the disorder is brain damage, as with mental handicap/learning disability, or the aftermath of a stroke, then it becomes impossible to achieve any meaningful kind of correlation, in our present state of knowledge.

One famous classification of the linguistic effects of adult brain damage (aphasia – see p. 165) illustrates this point well. Aphasic patients can be classified medically in terms of whether the part of the brain damaged is relatively forward or further back (the distinction between Broca's aphasia and Wernicke's aphasia – see p. 167). It is also possible to classify aphasic patients behaviourally, for instance in terms of whether their speech is relatively fluent or non-fluent. Some effort has been directed towards establishing whether there is a correlation between the two modes of description, and while there are indeed certain tendencies worth noting, there is plainly no necessary correlation. And the same conclusion is arrived at for any area of language pathology. As a result, so far, analysis of patients in medical terms has proceeded along largely separate lines from analyses in behavioural terms. The problems facing the clinician, who alone has to find a way of integrating the two areas in order to arrive at a self-consistent and systematic programme of individual therapy, are enormous. And for the language pathologist, interested in arriving at satisfactory conclusions about *groups* of patients, and thus developing a method of linguistic differential diagnosis, the problems are just as great. There are so many variables involved, of both a medical and a behavioural kind.

In the next chapter we will discuss a model of communication – the communication chain – which provides a way of drawing together medical and behavioural approaches. Then, armed with this model, we can examine the physical basis of communication (Chapter 4) and how the process of communication can be disrupted (Chapter 5).

Revision Questions

1. What have the medical sciences contributed to the study of language pathology?
2. What have the behavioural sciences contributed to the study of language pathology?
3. What 'levels' would a linguist describe in language?
4. What is cognition and what is its relevance to language behaviour?
5. How do the concerns of a linguist and a psychologist interested in language differ?

Tutorial Activities

1. Identification and elimination of causes of pathology is an important component of the medical model. Examine the case outlines and decide if knowledge of cause (both medical and behavioural) is significant in managing a condition.

   (a) The patient is a 4-year-old child with Down's syndrome. Testing the child's ability reveals that the child is functioning at an 18-month-old level in both language and non-language skills. Therefore the child has a severe delay in all areas of development.

   (b) The patient is a 6-year-old child. She comes from a home background in which there has been little language stimulation. This girl performs at about a 3-year-old level in language activities. In non-language activities she has only a slight delay, performing almost at a 6-year-old level.

   (c) The patient is a 54-year-old man, who has suffered a stroke as a result of high blood pressure (hypertension). Because of his stroke, he has difficulty moving the right side of his body due to paralysis. He has difficulties in understanding and speaking.

(d) The patient is a 5-year-old boy. His parents have brought him to the speech and language therapy clinic because they are concerned that he might be developing a stutter. All other areas of the child's development are entirely normal. A medical examination has revealed no problems. The parents report that no events have occurred recently to cause the child any anxiety.

(e) The patient is a 36-year-old physical education teacher. He has a voice disorder. His voice is very croaky and hoarse, and by the end of the day his voice has almost completely disappeared. He uses his voice a lot while teaching and likes to sing in a choir in the evenings. An ENT examination revealed that he has a small non-malignant growth on his vocal folds (part of his larynx). This can be removed by surgery, but is likely to recur if he does not modify his pattern of voice use.

2. A test which is often administered to children with difficulties in learning language is the Symbolic Play Test. The child is given a toy which is a miniature of a real object (for example, a tractor or a doll). The ways in which the child uses the miniature are then observed and recorded. Why do you think a speech and language therapist might be interested in such behaviours?

3. The parents of a child have decided that it is about time their child began to learn colour names. They sit down with a set of coloured blocks. There are red blocks, which happen to be circles; blue blocks, which are triangles; and yellow blocks, which are square. The parents patiently name the colours for the child, and by the end of the game the child is correctly naming the bricks as 'blue', 'red' and 'yellow'. The parents, delighted, are eager to demonstrate their child's prowess to a friend and reach for a different set of blocks. The parents hold up a red triangle and the child labels it as 'blue'; then a yellow circle, which is triumphantly labelled as 'red'; and then a yellow square, which is then correctly labelled as 'a yellow'.

(a) How could you account for this behaviour?

(b) Suggest an alternative way of teaching colour concepts to avoid the problem.

(c) What would be the effect on language of the absence of colour (or other) concepts?

Chapter 3
The Communication Chain

An often-used approach in an introductory book on language pathology is to detail the range of communication disorders that commonly occur, together with their typical characteristics. But before launching into a discussion of individual disabilities, it will be useful to try to get a general view of the field as a whole. A normal procedure in scientific investigation, especially when we are dealing with a new or unformed field of study, is to attempt to impose some organization upon it by constructing a 'model' of the field. The aim of the procedure is emphasized by the philosopher of science, Marshall Walker: 'the purpose of scientific thought is to postulate a conceptual model of nature from which the observable behavior of nature may be predicted accurately',[1] and a similar view is expressed by Stephen Toulmin: 'The heart of all major discoveries in the physical sciences is the discovery of novel methods of representation, and so of fresh techniques by which inferences can be drawn'.[2] Science, it has been said, is a continual search for fresh models, and language pathology is no exception.

Of course, this is not the everyday sense of the word 'model'. Clinicians constructing a model of linguistic disability do not get out their Plasticine and attempt to build a miniature copy of a brain or a palate! 'Model', in its scientific use, has a much more abstract sense – or rather senses, for the study of scientific models has itself a long, interesting and controversial history, as any text on the philosophy of science will show. A model is part of the process of scientific explanation. It is a visual way of expressing an abstract set of relationships, such as have been propounded by some theory. It is a way of physically representing the complex ideas which constitute a theory, so that they can become more intelligible. For example, it is possible to discuss the principles governing the number and nature of the elementary particles of matter in abstract, mathematical terms, but most of us who have grasped a little

---

[1] *The Nature of Scientific Thought* (Englewood Cliffs, NJ, Prentice-Hall, 1963), p. 5.
[2] *The Philosophy of Science* (London, Hutchinson, 1953), p. 31.

of what has been discovered by this branch of physics have managed to do so by applying our minds to the models of the elementary particles, as presented in introductory texts and television programmes. Take, for example, the model of the atom, 'containing' a nucleus, which 'consists of' protons and neutrons, and is 'surrounded by' electrons; these in turn are investigated to establish whether they may be 'built up' from even smaller particles of matter. Because we understand what notions such as 'building' and 'surrounding' mean, we can begin to make sense of the claims of particle physics; without this, we should be lost. And the same applies to all areas of scientific enquiry, such as the models of molecular structure, or of geographical terrain (a map is a simple form of model), or of historical relationships (as in a tree-diagram of the kings and queens of England).

One thing all models have in common: they are simplifications of the reality they represent. Features of the reality are left out, and other features emphasized. The model would not be a model if it did not do this. The reason, of course, is that the purpose of the model is to help our understanding. If all a model did was simply to reflect reality, containing all its detail, we would be no better off. If we look down on a battle scene, and ask you to explain to us what is happening, and you simply hand us a photograph of the battle scene, we are hardly helped! On the other hand, if you give us a diagram showing us the main dispositions of the troops, with each side coloured differently, and the movement lines marked by arrows, we are likely to be much illuminated. This diagram is a simplification, though. It omits innumerable details. There are no battle-scars or blood on our diagram. But the simplification was made for a purpose: the diagram tells us what we wanted to know, and therefore the omitted details do not bother us. All models are in principle like this one: their purpose is to illuminate an area of enquiry, and they are always designed for a specific purpose. Insofar as the features of reality which the model represents are the ones in which we are interested, the model will be helpful to us, and we will continue to use it. Insofar as the model gives us details which are not relevant to our aims, we shall find it unhelpful. For instance, there are many possible ways of modelling the human body – representing its muscular structure, its nervous system, its skeletal structure, its blood circulation, and so on. If we are trying to understand the neurological basis of a speech disability, we will be much helped by the model of the nervous system, but hardly at all by the model of the digestive system.

Of course, this simple account works only if we know what we want of our models in advance. If we *know* our problem is a neurological one, then we can select our neurological model to help us organize our ideas. But what if we do not know in advance which model is likely to help us? What if there are no models available at all to guide us in our research? How should we begin to model the functions of the internal structure of the brain, for example? or of social relationships within a community? In such cases we have no alternative (apart from giving up!) but to attempt to construct a model for ourselves, using whatever analogies we can find from other areas of experience with which we are familiar. There will be a lot of guesswork, but we can check our guesses by observing whether the patterns we see in our model actually turn up in reality. Putting this more technically: our model will generate hypotheses about reality, which we can then subject to experimental test. Insofar as our model suggests fresh hypotheses to us – brand new ideas – we will be well satisfied. Our model will be a 'fruitful' one. On the other hand, we must be cautious in using our model. The patterns we put into it may mislead us. They may make us think of reality in a fixed way, so that when we make our observations we end up seeing only what we want to see. This is a familiar danger. Scientist A says to B that B is 'blinkered', unable to examine data in any way other than the one B originally devised. What A means by this, of course, is that A does not think B's model is illuminating, and that A's own model is better. B, if we were to ask, might think the same about A's model! To a considerable extent, science involves this process of comparison of the claims of different models, building on their strengths and attempting to avoid their weaknesses. If the weaknesses of a model become so great as to continually distort reality, in the view of the majority of scientists, then it will be dropped – though this process often takes many years, involving a great deal of heart-searching on the part of those involved, and sometimes involving harsh judgements from society as a whole (as in the case of Galileo).

Models, then, do four things: (1) they provide an intelligible representation of a theory; (2) they generate hypotheses for scientific testing; (3) they provide us with insights about our field of study; and (4) they tend to make us think along fixed lines. We cannot do without models in our work, but we must always be critical of them, in case they lead us astray.

The medical and behavioural approaches described in Chapter 2 have each been described as 'models of enquiry', and one of the most convenient ways of drawing them together is to construct a model that is capable of incorporating the essential characteristics of both. This model is sometimes referred to as the 'communication chain', or the 'speech chain'. The latter is probably the more widespread use, reflecting the priority that most investigators give to speech over other modes of communication,[3] but it is important to recognize that the same model could be used for writing, signing or any other mode. Indeed, if we trace the history of ideas behind the use of this model, we will end up with the broadest possible view of the notion of communication, as developed within the field of *information theory*.

---

[3] The best reference is P. B. Denes and E. N. Pinson, *The Speech Chain: The Physics and Biology of Spoken Language* (New York, W. H. Freeman, 2nd edn, 1993).

Information theory developed in the late 1940s, primarily as the result of proposals made by an American electrical engineer, Claude E. Shannon.[4] 'Information' does not here refer solely to its everyday general sense of 'factual knowledge', but has a much more precise interpretation. Under the heading of 'information' is included the whole range of signals that can be transmitted from one place to another, such as by radio or telephone, or within the circuits of electronic computers, or within the nervous systems of humans and animals. The idea was to study the properties of these signals, and of the devices which send and receive them, to see if measures could be devised which would quantify the amount of information contained within a signal, the amount of information that a communication channel could transmit, and the capacity of a system to store and process information. The various practical applications of such studies are endless. An early application was in the field of telephone communication: how much speech sound could be omitted without the intelligibility or acceptability of the message being affected? Could several conversations be transmitted at once along the same channel? How much information could the channel cope with before it became overloaded? The analysis of the concepts involved required sophisticated statistical techniques, and the principles that came to be established were formulated in mathematical terms. The theoretical field involved is thus usually regarded as a branch of mathematics.

One result of this approach was an account of the information process in terms of a sequence, or chain of events – a chain that can be used as a basis for analysing what happens in *any* communicative activity. Basically, seven steps are involved. First, there must be an *information source*, which might be a human being, animal, machine, object (such as the sun, sending out radiation), and so on. This source has internal properties which enable it to construct a signal, or message: this process of construction is referred to as *encoding*, and this constitutes the second step in the chain. The third step is *production*: the encoded signal is made public – accessible to direct observation – through the use of some device (such as a nervous system, or a radio). The signal is then sent along a medium, or channel (such as the air, water, wires, nerves), and this constitutes the fourth step: *transmission*. Fifth, the signal is *received* by some other device (such as a radio receiver, or another nervous system). The internal properties of the device which receives the signal enables it to be *decoded*, and this constitutes the sixth step in the chain. The remaining step is the decoded signal arriving at its *destination*, where the significance of the message will be registered in some way. We can summarize this process in a single sequence, as follows:

---

[4]The classic textbook on the subject is C. E. Shannon and W. Weaver, *The Mathematical Theory of Communication* (Urbana, University of Illinois Press, 1949). An influential popular survey is C. Cherry, *On Human Communication* (Cambridge, MA, MIT Press, 3rd edn, 1978).

Information source → Encoding → Production → Transmission →
Reception → Decoding → Destination

Sometimes the whole process is collapsed into three main stages:

Production → Transmission → Reception

and this in fact will be the usual use of these terms below. *Production* will refer to the whole process of making a linguistic message ready for transmission. *Reception* will refer to the whole process that takes place once a linguistic message has been transmitted.

This model can now be applied directly to the various stages involved in human communication. In some cases, however, it will prove useful to break down the steps in the process into 'substeps', in order to make the model more usable for the investigation of linguistic disability. Each step in the communication chain will require detailed study, but to begin with let us look at the process in outline, to provide a general perspective. A representation of the communication chain is given in Figure 3.1. For communication to take place, a minimum of two human beings are required, and these are symbolized by the facing heads. Communication may proceed in either direction.

PRODUCTION   TRANSMISSION   RECEPTION
(ENCODING)   (DECODING)

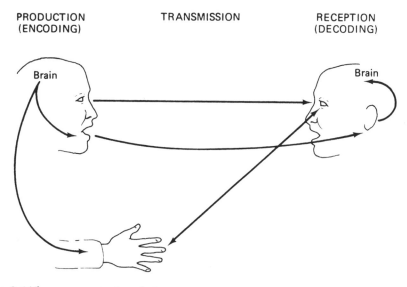

Figure 3.1 The communication chain

Figure 3.2 takes this general approach a stage further, introducing some additional features. It is this level of detail that is needed to discuss the physical basis of the communication chain (Chapter 4) and how this chain might be disrupted, resulting in disorders of communication (Chapter 5). This model is a development of the seven-step process in that several substeps of encoding and decoding are recognized. It also shows that communication does not just involve sending information in a linear way from one individual to another. Instead *feedback loops* are built into the process, which allow the message-sender to monitor the correctness and success of the message. This can include identifying errors in the encoding process or monitoring the receiver's reactions for signs of misunderstanding or misinterpretation (see further, p. 74).

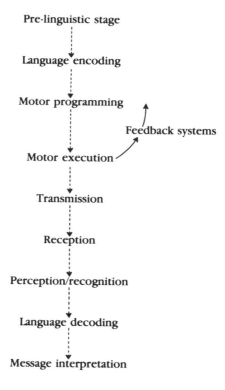

Figure 3.2 Stages within the communication chain

The Pre-linguistic Stage

The communication chain begins with an information source which is capable of constructing a message. These messages can be conceived of as ideas or thoughts, which we may, or may not, wish to communicate to others. Some of these thoughts will not be made public through the use of language and they will remain a part of our private mental lives. It is an important part of our social and interactional knowledge (sometimes called 'social cognition') to know which thoughts can be communicated to others, and which should remain private. Failure to acquire this social knowledge, with the resulting production of utterances which are untimely or inappropriate in their content, is likely to lead to interactional breakdown and social ostracism. Conversely, a failure to make ideas public when they are relevant and timely is also likely to lead to interactional failure. Individuals with such problems are likely to experience difficulties in forming and maintaining relationships, and may often find themselves in conflict with many of the major institutions of society.

We have termed the first stage in the communication chain the 'prelinguistic stage'. This suggests that the ideas and thoughts entertained by the information source exist independently of language. A second separate step, as we shall see, gives the idea a linguistic shape. This notion of thought without language is controversial and is undoubtedly an oversimplification, and we are confronted here with the thorny issue of the relation between language and thought. Can we think without language? The answer to this question depends on the kind of activity involved. If we reflect on our thinking, we have some awareness of highly conscious forms of thinking. When given a visual puzzle to complete, we have the sensation of thinking in shapes and colours, and mentally performing operations such as the rotation of images. The feelings we have in listening to music are not as a rule possible to 'put into words' and do not seem to be language-dependent. It would seem therefore an uncontroversial conclusion that we have different modes of conscious thought available to us. But, on the other hand, there seem to be a large number of thoughts which do seem to critically involve language. It is not usually possible to work out the stages of a moral or scientific problem without formulating the problem linguistically – and sometimes it proves essential to speak the problem aloud, or write it down, before our thinking can be clarified. Some forms of characteristically human thought therefore do seem to involve language. But what of less conscious modes of thought, perhaps akin to the state of 'daydreaming', where we are clear that we were thinking about something, but that the 'something' is intangible and the form of the thought is unclear. All of this suggests a notion of pre-linguistic thoughts and ideas, and the precursor stage to linguistic encoding. It may well be that encoding thoughts into language not only allows the opportunity to make them public, but even when they are not spoken aloud, language form gives them a permanence that pre-linguistic representation lacks.[5]

Before an idea or thought can be entertained, there must be knowledge of the thing that is to be thought about. Psychologists make a distinction between knowledge stored in autobiographical (or episodic) memory, and in semantic memory. Autobiographical memory is knowledge of specific events and their time-reference (i.e. knowledge of when, approximately, they occurred), while semantic memory is our knowledge store of facts, words and concepts. The size of information chunks

---

[5]For further discussion of these issues, see S. Pinker, *The Language Instinct* (New York, Morrow, 1994), Chapter 3.

in semantic memory varies from that of the individual concept, such as the meaning of 'two', to much larger structures such as 'how to behave at a funeral'. These larger knowledge structures are sometimes termed 'scripts' or 'schemas'. The difference between semantic and autobiographical/episodic knowledge is best displayed in trying to answer the following two questions: 'when did you first go to London?' and 'when did you first learn that London was the capital of the United Kingdom?' The first question may be relatively easy to answer as it addresses autobiographical memory, which is time-referenced, whilst the second is very difficult to answer as it addresses semantic memory, which is not so strongly time-referenced. The two types of knowledge are, however, linked. Our semantic or conceptual knowledge about dogs is built up through various encounters with dogs, experienced both directly and vicariously through hearing or reading about dogs. In the course of these encounters, we develop an abstract notion of 'dog', which is a synthesis of the common elements of dog encounters. Conceptual knowledge is likely to be fluid, as we constantly acquire new knowledge and modify past beliefs throughout our lifespan, and there is also the possibility that one individual's knowledge of 'dog' is a little different from another's. If you have been bitten by a dog, 'ferocious' may be a central component of your dog concept, but if your dog experiences consist only of interactions with a creature that wants nothing more than to have its tummy tickled, then your beliefs about dogs may be different. There is likely, however, to be a relatively stable core to concepts. If you were to hear of a fish that never entered water, you might find this surprising given that 'aquatic-living' is likely to be a core element of your concept of 'fish'.

In order to talk about dogs or entertain ideas about dogs we have to have knowledge or a concept of dog, and to a reasonable extent one individual's concept of dog has to be similar to another's concept of dog if the two individuals are to communicate with one another. If people have difficulty in learning about the things in their world, and forming abstract concepts from a variety of experiences, then this will limit both the thoughts they can have about their world and also what they can communicate. Individuals with learning difficulties (or mental handicaps, see p. 154) are likely to experience such problems.

In the clinical context, the separation of a pre-linguistic and linguistic stage in the model of the communication chain can be justified only if, in reality, we can identify disorders which involve a difficulty with thinking, or with language, but not with both.[6] Of course, we shall also find instances where both are impaired, as in many forms of learning difficulties.

[6]See, for example, S. Schaller, *A Man without Words* (University of California, Summit, 1991) for an account of a profoundly deaf individual, who had not been exposed to sign language, but who appeared rational and alert, behaved appropriately, and was able to work as a labourer.

Because the pre-linguistic stage is a precursor to linguistic encoding, we will also find instances of 'knock-on' effects – where thought is incoherent and disorganized, resulting in equally incoherent linguistic encoding of those thoughts. Psychiatric conditions that involve thought disorders, such as schizophrenia, are examples of such disabilities.

Language Encoding

The second step in the chain is that of language encoding. In discussing this stage in the processing of messages, the aspects of language structure and use that were discussed in Chapter 2 – syntax, semantics, phonology/graphology and pragmatics – are essential. Imagine that we are watching two children (A and B) playing, and we have seen A hit B. At the pre-linguistic stage, we have two elements (A and B), an action (hitting) and a particular event linking them together. In coding this idea into a linguistic form, we need to select words that correspond to the elements and the action. To do this, we need to access information in our semantic store and select appropriate words, such as *boy, girl, Mary, Nicholas, hit* or *punch*. In retrieving the words, we also access their sound or phonological structure – that *hit* is made up of an initial consonant /h/, a vowel /ɪ/ and a final consonant /t/. We also need to establish the relations between the units we have selected and so structure them into an accurate sentence structure. Who was the one who was hitting – Mary or Nicholas? Who got hit? Here we need our knowledge of sentence structure to capture the correct relation between the elements. We also need to decide the purpose to which our utterance will be put. For example, would we like to discover the reason for the event and maybe ask a question ('Why did Mary hit Nicholas?') or do we want to communicate this event in a statement to another who did not observe it ('Mary hit Nicholas'). The decision on the function that the utterance has to serve will affect our choices not only of sentence structure but also of words. When we come to examine *language disorders* (p. 162), we will see that the different layers of linguistic encoding can be differentially affected by disability. Thus we can identify individuals with problems in syntactic encoding or phonological encoding, and so on. These disabilities may be *developmental* – that is, the linguistic knowledge fails to develop; or they may be *acquired* – the individual previously possessed competence in an area, but this was lost following damage to the cerebral cortex of the brain (p. 150). As well as identifying individuals with specific difficulties in individual areas of language encoding, it is more common to find that a number of areas of language structure are impaired, so that, for instance, the patient may have both a phonological and a syntactic disorder.

The process of linguistic decision-making – what function will the utterance have? what sentence structure? what words? what sound structure? – is complex as it stands. But this complexity increases with the realization that these decisions are also linked to variables external to the language system. A few examples will illustrate such interrelationships. An important input to our linguistic decisions is an assessment of what the receiver of the message already knows. In our example, the event of two children fighting, if the recipient of the message also observed the event, it would be redundant to send the message 'Mary hit Nicholas' because this information would already be known. It might be appropriate to ask a question such as 'Why did Mary hit Nicholas?'. This ability to 'know what the recipient knows' is a very complex cognitive skill, and one that young children take some time to acquire. But, if the child is to achieve an adult-like level of communicative competence, it is cognitive skills such as these which have to be developed. A current and influential hypothesis of the cognitive impairment which underlies autism (see p. 161) suggests that these children are particularly slow in developing the ability to understand that the content of another's mind might be different from their own. The 'theory of mind' hypothesis suggests that many of the communicative impairments which occur in autism are a consequence of this inability to 'mind-read'.

The following examples illustrate the importance of our knowledge of social situations in linguistic decision-making. Awareness of such factors as the formality of a situation and the status of the participants is essential. These factors may influence a decision as to whether to speak or not to speak. For example, would you inform a senior professor that his trouser fly was undone? The perceived status of participants and the formality of a situation may also influence choices of words or even of the sound structure of words. For instance, in describing feelings of nausea to a doctor or an employer, most people would feel it more appropriate to select such expressions as 'to be sick' or 'vomit' than the more informal 'throw up'. Similarly, the influence of social variables on decisions of sound structure of words can be observed. The dropping of initial /h/ sounds is typical of informal speech and is found in a number of British dialects. Habitual '*h*-droppers' do not, however, always drop their *h*s. If placed in a situation which they perceive to be formal, or addressing a listener of perceived high status, the amount of '*h*-dropping' is likely to decrease. Indeed, women are reported to be more likely to modify their speech than men, although why they are more sensitive to such social variables is less clear.[7] One might even observe the phenomenon of *hypercorrection*, where /h/ starts to appear at the beginning of words where it is not usually found – often words that begin with a vowel, such as *idea* or *envelope*. The point here is that linguistic competence is interlinked with many other areas of cognition.

---

[7]These issues are discussed within the discipline of sociolinguistics. Introductory texts are P. Trudgill, *Sociolinguistics: An Introduction* (Harmondsworth, Penguin, 3rd edn, 1995) and R. A. Hudson, *Sociolinguistics* (Cambridge, Cambridge University Press, 2nd edn, 1996).

Encoding a linguistic message involves a series of decisions regarding language structures and uses, but these decisions are also influenced by external variables such as our social knowledge. There are cognitive disabilities, such as learning disabilities or mental handicap, which impair non-language competences but also have secondary effects on language. Limited social knowledge is one such example.

Linguistic encoding therefore involves pragmatic, semantic, syntactic and phonological processing, plus a series of external constraints on the encoding process. How, we might speculate, are these levels of language represented within the mind? Which comes first? Does the brain first of all 'generate' meanings, in the form of items of vocabulary, then put them into sentences, and then give them phonological shape? Or is a grammatical 'shape' first organized, into which vocabulary items are later placed? There are plainly many possibilities, and a great deal of research has taken place to find evidence which supports one or other of these models of language processing. These questions are addressed by the academic discipline of *psycholinguistics* – a field that bridges psychology and linguistics. The communicative behaviour of speakers is examined for clues as to how the human mind is organizing language. For instance, pausing and hesitation are informative. It is evident that we do not plan our utterances 'a word at a time': if this were the case, our 'mental planning' would be reflected by the way we would hesitate and melodically shape our utterances. There would be a pause after every word – or, at least, the same amount of pause after every word, with only occasional variations due to changes in our attention, tiredness, and so on. But speech is obviously not like that. We do pause and shape our utterances melodically, although these features do not seem to relate to word-sized units, but to larger units of grammar. In particular, the clause (compare p. 45) has emerged as a unit of speech that is more readily identified than any other as being phonologically 'shaped' by such features as pause and intonation. We are much more likely to pause *between* clauses than *within* clauses. And if we do pause within a clause, then again it is not just a matter of chance where the pause will occur: the likelihood is that the pauses will occur between the main constituents of clause structure (between Subject and Verb, and Verb and Object, for example).

Another technique which gives insights into mental processing of language is the study of speech errors. These can be the errors made by normal speakers or errors made by disordered speakers (though one must always be cautious when applying to normal brains the results of research into abnormal brains). The importance of information from speakers with communication disorders is, first, that they make more errors than normal speakers and so provide the researcher with more data with which to work. Second, certain types of language disorder – for example, *aphasia*, a language disorder that occurs after brain damage (see p. 165) – may selectively disrupt components of the language processing system. By detailed study of the errors made by an aphasic speaker, therefore, we can construct a picture of how the damaged components actually operate – insights that are not usually attainable from observations of normal speakers. Studies of speech errors also support the idea that the clause is a significant unit in the planning of speech. Certain types of speech errors, or *slips of the tongue* – those involving a switch around of words or sounds – occur within clauses: they typically do not cross clause boundaries. For instance, the following two examples illustrate, first, a likely tongue-slip, and second, a highly unlikely tongue-slip, happening to the (two-clause) sentence *John caught the ball, and Mary laughed*:

> John *b*aught the *c*all, and Mary laughed
> John *l*aught the ball, and Mary *b*aughed.

Speech errors are just one of the ways in which we can gain information about the way the human mind works, with reference to language. Despite some insights into the complex process of how language operates in the mind, so much is still unknown. Here, as in so many other areas reviewed in this book, there is a strong need for empirical research.[8]

Motor Programming

By the end of the linguistic encoding stage, a message will be fully speci- fied in terms of its sentence, word and sound structure. The next step in the chain is to convert the linguistically encoded message into a form which can be sent to some external receiver. The actual choice of channel (speech or writing) is likely to have already been made, as the choice of transmission modality influences many of the linguistic encoding choices (compare the social pleasantries with which a letter begins, to those that start a conversation). The stage of motor programming takes the linguistic message and converts it into a set of instructions which can be used to command a motor output system, such as the muscles used in speech or writing. The motor program can be conceptualized as the software program which drives the hardware of the vocal organs and their associ- ated nerves, if the output is to be speech. Motor programs are necessary for highly skilled, voluntary movements such as speech. In the event of loss of

---

[8]For more on tongue-slips, see V. Fromkin, *Speech Errors as Linguistic Evidence* (The Hague, Mouton, 1973). General texts on psycholinguistics include: M. Harris and M. Coltheart, *Language Processing in Children and Adults: An Introduction* (London, Routledge & Kegan Paul, 1986); I. Taylor and M. M. Taylor, *Psycholinguistics: Learning and Using Language* (New York, Prentice Hall, 1990).

the software programs – through brain damage or their failure to develop normally – complex movements are disturbed, even though the muscles that implement the motor programs are not weak or paralysed. Volitional movements are particularly impaired; involuntary movements, which require little programming, are relatively unaffected. Hence patients with a motor programming disorder may have no difficulty in chewing or swallowing normally, because these are involuntary or automatic activities. Similarly, such patients may be able to move their lips and tongue to remove crumbs from the lips or from between the lips and the gums, but when they are required to produce a /w/ sound, the motor programmer fails to instruct the muscles to operate. Fine movements required for speech become distorted into grosser movement – instead of pursing the lips, the patient may pull them apart into an exaggerated smile.

Motor Execution and Feedback

Once the message has been programmed, the motor execution system can implement the plan. The motor system is made up of the motor areas of the brain, and nerves which run from the brain down to muscles. In addition, in order to produce smooth and controlled movement, there is a need for sensory *feedback* on the location of a muscle or joint, and its degree and rate of movement. Thus the motor system also requires information to be relayed from the periphery (the muscle) back to the centre (the brain) for well co-ordinated movement. This is particularly important for finely controlled movements of speech and writing.

Feedback

Feedback is another concept that stems originally from information theory and which is of major importance in discussing several kinds of communicative pathology. The term technically refers to the way in which a system allows its output to affect its input. A thermostat is a classic example of the way feedback operates: this device monitors the output of a heating system, turning the system off when it reaches a predetermined level, and turning it on again when it falls below a certain level. The amount of heat which the system puts out is 'fed back' as information into the system, and the system thereby 'told' whether it is functioning efficiently. In the present model, the system we are dealing with is the human being, and here too output affects input. The sensory feedback we have mentioned above, which tells us about the location and amount of stretch of muscles and joints, is termed 'kinaesthetic' feedback. Knowing (at an unconscious level) where our tongues are in our mouths is an important factor in maintaining our clarity of speech. When this information is interfered with, as when we lose sensation following a dental anaesthetic, or obtain novel sensations from a new set of false teeth or other dental appliance, our speech becomes distorted.

Similarly, our ability to write also relies on kinaesthetic feedback, along with visual feedback, from our hand movements and the shapes we make on the page.[9]

The most noticeable way in which we monitor our speech is, however, via the ear: while we speak, we are continually monitoring what we say. At a partly conscious and partly unconscious level, we are aware of what we are saying, and how we are saying it, and can compare this with what we intended to say. When there is a mismatch, we introduce corrections into our speech – correct any slips of the tongue, change the direction of the sentence (perhaps using such phrases as *I mean to say*, or *what I mean is . . .*), and so on. These are examples of conscious self-correction. But at an unconscious level, feedback is continuously in operation, as can be demonstrated by experimentally interfering with the normal course of events. This can be done by delaying the time it takes for the sound of speakers' own voices to be 'fed back' to their own ears. The process is called *delayed auditory feedback*. What happens is that, as speakers talk, their voices are stored for a fraction of a second on a recorder, and then played back to their ears through headphones, sufficiently loudly that it drowns out, or *masks*, what they are currently saying. If the delay is of the order of one-fifth to one-tenth of a second, the effect can be remarkable: speakers may begin to slur their voice and stutter in quite dramatic ways, and after a while may become so unconfident that they stop speaking altogether. Evidently, the delay between the time it takes for the brain to initiate the right sequence of sounds and to interpret the feedback has upset a very delicate balance of operation. The experiment demonstrates our reliance on auditory feedback in normal everyday speech.

One theory regarding the cause of stuttering behaviour (p. 193) suggests that some stutterers have inherent delays in their auditory feedback loop. A form of treatment for stuttering, which stems from this theory, is to mask the sound of the stutterer's own voice with a burst of white noise. The masking noise is triggered by a microphone attached to the stutterer's neck. When this picks up the stutterer's speech, the white noise is activated, so drowning out the sound of the voice as they speak. This eliminates all auditory feedback, whether or not it is delayed. As soon as the stutterer stops speaking, the masking stops, enabling the person to listen to the contributions of other participants in the conversation. This rather drastic treatment is, however, successful with only a small proportion of stutterers, which suggests that not all suffer from a problem in delayed auditory feedback, and that this disorder may stem from a variety of sources.

A second form of auditory feedback which operates in speech arises from the fact that we hear our own voices in two different ways. We hear

---

[9]For more on feedback, see R. Schmidt, *Motor Control and Learning* (Illinois, Champaign, 1988), Chapter 6.

ourselves and other speakers through vibrations in the air (*air conduction*), but we can also detect vibrations through the bones and tissues of the skull (*bone conduction*) (Figure 3.3). In fact we hear most of our own voice through this means, and not through the air: this is why we are usually surprised when we hear our voices on a tape-recorder for the first time – we may not recognize ourselves, or we may dislike this 'squeaky' voice. As bone vibrates at a slower rate than air particles, our perception of the pitch of our voice may differ from that of our listeners, who hear us very largely through air conduction.

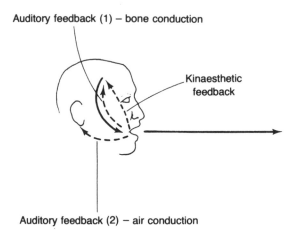

Figure 3.3 Feedback in speech

Speech is produced, however, at a very fast rate (in conversational speech, five syllables can be produced in a second). It is therefore unlikely that feedback has an important role in the moment-to-moment control of speech movements, as there is simply insufficient time for information from the periphery to reach the brain and be utilized in movement control. Feedback is likely to be important in the learning of movements, hence individuals with profound hearing impairments from early in life have considerable difficulty in acquiring fully normal speech patterns. Feedback may also be important in determining the general 'settings' for speech such as loudness level, and prolonged loss of feedback, whether auditory or kinaesthetic, may result in gradual loss of movement accuracy.

In recent years, the term 'feedback' has also come to be used in a looser, extended sense, which ought to be kept clearly distinct from the discussion so far. Here it refers to the way in which we monitor *other* people, as opposed to ourselves. It is plain that while we are talking to someone, we are constantly obtaining information from them as to how we are doing – whether our message is getting across, whether it is being misunderstood, objected to, and so on. The main means involved is our observation of the listener's face, but a very important factor is the way in which we tune in to how our listener verbally acknowledges the success of our message. Listen to a conversation, and you will notice that it does not consist of a sequence of monologues: person A speaks and then B and then A, and so on. While any one person is speaking, speech is punctuated by an accompaniment of noise from the listener – a sequence of words which express such notions as agreement, 'I'm listening', 'carry on', and the like (*mhm, m, yes, sure, uh-uh* etc.). These become particularly crucial when one speaker cannot see the other (as in a telephone conversation, where to withhold these noises will soon elicit an enquiry from the person speaking as to whether you are still there!). But they are an important feature of all conversational situations – and one, incidentally, which some individuals with linguistic disabilities find difficult to maintain or acquire.

Speech production

The motor and sensory systems involved in communication differ, depending on the nature of the output: whether it is speech, writing, signing or non-verbal communication. Speech is produced by the integrated functioning of three systems: *respiration, phonation* and *articulation*. The structure of each of these component systems and their function in speech will be considered in detail in Chapter 4, and we present only a brief overview here. The *respiratory* system provides the power source for speech. The movements of muscles inside the chest force air either into or out of the lungs. The *phonatory* component of speech involves the action of the larynx. If you place your fingers lightly around the Adam's apple in your neck and make a /z/ sound, you should feel a vibration beneath your finger tips. Here you are feeling the action of the *vocal folds*, or *vocal cords*, which are vibrating at a very rapid rate inside the larynx. Contrast this to the sensations in your fingers when you make the sound /s/. You should feel nothing. These two states of the vocal folds – vibrating and not vibrating – produce two classes of sounds: voiced sounds (produced with vibration) and voiceless sounds (produced with no vibration). The action of the vocal folds is also impor-tant in the control of pitch, loudness and several tones of voice. Changes in the length of the vocal folds alter the frequency of vibration. Tense vocal folds vibrate more quickly, producing high-pitched sound; lax folds vibrate more slowly, producing lower-pitched sound.

The *articulatory* component in speech production involves various structures within the mouth, including the tongue, lips, palate and teeth. The airstream, which has been set in motion by the action of the lungs and chest muscles, and which may or may not have vibration super-imposed on it by the action of the larynx, is shaped by the various articulatory structures to produce different sounds. If you compare the sounds /d/ (as in *dog*), /n/ (as in *nine*), and /g/ (as in *go*), you will notice that two of them (/d–n/) are made with a similar tongue position, but they differ in that for /n/ the airflow is directed down the nose by the action of the palate (try producing /n/ with your fingers pinching your nostrils), whilst with /d/ the palate is raised, thus directing the airstream through the mouth. The /d–g/ pair differ in their tongue position, rather than the route of the airflow through the mouth or nose. If you contrast them, you will feel that the /g/ sound is made by the tongue moving to the back of the mouth, while in /d/ it touches the bony ridge just behind your teeth. You may by now begin to appreciate the complexity of speech. It requires very finely controlled movements and integration of a number of component systems, and all this must occur within a very short time-frame.

Other muscle systems are involved in writing, signing and non-verbal communication. Writing and signing require fine control of finger movements, but also demand postural changes in the torso, and control of the arm and hand. The movements involved in non-verbal communication are many and varied, depending on the type of non-verbal communication which is being considered. Posture, gesture, facial expression and eye contact all involve different muscle systems.

Transmission

The transmission stage of the communication chain is the sending of the message through some medium to another human being. In the case of speech, the medium of transmission is air; vibrations produced by the movement of the vocal organs are translated into the molecular movement of air particles, which form sound waves. In more complex communication situations, such as those involving telephone or radio, the sound waves are further encoded into electrical signals and transmitted using the devices available; but these aspects of the process are not really germane to the present volume. Communication problems may occur during the transmission stage, but generally these arise from circumstances outside the speaker – for instance, high noise levels in the environment (*ambient noise*), which mask the speech sound waves. Another possibility is transmission across a large physical space, where the sound wave decays and cannot reach the intended recipient. There can be an interaction with speakers' abilities. If, for example, speakers have voice or respiratory disorders and so are unable to increase the volume of their voice, then communication may fail – such as in situations where there is a higher-than-usual level of ambient noise, or where communication is required over larger spaces than those involved in a one-to-one conversation. This problem has often been noted in teachers, for example, who are required to project their voice to the back of a classroom.

If modes of communication other than speech are used by the sender, then the medium of transmission will differ. In the case of writing, visible marks have to be made on a surface of some kind – a graphic step in the chain. In the case of signing, configurations of hands, arms and face are set up and transmitted purely through the medium of light – a wholly visual step in the chain. Just as noise or physical distance may impair the efficiency of transmission of speech, so other variables may affect the efficiency of transmission of written or signed messages; for example, it is impossible to transmit a signed message through barriers that are opaque – like walls.

Reception

Whatever the medium of transmission, there comes a point where, if communication is to take place, the message has to be picked up by another human being. Reception of the message is the first stage in the decoding process. The sensory organ which registers the incoming message, and the pathway which is used to relay this information to the centre (the brain), vary in relation to the modality of communication that is used. The eye and visual pathways receive and relay incoming visual information to the brain, as in the case of written, signed and non-verbal communication. The ear and auditory pathways receive and relay speech. The loss of these sensory receptors and their pathways, as in hearing and visual impairment, will clearly have profound implications for the reception of messages. If, however, other processing routes are operative – for example, the ability to register tactile information in the case of individuals with visual impairments – alternative means can be found of coding linguistic messages, which will permit information to be transmitted to the brain for decoding.

Perception and Recognition

At this step in the communication chain, information is received by the brain and the decoding of the incoming information begins. The perception phase involves the identification of the physical characteristics of the incoming message – for example, is an input *bill* or *pill*? At this stage, the meaning of the input is not accessed, but solely the acoustic or visual characteristics of incoming stimuli, including the identity of the units and their sequence. Once these have been established, the perceived stimulus is matched up to information stored in memory to see if it is an instance of an input that has previously been experienced – the recognition phase.

The first stage in this process might be to decide whether the input is linguistic or not. The word *dog* would be fed into a linguistic processing and decoding system, whilst the sound of a dog barking would be processed by a different memory store dealing with non-linguistic auditory inputs. If the input is the word *dog*, and the first stage of decoding is successful, its corresponding entry in memory will be activated. At this point the input has been recognized. If you are presented with a series of 'words', some of which are real words and others that are non-words, and you are asked to categorize them as either real or nonsense words (a task that is called *lexical decision*), you are being asked to decide if the form has been encountered previously and stored in memory. Hence, whereas you have entries for *pill, date*, and *paper*, you do not possess them for *lilp, tade*, or *repap*. It is possible to establish that this process of recognition is independent of accessing the meaning of the word, as most of us have had the experience of knowing that a word is a word in our language – maybe we have read it in textbooks – but we do not know what it means and have not yet got round to looking it up in the dictionary. *Iconoclast* or *telemetry* might be words that fall into this category.

This process of identifying the characteristics of the input and matching it up to stored knowledge may be achieved by the combined action of two routes. A *bottom-up* route starts with the lowest level of analysis and works upwards to higher levels of analysis – as in a letter-by-letter or word-by-word decoding strategy. This kind of processing is very accurate, but has the disadvantage of being very slow. The alternative strategy, a *top-down* route, is a much quicker way of processing information, but is potentially less accurate. A top-down process uses higher-order information, and attempts to predict or guess the incoming information. If we are presented with the message *The caterpillar turned into a beautiful —*, it is relatively easy to guess the final word, using the meaning of *caterpillar* and *turned into*, and our knowledge of the world – caterpillars usually turn into butterflies and not dinosaurs. Similarly, if we read or hear *caterpillar*, we do not need to wait until the end of the word before we can match the fragment (e.g. *caterpi—*) to a stored entry. It seems that a great deal of our language processing combines a scan of the input (bottom-up) and then a rapid guess as to its likely identity (top-down). In the case of language, knowledge of context – what is likely to be said or to happen in a particular situation – may help us to predict what is being said.

It is through such contextual knowledge, and also through our ability to handle non-verbal information, that we can gain some understanding of communicative situations when we are addressed in a foreign language, even though we are unable to recognize or decode many of the words. We know conversations start with greetings, and so can return them with smiles and nods. We can read the non-verbal information which suggests friendliness or hostility. Often we can detect the features of voice which suggest humour or irony. In a similar way, individuals with often quite severe problems in understanding language can read the context and various non-verbal and voice quality cues in a situation, in order to gain some understanding of what is being said to them. One meets adults who have considerable language processing problems following brain damage, but who are still able to laugh at verbal jokes. When their language comprehension is formally tested, however, their ability to understand even single words may be radically impaired. If these linguistically-impaired individuals are placed in a context where there is a high degree of routine – in particular, institutional settings such as hospitals – they often appear to have excellent understanding of language. Their family, friends and even professional carers may be misled as to their level of ability, and may disagree with the language pathologist when they are told that their family member has language comprehension problems. The clinician has to explain very carefully that the patient does have some understanding of communicative situations, but when comprehension requires decoding of language, then there will be difficulties. This issue can assume considerable importance when patients are required to make important decisions on the basis of understanding what is being discussed with them – for example, deciding to sell a home and go into long-term institutional care, or giving someone power of attorney over their affairs.

Language Decoding

This heading is perhaps somewhat arbitrary, because in the perception and recognition phase some decoding – particularly of phonological information – has already occurred. At this stage, the meaning of the message is derived. This meaning is not just the sum of the word meanings: *The bird ate the snake* and *The snake ate the bird* describe very different events, and information from sentence structure – whether *bird* is acting as a Subject or an Object – has to be decoded as well as the meaning of the word units. Furthermore, any grammatical affixes attached to the words need to be decoded – for example, information on tense attached to verbs, or number information (singular or plural) on nouns. The linguistic decoding stage therefore involves the interpretation of semantic, syntactic and morphological information. And just as top-down processing can be used at the recognition stage, it may also be used to speed up linguistic decoding. This is why individuals with difficulties in grammatical or semantic decoding may none the less display apparently good language comprehension abilities.

The complexity of the situation may be illustrated as follows. Imagine we are investigating someone's ability to decode sentences, and wish to give them an instruction of the type *Put the spoon in the cup*. We have placed a series of objects in front of the patient, and explained and demonstrated the task we wish to be completed. We have presented commands such as *Put the key in the box* to the patient, and have ourselves performed the corresponding action to avoid any misunderstanding of the task. We then give the instruction *Put the spoon in the cup* and the patient follows the command accurately. What can we claim on the basis of the patient's performance? How much information does the patient need to decode to respond correctly to this command?

It is surprisingly difficult to answer this question. We might first count the number of words in the command (six) and suggest that this is the number of units that have to be interpreted. But we might then decide that not all are essential in performing the command: perhaps we can eliminate *the* and still successfully complete the task (leaving *Put spoon in cup* – four units to decode). We might remember the suggestion above that decoding utterances is not just about understanding word meanings, but also about syntactic structure. Thus the patient needs to understand that the sentence has a command/imperative structure ('Put X in Y'), that the order of the units (*spoon* and *cup*) is significant, and that the preposition *in* introduces the phrase *in the cup*. All of these features would suggest that, in order to respond to this command, the patient must have considerable linguistic processing ability.

But let us re-examine this assumption. First of all, consider the issue of decoding the imperative structure of the command. If we have already demonstrated to the patient the activity required, by relocating a trial set of objects on the table, and if the patient has closely observed our behaviour, then the syntactic information may well now be redundant. Second, we may question the number of units that require semantic decoding. We have already reduced this to four, but in view of the above comment, does the patient have to decode *put*? We have already put a variety of objects in a variety of locations, and so the patient may assume that any commands will involve the relocation of objects. It may be that the patient is processing only three units, still in a strict sequence: *spoon in cup*. Next consider the preposition *in*, and consider, from our knowledge of the world, what we would do if we were presented with a spoon and a cup and were asked to place them in some spatial alignment. From our knowledge of the way in which spoons normally relate to cups, we are likely to place the spoon inside the cup. Perhaps then only two units are being processed, still in a strict sequence: *spoon cup*. We may want to argue further that even the sequential information is unimportant, because our knowledge of the world tells us already how these two objects relate to each other; but the point should by now be clear – the testing of language comprehension is an exceedingly complex task, and it is difficult to disentangle patients' language-decoding abilities from their knowledge of the context of the utterance (the demonstration of the task) and of how objects are used in the world.

Message Interpretation

The final stage of the communication chain is perhaps self-evident from the discussion of linguistic decoding. At this point the information gained from linguistic decoding is integrated with other information available to the listener. This could include information regarding the context in which the communication takes place, or broader knowledge of the world. It can also involve the interpretation of non-verbal communication and voice quality information. Imagine a situation where we have out-stayed our welcome at a party; it is two o'clock in the morning, and our hosts have been yawning and looking at their watches for the last half-hour. As we make ready to depart, we are asked *Must you leave so soon?* We now have a great deal of information to synthesize, some of it conflicting, in order to interpret this utterance. The features of voice quality are likely to be important in our ultimate interpretation – was it said ironically or not? Our decoding of the speaker's intent behind the utterance – a conventional politeness, a sincere invitation, or a rebuke – relies on a subtle synthesis of several kinds of information, some of which is linguistic, some of which is not.

It is of course possible that we shall fail to decode the speaker's intentions satisfactorily. A listener's interpretation of a message may be quite different from that intended by the speaker. This may be because listeners misinterpret an aspect of the message, or because their understanding of the context, or their knowledge of the participants or the topic, differs from that of the speaker. Because of the lack of shared assumptions, the derived listener meaning may be very different from the intended speaker meaning.

The point of message interpretation constitutes the destination of the signal, in the sense that it is here that the decoding process comes to an end, and the signal's meaning is interpreted. If all has gone well, the meaning that was in the mind of the first human being will have effectively been conveyed to the mind of the second. If it has not – if, that is, a wrong or misleading message has been conveyed, or no message at all – then the task facing the communications analyst is to find out why. Was the failure due to a breakdown in the communication chain at one or more points? If so, which? And what can be done about it? We are now plainly within the subject matter of this book.

But before we proceed to look at these steps in communication in terms of their physical basis and their potential disruption, a few cautionary remarks are in order. The model in Figure 3.2 may seem the obvious way of investigating the communication process, but we must not forget that it is only a model, illuminating certain aspects of reality and distorting others. For example, the model suggests clear dividing lines between the various subcomponent processes, but in reality these steps shade into one another. For instance, it is very difficult to identify sharp distinctions between the pre-linguistic, ideational stage and the language, encoding stage. The model is a highly abstract representation. Its usefulness can be judged by the extent to which it imposes order or an overall structure on the field of communication disorders, and by the extent to which it produces testable hypotheses. For example, when we come to examine the range of communication disorders, do we find disabilities which correspond to the stages proposed by the model? The reader therefore needs to be aware of some of the limitations of this model and to appreciate where there is need for expansion.

Limitations of the Model

The model of the communication chain, in addition to containing some simplifications, also has some serious limitations. These limitations stem from the difficulty of fitting into a first-stage model all the detail that is necessary to account for the complexities of human communication. In fact, inclusion of such detail would diminish the usefulness of the model in giving us a broad overview of the field. An awareness of the more obvious limitations of the model, however, will permit understanding of the type of information that needs to be included in subsequent and more detailed characterizations. Two major issues will be examined here. First, there is the fact that this model is a *macro-model*: that is, within the various stages of the communication chain it gives little detail about the type of processes operating within each level. Second, it focuses on the stages involved in sending and receiving messages, but neglects the other issues that were discussed under the holistic approach in Chapter 1.

Macro-model

The model outlines a series of stages in the process of sending and receiving messages. However, the stages that have been identified have been only sketchily drawn. This is partly due to the state of our knowledge; in some areas the processes involved are as yet unclear. In others, though, we do have more detailed theories or descriptions about the processes involved. One such example is of *word finding*, or *lexical retrieval*, which is part of the stage of linguistic encoding. If we examine this task in more detail, we can illustrate the way a macro-model can be progressively refined, resulting in a more specific and testable *micro-model*.

The use of speech error data, whether from normal or linguistically disabled speakers, has already been discussed in terms of its value in identifying how the human mind processes language (p. 72). In describing the stages involved in word retrieval, let us start with three different types of speech error. All the errors were made by supposedly normal speakers.

1. The speaker is looking for the washing-up *sponge* and says 'Where is the *cushion*?'.
   (Error: sponge → cushion)

2. The speaker is reporting on a *professional* group's campaign for higher salaries and says 'All members of the *procession* will be balloted'.
   (Error: profession → procession)

3. A famous error from the Oxford don, Dr William Spooner, who gave his name to 'spoonerisms': intending to say 'God bless the *dear* old *queen*', he is said to have produced 'God bless the *queer* old *dean*'.
   (Error: transposition of the initial sounds of *dear* (/d/) and *queen* (/kw/))

What do these errors tell us about the process of word finding? The first thing to note is that they are very different *kinds* of error. In (1) we can see that there is a meaning-based relationship between the target word (*sponge*) and the error (*cushion*). Both are soft materials, often with an identical physical structure, but they differ in their function – the sponge is used for washing, the cushion for sitting on. When we examine (2), we can observe no similarity in meaning, but a similarity in form, or structure. This target-error pair have the same number of syllables, identical initial and final syllables, and the same stress pattern; they differ only minimally in the structure of the middle syllable. By contrast, there is no obvious formal or structural similarity in the *sponge–cushion* pair.

The existence of such qualitatively different errors suggests that there are different stages involved in the process of word retrieval, and that failure at these stages results in the different types of error. There seem to be two distinct phases in the lexical retrieval process: one involves retrieval of a meaning representation, and the other involves access to a particular word form. Errors are possible at either stage: the *sponge–cushion* pair suggests access to a related but incorrect meaning representation, whilst the *profession–procession* pair indicates access to a related but incorrect word form. We would predict that, if normal speakers can make such errors, similar errors (although maybe more frequent) will be identified in the speech of people with language disorders. And indeed this is what we find when we analyse the errors made by *aphasic* speakers – that is, speakers who have suffered brain damage which has affected their ability to encode and decode linguistic messages (p. 165).

The third type of speech error is of a very different order to the meaning-based and form-based errors described above. In this example, both meaning-based and form-based retrieval stages have occurred successfully; but subsequent to this retrieval, switches between the initial sounds of *dear* and *queer* have taken place. Notice the importance of the clause-sized unit here: the changes have taken place within the clause boundary, and not across a clause boundary (p. 73). This error would suggest that the clause is placed in some short-term memory store, and that, while in this store, actual sounds are allocated to their correct slot in the utterance. Errors can occur and sounds can be misplaced, thus producing a spoonerism. Again, if we look in language pathology data for this pattern of error, we will find many instances of patients who switch sounds in this way.

These errors give considerable insight into the processes involved in word retrieval and the assembly of a message before it is transmitted. Speakers have to locate the correct meaning they wish to convey – in the case of (1), is it to be a soft, absorbent substance for sitting on or for use in washing? Once the correct meaning has been accessed, it has to be given a corresponding word form. (If we look at how entries in a dictionary are organized we see the same kind of organization, but in reverse. A dictionary lists a word form and then gives a definition – a semantic representation of that form. In encoding speech, it is the semantic information which is first located, and subsequently linked to a word form – more like the organization of entries that can be found in a thesaurus.) Once the word selection process is complete, a unit the size of a clause is assembled in a memory store, and all the appropriate sounds are allocated to their appropriate positions. Once this phase is complete, the linguistically specified message would be passed on to the next stage in the communication chain, the motor programmer (p. 73). We begin now to see the type of detail that is required if our model of the communication chain is to be a detailed and specific micro-model.

Holism

In Chapter 1 we discussed the importance of a holistic approach to communicative disability. A criticism that a language pathologist might make of the communication chain model is that it fails to take this broader perspective into account. In particular, it proves difficult to introduce a cognitive perspective into the model. Although in previous chapters we have emphasized that language and communication do not operate in isolation from other cognitive abilities such as memory and attention, the model presents the act of communication in isolation from these abilities (except insofar as they are implicit in the pre-linguistic stage). There are hints at the importance of other knowledge bases in linguistic encoding and decoding – for example, social knowledge and knowledge of objects in the world – but these are not made explicit. We can see this limitation of the model if we look briefly at the way attention is essential for communicative functioning, and thus needs to be incorporated at various points within the communication chain.

Attention is an ability which allows us to select stimuli from the mass of information that is constantly bombarding us. We can 'lock on' to the selected information and ignore distracting background information. We can decide to switch our attention when a new and more interesting piece of information presents itself. Without this ability to select, focus, and switch our attention when necessary, communicative functioning becomes difficult. Some patients would be unable to ignore background information, so making them highly distractible; others would remain 'locked on' to a piece of information, and fail to notice a new and important stimulus – for example, they might be talking obsessively about a topic, and failing to see that their listeners are becoming bored and uneasy. Virtually all stages of the communication chain require the ability to control attention to the information which is currently being processed. This is true of message encoding as well as decoding. In encoding, it is necessary to hold on to the idea that is to be communicated, and not be distracted by irrelevant stimuli – whether they be internal (e.g. other ideas) or external (e.g. somebody new walking into the room). In decoding, the receiver must attend to the incoming stimulus in order to process it and derive its meaning. However, the model of the communication chain as it now stands does not incorporate such interactions. It is thus important that the reader is aware of them, and attempts to place the model in a broader cognitive framework.

Another criticism, from the holistic point of view, is that the model does not take into account the broader context in which individuals find themselves. It focuses only on the efficiency of people as senders and/or receivers of messages. It does not deal with what patients feel about their abilities, or the role of carers in either facilitating or inhibiting communication. Apart from passing mention of the way environmental conditions can affect the efficiency of transmission of messages, there is little consideration of how different communicative environments may influence communication and its development. Such a perspective is critical, particularly when dealing with disorders of language acquisition. When a clinician meets children who are slow to learn language, the initial aim of assessment is to identify whether such children have the necessary cognitive, auditory, phonetic and social prerequisites to acquire language. In the event of children proving adequate on all these aspects, the clinician may then direct attention to the learning environment, and ask if such children receive adequate stimulation appropriate to their level of ability and whether there are sufficient opportunities for each child to learn and practise new behaviours. Where the children's environment is found to be inadequate, the clinician might intervene to provide more opportunities for language learning within the environment – the therapeutic intervention being directed at parents and other carers, rather than directly at the children. All these factors are vital for that full clinical perspective which the communication chain model cannot provide.

The limitations of the communication chain model are several, but they are far outweighed in our view by its strengths. It enables us to recognize certain fundamental factors which will provide the basis for a classification of communication disorders (Chapter 5), and suggests a way in which these factors might be related. It gives us an overview of a large part of our field of enquiry, and suggests a way in which our medical and behavioural modes of knowing might be integrated. It also makes us broaden our perspectives of analysis, by making us relate the findings of the different disciplines of study involved (anatomy, physiology, phonetics etc.), and thus helping us get to grips with the terminological, methodological and conceptual differences which separate these disciplines.

Revision Questions

1. What are the benefits and dangers of developing and using models in scientific inquiry?
2. What are the stages involved in producing a linguistic message?
3. What are the stages in understanding a linguistic message?
4. What are the most obvious limitations of the model of the communication chain?

Tutorial Activities

1. Where should modifications be made in the model of the communication chain in order to account for:
   (a) reading and writing;
   (b) aspects of non-verbal communication such as facial expression, arm and hand gesture, and posture?
2. Over a period of a week, record all instances of speech errors that you hear. These can be errors made by yourself, family and friends, and lecturers. Identify the level of language organization that is affected in each error – for example, can you find instances of syntactic and morphological errors, word retrieval errors (meaning-based and form-based errors), or errors involving changes in the sound structure of words? Record the conditions in which the speaker made the error – for instance, were they concentrating on what they were saying or were they distracted? tired or alert? relaxed or nervous? rushed or unhurried? Are you able to identify a set of conditions which make speech errors more likely to occur?
3. Testing a patient's language comprehension ability is a complex undertaking. In addition to the linguistic information presented to the patient, there is other non-language information which may assist him or her in decoding the meaning of the message. The ability to use non-linguistic information to decode linguistic messages is of great significance, as it may mean that the patient with severe language comprehension problems can still gain some understanding of communicative events. The language pathologist may, however, want to

identify the exact level of ability in decoding specifically linguistic information. This requires careful control of the stimulus item (the word or sentence presented to the patient for decoding) and the distractor items present (other alternatives presented to the patient). If, for instance, clinicians wish to discover if patients understand single words, they might present them with a target word (e.g. *black*) in the presence of a number of distractors. These distractors may be unrelated both in form and meaning to the target (e.g. *bottle, fat, window*) or related either in form (*sack, tack*) or in meaning (*white, grey*). Consider the following:

(a) Is a test that uses related or unrelated distractors likely to be more sensitive to comprehension problems?

(b) What is the significance of the patient consistently selecting one type of related distractor?

(c) What non-linguistic clues to the answer to the test could possibly 'leak' from the examiner, which might allow the patient to complete the test correctly?

(d) If you wished to set up a test of the patient's ability to understand Subject–Verb–Object sentences (e.g. *The lady is drinking coffee*), what distractor items would you select for your stimulus sentence?

Chapter 4
The Physical Basis of the Communication Chain

The communication chain has, so far, been described as a process containing a number of behavioural steps. In this chapter, we look at the physical bases of this process – that is, at the anatomical structures which underlie the behaviour, and at their physiological function. We shall discover that the amount we know varies between the stages within the chain. More is known about the structures involved in motor execution and message reception than about those underlying the end-points of the chain – language encoding and decoding, and the pre-linguistic formulation of messages and their ultimate interpretation. The organ which controls all of the stages of the communication chain, and which is fundamental in the key stages of message formulation, encoding and decoding, is the human brain. It is with this structure that we shall begin, and later end, our discussion of the physical basis of the communication chain. The relevant disciplines are *neuroanatomy* and *neurophysiology*, from which the following perspective derives.[1]

The Brain

If the human brain is compared to the brains of other species, there are two major differences that will be noted. First of all, the size of the human brain is relatively large. This statement is perhaps obvious if one were to compare a mouse brain to a human brain; but even if brain size is considered in relation to body size, the human brain is still comparatively large. In addition to differences in size, the human brain differs from the mouse brain in shape. In particular, the *cerebrum* of the human brain is much larger (Figure 4.1). This enlargement is especially evident in the front lobes of the brain. This difference in human brain size and structure is the physical basis of the many behaviours – for example, language – which differentiate humans from other species. The first stage in our consideration of the physical basis to communication is to

---

[1]An introductory account can be found in S. Greenfield, *The Human Brain: a Guided Tour* (London, Weidenfeld & Nicolson, 1997).

explore the human brain. We can do this on both a macro- and micro-level. At a macro-level we can see how the brain can be divided into a number of component structures – for example, its hemispheres and lobes. We can then go on to look at its micro-structure, investigating the brain at the level of the cell. Just as the brain can be divided into different structures, so too can brain cells, which belong to different families, and vary greatly in structure. We shall begin our consideration of the brain at the level of its macro-structure.

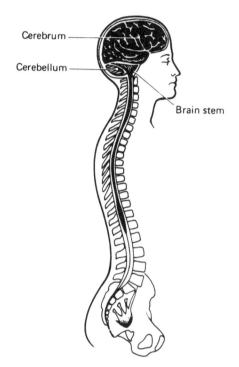

Cerebrum

Cerebellum

Brain stem

Figure 4.1 The brain and spinal cord

The network of connections whereby signals can be transmitted from one part of the body to another is known as the *nervous system*. This system is subdivided into the central nervous system (CNS) and the peripheral nervous system (PNS).

Central nervous system

The CNS consists of the brain, the spinal cord which connects to it, and their associated membranes and fluids. The system is immensely complex, and its potential for processing information needs to be appreciated. It contains billions of nerve cells, some of which relay information to and from connections with the peripheral nervous system, others of which transfer information within the central nervous system. The brain is contained within the skull, or *cranium*, whilst the spinal cord is the elongated tube which runs for some 45 cm within the vertebrae of the spine. The relationship of the brain to the spinal cord is illustrated in Figure 4.1.

Peripheral nervous system

As its name suggests, this system of nerves links the CNS with the rest of the body. Sensory information is relayed from a variety of *receptors* (e.g. touch, taste, kinaesthetics, pain) to the junction with the CNS. In addition, instructions from the central system are transferred to nerves for transmission to the appropriate *effectors*, e.g. a muscle. Peripheral nerves which leave the CNS from the spinal cord are known as *spinal nerves*. There are 31 pairs of these nerves – each pair leaving the spinal cord at the level of each vertebra. A second set of peripheral nerves leave the CNS from within the cranium and are attached directly to the brain. These are called *cranial nerves*. There are 12 paired cranial nerves, and they are essential for the control of speech, and for relaying information from the ear back to the brain.

We now need to proceed to a more detailed study of the brain, because in Chapter 5 we shall be referring to several categories of disability that are the result of damage to specific brain areas. But it will be useful, first, to introduce a terminological preliminary. In order to describe any area of human anatomy, it is necessary to use a terminology about which there is universal agreement, otherwise there would be ambiguity in knowing which specific part of the brain, for example, was being referred to. What would 'on the left side' mean, for instance? 'Left', from the point of view of the observer, or of the person whose brain it is? To avoid such problems, it is conventional to see the human body as capable of being divided along various lines, or *planes*. Thus, we can imagine a line vertically dividing the front part of the body from the back part, as in Figure 4.2a: this is known as the *coronal* or *frontal* plane; and it divides the body into *anterior* or *ventral* (i.e. front) and *posterior* or *dorsal* (i.e. back) parts. Second, we can imagine the body being divided vertically into left and right sides, as in Figure 4.2b: this is known as the *sagittal* plane; and if the division has been made exactly in the middle (in the *midline* or *median*), it is referred to as the *medial sagittal* plane. *Lateral* refers to a plane further away from the midline; *medial* to a plane closer to the midline. The terms 'left' and 'right' are always used from the point of view of the body being described, and not as from the observer. Third, we can imagine a line dividing the body horizontally, at right angles to its vertical axis, as in Figure 4.2c: this is referred to as a *transverse* or horizontal plane. Fourth, relative position on the vertical axis is referred to using the terms *superior* (for higher up) and *inferior* (for lower down). Fifth, a view of the body from underneath, looking upwards, is referred to as a *basal* view: see Figure 4.2d. Lastly, a feature further away from a point of origin is said to be *distal*; one nearer to the point is *proximal*.

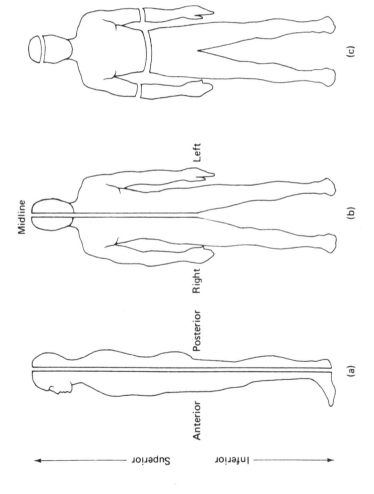

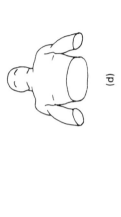

Figure 4.2 Anatomical planes: (a) coronal; (b) sagittal; (c) transverse; (d) basal

Using this terminology, we can now begin to identify those areas of the brain that are of particular importance for the study of linguistic disability. A general point to be made, first of all, is that the brain is not a single, undifferentiated structure, but contains several anatomically distinct regions. The largest part of the brain is known as the *cerebrum* (Figure 4.1). Its most noticeable feature is the way it is divided sagittally into two great lobes of similar size, the *cerebral hemispheres*. There is, accordingly, a *left hemisphere* and a *right hemisphere*, the differential function of which we shall discuss below. *Unilateral* refers to one of these hemispheres alone, *bilateral* to both hemispheres; *contralateral* to the opposite side of the body from a particular hemisphere. Beneath the hemispheres is a thumb-sized midline structure, the *brain stem*, which connects the two hemispheres to the spinal cord. It is described as having three parts: the *midbrain* (from which the hemispheres spring), the *pons* and the *medulla oblongata*, which continues below as the spinal cord. Arising dorsally from the pons is another major structure, the *cerebellum*, which is responsible for the maintenance of body posture and the smooth co-ordination of all movements, including walking and speaking. Buried deep within the hemispheres are further masses of nerve tissue, the *basal ganglia* (which help to control movement), the *limbic system* (which consists of structures such as the *hippocampus* and *amygdala*, important for memory) and the *thalamus* (which relays information to and from the *cortex*, and helps to analyse sensory information). The relationship between the hemispheres is shown from above in Figure 4.3a, laterally in Figure 4.3b, and that between the other structures is shown in medial sagittal section in Figure 4.3c.

Most research relevant to language processing has focused on the structure and function of the cerebrum, and in particular on its surface layer of grey matter (grey, because the cell bodies of the cerebral neurons are concentrated here) known as the cerebral *cortex*.[2] The reason for this emphasis is that the cortex is the part of the brain which seems to be primarily involved in the decoding of information from the senses and in the control of voluntary movement and intellectual functions. It is also the area of the brain most amenable to direct observation and investigation. It contains about 10 billion cells and some 200 million fibre processes. Beneath the cortex is a body of white matter, which transmits signals between cortex and brain stem, and from one area of the cortex to another. The most noticeable feature of the cortex is its lack of a smooth surface: what has happened is that, during its course of development (from between the third and fourth months of life in the womb) the surface of the brain has folded in upon itself along certain

---

[2]Different areas of the cortex may be distinguished, such as the sensory cortex or the visual cortex (p. 105). If several cortical areas are being referred to, the plural form *cortices* may be used.

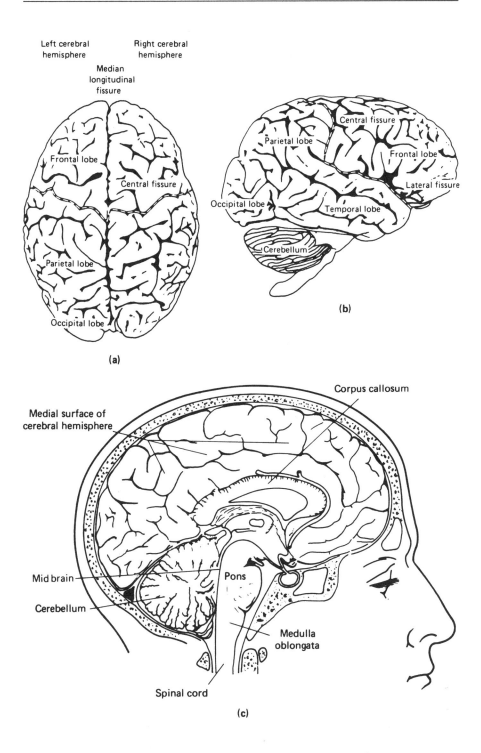

Figure 4.3 (a) The brain from above; (b) right lateral view; (c) relationship between the main brain structures

genetically predetermined lines. A large area of cortical tissue is thus packed into a relatively small anatomical space. The various folds that have been produced are known as *convolutions* or *gyri* (singular: *gyrus*). The furrows on either side of the gyri are known as *sulci* (singular: *sulcus*). Each has a precise anatomical designation, but for present purposes we need concern ourselves only with the most dominant features, and those which are most relevant for language.

The brain is most commonly represented diagrammatically from above and laterally. The former view has been given in Figure 4.3a; a lateral view (left lateral) is given in Figure 4.4. The dominant feature of the former view is the deep fissure, known as the *median longitudinal fissure*, which separates the hemispheres. It does not, however, extend the whole way down through the cerebrum; the two hemispheres are in fact joined deep within the cerebrum by a thick bundle of nerve fibres, known as the *corpus callosum* (see Figure 4.3c) the means whereby information from one hemisphere can be transmitted to the other. The dominant features of the lateral view are also fissures, or sulci:[3] the *central sulcus*, *fissure of Rolando*, or *Rolandic fissure* (named after the Italian anatomist, Luigi Rolando (1733–1831)), and the *lateral sulcus*, or *Sylvian fissure* (after the Flemish anatomist, François de la Boë Sylvius (1614–1672)). These fissures are of particular importance, because they are used as the primary

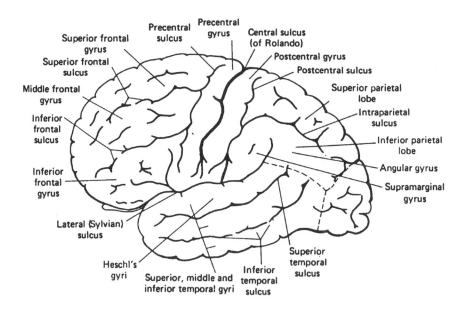

Figure 4.4 Superolateral surface of cerebral hemisphere

---

[3]'Sulcus' is the more general term. Originally, the difference was that a sulcus was a relatively shallow furrow in the surface of the hemisphere, whereas a fissure was much deeper.

anatomical basis for dividing the brain up into different major areas or *lobes*. Four such lobes are universally recognized, within each hemisphere, based on the topographical relation of these areas to the skull (the temporal lobe corresponds to the temporal bone, etc.):

1. The *frontal* lobe – from the front of the brain above the Sylvian fissure and extending as far back as the fissure of Rolando. The frontal lobe is crossed by three main sulci (superior, inferior and precentral), and four main gyri (superior, middle, inferior and precentral).
2. The *temporal* lobe – the area beneath the Sylvian fissure, extending posteriorly until the junction with the occipital lobe. It is crossed by two main sulci (superior and inferior) and three main gyri (superior, middle and inferior).
3. The *parietal* lobe (pronounced /pə'raɪətəl/) – extending from behind the fissure of Rolando to the occipital lobe. It is crossed by two main sulci (postcentral and intraparietal) and three main gyri (superior, inferior and postcentral).
4. The *occipital* lobe (pronounced /ɒk'sɪpɪtəl/) – a relatively small lobe in the most posterior part of the cerebrum. Its anterior boundary, seen on the medial surface, is the parieto-occipital sulcus, and the main sulci are the calcarine and post-calcarine sulci, also on the flat medial surface. On the lateral surface, this lobe merges with the parietal lobe.

These are all indicated in Figure 4.4.

Up to this point, our discussion of the CNS has been in terms of macro-structure. But we can also examine the component parts of the nervous system and study their internal structure. A nerve cell is known as a *neuron* or *neurone* (both spellings are in current usage). The actual structure of the cell varies across regions of the CNS – for example, distinctive cells can be found within the thalamus or basal ganglia. But all cells share certain common characteristics; and their function is to conduct electrical impulses. The structure of a neuron is illustrated in Figure 4.5. Each neuron has two main constituents: a cell body (sometimes called the *soma* or *cyton*), which contains the nucleus of the cell; and one or more branching processes[4] which conduct impulses to and from the cell body. These processes are generally referred to as *nerve fibres*; they vary in length from a few thousandths of a millimetre (or micrometre) to over a metre, the longest connecting the spinal cord to the extremities of the hands and feet. One process conducts impulses away from the cell body; this is known as the *axon*, which is readily identified by its relative lack of branches along most of its length. The other processes conduct impulses into the cell body: these are usually several in number, much shorter than the axon, and containing several

---

[4] *Process* is an anatomical term for any prominence or outgrowth from a central area.

branches; these processes are known as *dendrites*. The type of neuron illustrated in Figure 4.5 is one that constitutes the majority in the nervous system (it is known as a 'multipolar' neuron).

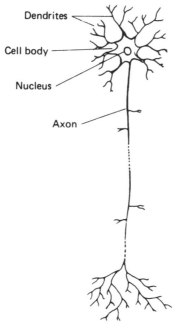

Figure 4.5 Structure of a neuron

The direction in which impulses flow provides the basis for a binary classification of neurons into motor and sensory types. *Motor neurons* (or *motor nerves*) carry signals *away from* the CNS (i.e. they are 'efferent' nerves),[5] either to muscles which they cause to contract, or to glands which they cause to secrete. Muscles and glands are *effector* organs – they produce the effective end result of nerve impulses. *Sensory neurons* (or *sensory nerves*), by contrast, carry signals from *receptor* nerve endings in the skin and other tissues, which respond to different stimuli (pain, touch, temperature, etc.) *into* the centre (i.e. they are 'afferent' nerves). One sequence of neurons transmits a signal from receptors to the brain; another sequence transmits signals in the reverse direction. This binary classification, however, is not exhaustive: another group of neurons exist that have relatively short axons and are responsible for sending signals within the CNS. Neurons connect at junctions known as *synapses* (singular: *synapse* /'saɪnæps/): a neuron is said to synapse with another neuron, or with a receptor cell, or an effector cell (such as a muscle fibre). The electrical impulse carried by the neuron

[5]From the Latin, *e* + *fero*, 'to carry away from', compare below, *ad* + *fero*, 'to carry towards'.

triggers the release of transmitter substances at the synapse (these substances are known as *neurotransmitters*). These travel across the junction and influence the second neuron. The effect may be *excitatory*, encouraging the firing of the second neuron, or *inhibitory*, decreasing the likelihood that the second neuron will fire. The second neuron receives a very large number of synaptic inputs, some of which may be excitatory and others inhibitory. Thus neuron relays are not simple systems: whether the second neuron fires is dependent on a complex interplay of excitatory and inhibitory impulses.

If a neuron does fire, the electrochemical impulses last for about a thousandth of a second. The speed at which they travel along the neuron is very variable – some impulses travel at less than a metre per second; others are much faster, reaching speeds of around 100 metres per second. The factors that govern the rate of impulse transmission are several – the type of fibre involved, its general environment, and above all the nature of its protective covering. Most fibres are covered in a white, fatty substance called *myelin*; the covering as a whole is referred to as a 'myelin sheath'. The sheath is about one millionth of a centimetre thick, and acts as an insulator for the fibre. However, this surface covering is not total: every half millimetre or so the covering is broken, at points known as 'nodes of Ranvier' (after the French pathologist, Louis-Antoine Ranvier (1835–1922)), and there are also variations in the thickness of the sheath along different fibres. The significance of this is that the presence of myelin affects the rate at which impulses travel: the greater the distance between the nodes, the faster the rate of transmission; also, the thicker the fibres, the faster the rate of transmission. Moreover, nerves develop their myelin sheaths (or become 'myelinated') at different periods in human development. All fibres are 'unmyelinated' to begin with; the process of myelination continues into adolescence, and proves to be an important factor in the extent to which the nervous system is capable of transmitting efficiently several of the more complex voluntary movements. For example, it is possible that the relatively late appearance of certain types of sound in speech (e.g. with high acoustic frequency, such as [s]) may be due to the degree of myelination of the auditory nerve and the cortical areas to which it connects (see further below), controlling the ability of the child to discriminate these sounds auditorily.[6] It should also be noted that there are a range of diseases which specifically affect myelin, the most well-known of these 'demyelinating diseases' being *disseminated (multiple) sclerosis*.

Language and the Brain

At this point, we will try to relate what we have said about a particular human behaviour – language – to what is known about the structure and

---

[6]The point is argued in P. H. and M. W. Salus, Developmental neurophysiology and phonological acquisition order, *Language* 50 (1974), 151–60.

function of the brain. There has been an enormous amount of research in this area, but despite this there is much which is still unknown or speculative in our understanding of language–brain correlations. What is quite clear is that many production and reception stages of the communication chain are mediated by the brain. Messages are planned and linguistically encoded in the cortex; a number of regions of the brain are involved in motor programming and execution; and similarly, much of message decoding, from perception to interpretation, is mediated by the brain. It follows, therefore, that damage to the brain has the potential to cause failures both in message encoding and decoding.

Lateralization of functions

The most notable feature of the cerebrum, referred to above, is the way in which it is split into two hemispheres, of roughly equal size and proportions (there are certain asymmetries between the hemispheres, but these need not concern us here). The functions of the two hemispheres are not identical. Certain functions – for example, movement and sensation – are largely *crossed* functions: that is the left-hand side of the cerebrum controls the right-hand side of the body, and vice versa. Similarly, with sensory abilities – such as touch or vision – information from the right side travels, very largely, to the left hemisphere for processing. In addition to controlling and receiving information from different halves of the body, the cerebral hemispheres differ in other ways. In the past, the left hemisphere has been described as the *dominant* hemisphere, and the right relegated to a more minor role as the *non-dominant* hemisphere. This view was influenced by the fact that most people are right-handed – thus, it is argued, a right-hand, and so left-hemisphere, preference in handedness reflected a left-hemisphere dominance in all functions. Similarly, damage (or *lesion*) to the left hemisphere was observed to have catastrophic effects on that most public of functions – language; whilst lesion of the right hemisphere led to more subtle deficits which can often be revealed only by careful and sophisticated assessment. There have been changes in this view over the years, and it is now recognized that each hemisphere has specific processing strengths or patterns of dominance.[7] The left hemisphere is important for language processing – an observation first made by Pierre Broca (see p. 107) in 1865, who noticed that brain lesions which caused language difficulties followed damage to the left hemisphere. Individuals who suffer right-hemisphere lesions do not experience obvious language deficits. The right hemisphere is important in processing visual and spatial information, such as knowing where we are, or using a map, and other complex visual abilities such as recognizing faces. It also plays a role in processing emotional information.

---

[7]See, for example, S. Springer and G. Deutsch, *Left Brain, Right Brain* (New York, W. H. Freeman, 4th edn, 1993).

Evidence for this *lateralization* of functions comes from a variety of sources. The earliest methods were lesion studies – such as Broca's – where patients who had suffered strokes or head injuries were the source of data. The behavioural deficits of patients with *unilateral* brain lesions (i.e. to the left or right hemisphere) were investigated, and behaviours which were absent or impaired were viewed as being controlled by the damaged hemisphere. Thus, as language deficits were identified following left-hemisphere damage, language was seen as a left-hemisphere function. Conversely, damage to the right hemisphere was typically associated with complex spatial disturbances – individuals had difficulty in copying designs or drawing, showed problems in navigation even within familiar environments, and had impairments of recognizing familiar faces.

This model of the functions of the two cerebral hemispheres is, however, not yet adequate. There is a further factor which needs to be considered – that of handedness, or *laterality*. This model of the left hemisphere as the language-mediating hemisphere and the right as a non-linguistic hemisphere holds for the vast majority of right-handed people (98%). But the situation in left-handed people is less clear. A significant proportion of left-handers are also left-hemisphere dominant for language (about 60%). The remaining 40% of left-handers are either right-hemisphere dominant for language and so can suffer from a language impairment following a right-hemisphere lesion, or appear to have bilateral language representation and experience linguistic difficulties following either a left- or right-hemisphere lesion. The relation between language and hemispheric organization is therefore complicated. The situation becomes yet more complex in the light of recent research which shows that damage to the right hemisphere, even in right-handers, can result in subtle impairments in communicative abilities. The type of behavioural deficits that have been identified in these patients include conversational disabilities – the patient's conversation is described as rambling and irrelevant. Abnormalities in prosody, facial expression and eye contact have been recorded. Subtle aspects of language understanding such as interpreting humour and metaphor are impaired.[8] It is not yet clear, however, whether the communicative difficulties which follow damage to the non-language dominant hemisphere are impairments specific to language, or whether they result from disruption of the cognitive functions such as attention and planning which are necessary to support the normal use of language.

In addition to the study of the effects of naturally occurring lesions, there are other sources of evidence regarding hemispheric specialization. One results from the surgical removal of a diseased hemisphere

---

[8]A review of the role of the right hemisphere in language and communication can be found in E. Perecman, *Cognitive Processing in the Right Hemisphere* (New York, Academic Press, 1983).

(*hemispherectomy*), or temporarily anaesthetizing one hemisphere (for instance, by injecting sodium amytal into the artery supplying the hemisphere); another results from the study of severely epileptic patients who have undergone surgery to cut the corpus callosum, the fibres connecting the two hemispheres (*commisurotomy*), in so-called 'split-brain' studies. In these instances it is possible to present stimuli to a single hemisphere, either because its fellow is anaesthetized, absent, or disconnected, and see how efficiently the isolated hemisphere can process information of a certain type – for example, linguistic or spatial information. The problem with all these procedures is that the patients who are subjected to them have a history of early brain damage. The young brain has a degree of plasticity of function; hence, if an important function is disrupted by a lesion early in life, other brain areas will take up the lost function. This means that the patterns of brain organization in individuals who undergo the major surgical procedures of commisurotomy and hemispherectomy are likely not to be typical of those of normal or undamaged brains. The validity of the assumption that the findings of studies with such subjects can be generalized to the normal brain is therefore questionable.

Other techniques have been developed to investigate processing in the normal, undamaged brain. The *electroencephalograph* (EEG) measures the electrical activity of the brain. Different types of stimuli can be presented to subjects and subsequent electrical activity of the brain monitored by sensors placed on the scalp. Activity can be compared between hemispheres or within a hemisphere. More evidence is drawn from experiments which exploit the crossed organization of the two hemispheres – the transmission of sensory information from the right side of the body to the opposite (or *contralateral*) hemisphere, and vice versa. Auditory, visual or tactile stimuli can be presented to one side of the body on the assumption that it is most rapidly processed by the opposite hemisphere. In a *dichotic listening task*, for instance, competing auditory stimuli are played simultaneously into each ear. Subjects are required to report what they have heard. The accuracy of their report varies with the nature of the stimuli. If the stimuli are words, then those played to the right ear (and hence the left hemisphere) are better reported whilst if the stimuli are complex tonal or musical information, these are more accurately reported via the left ear (and hence the right hemisphere).

An exciting new development in studying the areas of the brain responsible for certain types of processing is new techniques of brain scanning or brain imaging. It has been possible since the 1970s to produce images of living brain structures through the use of CT (*computerized tomography*) and, more recently, MRI scans (*magnetic resonance imaging*). A new generation of brain imaging techniques permits the recording of brain function. Functional MRI scanning and

PET (*positron emission tomography*) scanning measure the activity of different regions of the brain. PET works by radioactively labelling substances, such as glucose, which are necessary for cell metabolism. The labelled substances are then administered to the patient and their uptake by regions of the brain is recorded. Areas which are active in processing have a greater demand for the radioactively labelled substance than those which are not. Functional MRI is a technique which does not involve exposing a subject to radioactive material. The technique rests on the fact that oxygenated blood and deoxygenated blood respond differently in strong electromagnetic fields. It is possible, therefore, to detect areas of the brain which have high concentrations of deoxygenated blood, which in turn suggests that the brain cells in that region have been particularly active in processing information. Both techniques allow brain activity to be measured, and the patterns of brain metabolism can be compared across activities – for example, differences between a resting state and a time when the patient is listening to words. Where an increase in activation occurs, it would be hypothesized that these regions are involved in the processing of a particular type of information. Functional brain scans show that, during language processing, large areas of the left hemisphere around the lateral sulcus are active, and that there is also activation in the parallel areas of the right hemisphere.

The methodological and theoretical problems of doing research in this area are very great. All the techniques that we have discussed have limitations attached to them. Ideas about lateralization of functions in the cerebral hemispheres have undergone much change. From viewing the right hemisphere as 'non-dominant', researchers recognized that the right hemisphere is specialized in processing certain types of information, while the left specializes in others. In particular, language was regarded as a left-hemisphere function. Contemporary investigations are now suggesting that the role of the right hemisphere in communication has to be re-evaluated in the light of evidence of conversational disability and subtle language impairments in patients with right-hemisphere lesions. In all of the above, there is a complex interaction between hemispheric specialization and handedness – that is, left- and right-handers may differ in their patterns of cerebral dominance.

Localization of functions

We have seen that the hemispheres of the cerebrum do not have duplicate functions. The next stage is to ask whether, within a single hemisphere, regions have identifiably different functions – that is, can functions be 'localized' to different parts of the hemisphere? The answer to this question seems to depend on the type of function that is under consideration. In our discussion of neuropsychology (p. 56) we have already touched upon the controversy over the extent to which cognitive functions can be precisely localized within a hemisphere. It would seem that some aspects of lower-level functions, such as movement and sensation, are capable of quite precise localization. For example, the area of the cortex which governs movements of a particular group of muscles can be identified with some precision (p. 108). But even with functions such as movement, a number of brain areas are involved in the planning and implementation of actions. Models of movement control usually include areas of the frontal lobe near to the central sulcus, the cerebellum, and basal ganglia, together with the various neurons that run between these areas and on down to the muscles. The brain areas involved in controlling higher cognitive functions such as language, memory, and thinking are even more complex. The discussion of models of language in Chapter 2 suggested that language can be subdivided into components such as grammar, semantics, phonological form and pragmatics. These different components may be underpinned by different brain systems, often in widely distributed locations. Thus it is possible to disrupt a complex function such as language through damage to any of the sub-component processes.[9] A useful analogy here is that of the car engine. The motion of the car is caused by the action of the engine, and this consists of a number of sub-component systems. It is possible to interfere with the engine's ability to move the car through damage to any of these systems. A blocked fuel line would prevent fuel reaching the engine; faulty spark plugs would interfere with the ignition of fuel. Disruption of any of the sub-components would have the result that the car would cease to move. The function would be destroyed – but the function of the engine cannot be localized to just one site. Spark plugs are necessary for motion, but they are not the 'centre' or the site at which motion is controlled. The same situation holds for even more complex systems such as language. Damage to an area of the left temporal lobe may impair language ability – but the lost behaviour is not necessarily underpinned by that cortical site alone. It may be that the site was responsible for one, albeit vital, sub-component of the complex behaviour. Simple localization is unrealistic – the best we can hope for is to attempt to identify the location of the sub-component processes which operate together to produce the complex function.

The investigation of the localization of functions within a hemisphere uses a number of techniques. Lesion studies are common. After an individual has suffered a brain injury, the pattern of behavioural preservation and loss is documented and then the control of the lost behaviours is attributed to the site of the brain damage (i.e. the actual site that was deprived of a blood supply during a stroke, or the location of a tumour). In the past, the location of a lesion in a human subject was

---

[9]The work of A. R. Luria is influential in many of these ideas. For example, A. R. Luria, *Higher Cortical Functions in Man* (New York, Basic Books, 1966).

established at autopsy, but advances in neuroradiography permit identification of the lesion site soon after the onset of the condition, and in the living patient. Techniques used have included CT scanning (computerized tomography) and, more recently, MRI imaging. These techniques differ from those of functional brain imaging (p. 102) in that they record images of brain tissues and structure, and not the levels of activity within different brain regions. The new generation of functional brain imaging techniques suggest that the results of lesion studies, in which lost functions are attributed to the lesioned brain area, should be treated with some caution. Functional brain scans often reveal that the region of reduced brain metabolism which is the consequence of brain damage extends beyond the actual extent of the structural lesion. This reflects the connectivity of a brain region with other cortical sites: a lesion at one site can disrupt the flow of impulses to and from connected brain regions, with knock-on effects on the functions of the distant areas.

Lesion studies and the various methods of brain imaging have revealed that the regions of the cerebral hemispheres are specialized for different functions. For example, the anterior part of the frontal lobes, sometimes labelled the *pre-frontal* cortex, is involved in the planning and initiating of behaviour. The functions of the pre-frontal cortex are gathered together under the umbrella term of the *executive* function. The executive system (like an executive or manager in a business) is hypothesized to have an oversight of the activities of the individual. Other brain systems will control and organize behaviour in situations that are routine; but where the situation is novel, or routine operations have not been successful, the executive system will intervene and plan and control behaviour. For example, in routine language tasks such as naming pictures, functional brain scans reveal an increase in activity in the left superior temporal lobe, the boundary between the temporal and the parietal cortex, and in the movement control regions of cortex. If the word retrieval task is less routine, such as naming as many items as possible in a two-minute period from a category such as animals or words beginning with 'f', then there is an increase in pre-frontal cortex activity. Patients with pre-frontal damage display a range of personality and intellectual difficulties: aggression, antisocial behaviour and impulsiveness, under the former heading; poor memory, slow learning and impaired thinking, under the latter. A classic lesion study of the effects of pre-frontal cortex damage was reported in 1868 and concerned a railway construction worker, Phineas Gage. Following an explosion that drove a metal rod through his left cheek and up into the cranial cavity, damaging the left pre-frontal cortex, Gage's personality was reported as changed. Although previous to the accident he had been a diligent worker, he became rude, uncaring of others, and constantly made plans which he never enacted. He was unable to keep a job and became an exhibit in a freak show in a travelling circus.

The functions of the pre-frontal cortex are complex, and faculties such as thinking and personality are difficult to study. The investigation of other functions is perhaps more straightforward. There are regions of cortex which receive sensory information and which are responsible for the first stages in the decoding and perception of the input. Visual information is relayed to the primary visual cortex in the occipital lobe, and lesions in this area can cause loss of visual perception, or abnormalities in various components of visual information such as colour, form and motion. Kinaesthetic information from a variety of skin and muscle receptors is processed in the parietal lobe in the region of the postcentral gyrus. This area is referred to as the *primary somatosensory cortex* and damage in this area causes loss of sensation (or *hemianaesthesia*) on the contralateral side of the body. The temporal lobe is important in the processing of auditory information, and the superior temporal gyrus is the location of the primary auditory cortex, the integrity of which is particularly important in the understanding of speech. The medial regions of the temporal lobe also contain structures which are important for the consolidation of new information into memory. These deep regions of the temporal lobe form the *limbic* system, and consist of structures such as the *hippocampus, fornix* and *amygdala*. Damage to these structures results in various forms of *amnesia*. The primary motor cortex is located in the posterior part of the frontal lobe, in the area of the precentral gyrus. This region is important in the control of movement. Lesions here will result in a loss of voluntary movement on the opposite side of the body. If both the upper and lower limbs are affected, this is labelled *hemiplegia*; if just one limb is involved, the disorder is labelled *monoplegia*. Involvement of all four limbs is *quadriplegia*.

Surrounding the areas of the primary motor cortex and the various forms of sensory cortex are very large areas of *secondary* or *association* cortex. These regions are involved in higher-order processing of information from the related primary cortex. The secondary motor cortex lies anterior to the primary motor cortex. Electrical stimulation of this region does not result in simple muscle twitches at the periphery; rather, complex and integrated patterns of movement occur – for example, the subject may reach out and grasp, and this region may be involved in the organization of speech movements. These plans are then relayed to the primary motor cortex for implementation. Lesions of this area do not cause paralysis of muscles; rather, movement is difficult to initiate and is poorly executed. This disorder is labelled *apraxia* (or *dyspraxia*, see p. 182).

Areas of secondary sensory cortex also lie near to all the cortical zones responsible for receiving incoming information. Electrical stimulation of these zones results in a subject reporting complex patterns of sensory experience, whereas stimulation of the primary sensory cortex results in simpler sensory experiences (for example, following stimulation of the secondary visual cortex, the subject might report complex hallucinations, whilst stimulation of the primary cortex results in perceptions such as flashes of light). The function of the secondary sensory areas is seen as one of perceiving, integrating and categorizing incoming information. Lesions in these areas typically result in patients reporting that, for example, they can see an object in the visual domain, but they are unable to recognize what it is. In the auditory domain, patients might report that they can hear speech, but it sounds like a foreign language. These disorders are labelled *agnosias* (see p. 219).

We can begin to see from this outline why large areas of the left hemisphere in particular are active during language processing. Sending a message involves decisions to initiate behaviour and the formation of a communicative plan. Sending messages – whether spoken or written – requires planning and implementing movements. Movement results in feedback from a range of sensory receptors – auditory, tactile and kinaesthetic. Receiving linguistic messages from others will involve either visual or auditory processing in both primary and secondary cortex. Then, in addition to brain regions involved in movement control and sensory processing, two brain regions have been claimed to be especially important in the encoding and decoding of linguistic messages. A number of researchers suggest that the anterior regions of the left hemisphere – areas within the frontal lobe in particular – are important in the formulation of messages, whilst regions of the temporal lobe are essential in message decoding. These ideas were established in the middle to late nineteenth century by the European neurologists Pierre Broca (1824–1880) and Karl Wernicke (1848–1905). Broca identified an area within the frontal lobe (the third frontal convolution), subsequently named after him as 'Broca's area', which was important in the control of speech. Patients who suffered damage to this area were thought to have difficulties in formulating speech, but few difficulties in understanding messages. Wernicke identified an area of the temporal lobe (the first temporal convolution, or subsequently 'Wernicke's area') which he suggested was important in the decoding of speech. Damage to this area resulted in fluent speech but great difficulties in the understanding of spoken messages.

These precise localizations of components of language processing have been debated ever since they were established. Hughlings Jackson (p. 57) was an early critic, and the debates continue to the present day. But as we increase our understanding of language as a complex higher cognitive function, and also our ability to record patterns of brain activation during language processing, our models of localization of language processing in the brain will become more sophisticated – recognizing the importance of large areas of the left and possibly also the right hemisphere, and even of subcortical structures. Other stages within the communication chain are capable of much more precise localization within the brain and it is to these we will now turn.

Speech and the Brain

It is evident from the discussion of localization of functions within the cortex that the brain areas involved in the control of movement and sensory feedback from skin and muscle receptors have been quite precisely localized. Control of voluntary movement by primary and secondary motor cortices is centred in the region of the cortex immediately anterior to the Rolandic fissure, and kinaesthetic information is processed by the primary and secondary sensory cortex in the area of the brain lying immediately posterior to the Rolandic fissure. One of the earliest findings of neurological investigations of the brain was that there was a stateable relationship between peripheral parts of the body (for example, the fingers) and parts of the primary motor and sensory cortices. Hence, electrical stimulation of a specific part of the motor or sensory cortex results in specific consequences at the periphery. Thus, if the area of the motor cortex which controls finger movement is stimulated, then the muscles of the fingers on the opposite side will twitch. The motor activities of the body are represented within the motor cortex in an 'upside-down' order: the uppermost part of the region seems to control the legs, and the lowest part the face. A common way of representing the relationship is to draw the 'motor homunculus' – an invention of the American neurologist, Wilder Graves Penfield.[10] This is a figure of a human form in which the size of the parts of the body is made proportional to the extent of the brain area which is involved with them (Figure 4.6a). Notice the large area serving the muscles of the hand (especially the thumb), the face, the tongue, and the eye. Remember also that we have said that the motor cortex in each hemisphere controls the movements on the *opposite* side of the body. This is because the bundles (or 'tracts') of nerve fibres from the motor cortex, known as the *pyramidal tracts*, cross over each other on their way down through the brain stem, when they reach the medulla oblongata. It is this that accounts for the fact that brain damage to one hemisphere is correlated with effects, such as paralysis, on the contralateral side of the body. The sensory cortex shows a similar organization to the motor cortex, and a 'sensory homunculus' has likewise been drawn (Figure 4.6b). Notice here the large area devoted to the skin of the fingertips, the mouth area and tongue, and the tiny area given to the skin of the trunk. As with the motor cortex, the sensory cortex receives input from the opposite side of the body, so that damage to the left cortex results in sensory deficits on the right side of the body.

---

[10]See, for example, W. G. Penfield and L. Roberts, *Speech and Brain Mechanisms* (Princeton NJ, Princeton University Press, 1959)

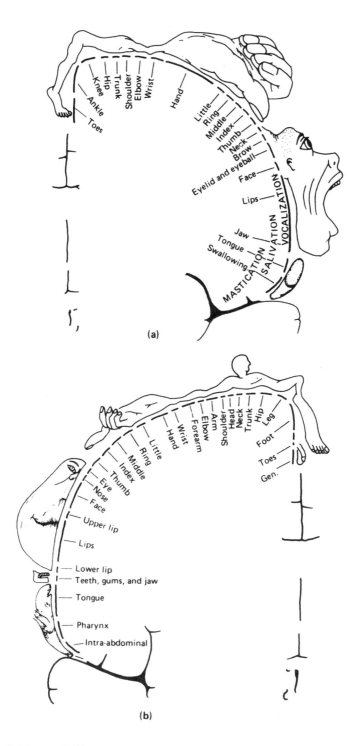

Figure 4.6 (a) Penfield's motor homunculus; (b) Penfield's sensory homunculus

The organization of motor and sensory systems within the cortex, however, is not a simple system. The areas of secondary cortex, both motor and sensory, modulate and integrate the action of the primary cortices in a complex way and do not share the homuncular pattern of organization (see p. 107). But the complexities do not end here. Both the sensory and motor systems are linked to subcortical zones that run through areas buried deep inside the hemispheres and on through the midbrain to the medulla oblongata and brain stem. An important structure in the processing of sensory information is the *thalamus*. This structure lies at the base of the hemispheres. Tracts of sensory fibres run into this structure, and it acts as an important relay of information to and from the cortex. The thalamus, however, does not just act as a relay station. It is important in the processing of sensory input – particularly pain stimuli.

The motor system of the brain also has important subcortical components. The basal ganglia, which are located close to the thalamus deep within the hemispheres, form the *extra-pyramidal system* (the *pyramidal system* is the component of the motor system running from the motor cortex). They allow us to maintain an upright posture at an entirely unconscious level. Muscle tone is set so that we are not rigid or totally floppy. A number of diseases affect the basal ganglia – for example, Parkinson's disease and Huntingdon's chorea. A characteristic of these disorders is disruption of baseline tone: in Parkinson's disease there is noticeable tremor, whereas in Huntingdon's chorea muscles show involuntary movements. The cerebellum is another subcortical structure that contributes to the motor system. It is important in integrating sensory and motor information in order to produce smooth, co-ordinated movement. Lesions in this region cause tremor or shaking in hand movements. Walking is clumsy and poorly co-ordinated. The finely controlled movements of speech are also disrupted.

The final component in the motor system necessary for speech comprises the cranial nerves (part of the peripheral nervous system) which run down to muscles and also carry sensory fibres in the reverse direction, to the brain. Neurons from the motor cortex (called *upper motor neurons* or *UMN*) synapse with cranial nerves (the *lower motor neurons* or *LMN*) in the brain stem. The cranial nerves then leave the cranium at various points and run to muscles in the head, neck and chest (or thorax). Many of these muscles are vital for speech. There are 12 cranial nerves, supplying the following areas:[11]

I   *olfactory* nerve (sensory), from the nose
II   *optic* nerve (sensory), from the eye
III *oculomotor* nerve (motor), supplying certain muscles of the eye
IV   *trochlear* nerve (motor), supplying certain muscles of the eye

---

[11]It is conventional to use roman numerals in listing the cranial nerves – referring to the VI nerve, the XII nerve, etc.

V   *trigeminal* nerve (mixed, i.e. motor and sensory) motor to muscles of mastication (chewing) and the soft palate; sensory to the face and tongue

VI   *abducent* nerve (motor), supplying certain muscles of the eye

VII *facial nerve* (mixed), supplying all muscles of the face; sensory to areas of the tongue and palate

VIII *acoustic, auditory*, or *vestibulocochlear* nerve (sensory), from the ear

IX   *glossopharyngeal* nerve (mixed), supplying the back of the tongue and the throat

X   *vagus* nerve (mixed), motor to the pharynx and larynx; motor and sensory to organs in the chest and abdomen

XI   *accessory* nerve (motor), supplying certain neck muscles and the soft palate

XII *hypoglossal* nerve (motor), supplying muscles of the tongue

It should thus be apparent that damage to the V, VII, IX, X and XII nerves will have direct consequences for our ability to control the muscles necessary for speech; damage to the V, VII and IX nerves will interfere with the tactile and kinaesthetic feedback systems for speech; and damage to the VIII nerve will disturb our ability to receive auditory information. Damage to the motor control systems of the brain and to the sensory systems involved in providing kinaesthetic feedback from actions result in a spectrum of disorders, which are gathered together under the label of *dysarthria* (see p. 186).

Causes of Brain Pathology

In the sections above, we have illustrated the function of areas of the brain by reference to damage from disease to these regions. There is, then, a range of disorders that can be associated with damage to specific areas of the brain (often termed *focal* lesions). There are also conditions which have widespread (or *diffuse*) effects on brain structure and function. There are many possible causes of brain disease, but the main categories include:

- diseases of genetic origin, such as Down's syndrome
- congenital malformations (i.e. any structural defects in the nervous system present at birth), such as spina bifida
- vascular lesions (i.e. lesions resulting from interference in the normal blood supply to the brain), as in strokes, or lack of oxygen in the blood (*anoxia*) following, for example, carbon monoxide poisoning
- injuries (or *trauma*) to the brain following falls, blows, and impact injuries as in road accidents
- infections caused by bacteria, viruses, or fungi, as in meningitis
- diseases of abnormal cell growth, as with tumours (or *neoplasms*)

- metabolic, nutritional and toxic disorders, as in a form of dementia which follows prolonged alcohol misuse, Wernicke–Korsakoff syndrome
- degenerative conditions where there is abnormal ageing of brain systems, as in Parkinson's disease and Alzheimer's disease

One of the commonest causes of brain pathology is a vascular lesion. The brain is a greedy organ, making heavy demands on the body for a constant supply of blood carrying oxygen and other products necessary for cell metabolism. Although the brain may constitute 2% of total body weight, it consumes 25% of the body's oxygen intake when at rest. If deprived of oxygen for more than three minutes at normal temperatures, the brain cells die. Consequently, any diminution in the blood supply (or *ischaemia*) to an area of the brain will lead to the death of cells (or *necrosis*). Medical textbooks will refer to ischaemic necrosis (or *infarction*) of the damaged brain region.

The blood supply to the brain is illustrated in Figure 4.7. It is carried by two pairs of arteries:

1. The internal *carotid* arteries, which pass through the petrous bone in the base of the skull and divide into the *anterior cerebral arteries*, which supply much of the medial surface of the hemispheres, and the large *middle cerebral arteries*, which supply much of the lateral surface of the hemispheres.
2. The *vertebral* arteries, which pass along bony channels in the cervical vertebrae, join to form a single *basilar* artery which lies on and supplies the brain stem and cerebellum, and then redivide to form the *posterior cerebral arteries*, supplying the occipital lobes and parts of adjoining areas.

The two systems are not isolated, however: the carotid and vertebral systems are joined by *communicating arteries*, to produce a complete circle of blood vessels on the inferior surface of the hemispheres. This is known as the *circle of Willis* (after the British physician Thomas Willis (1621–1675), whose major work on the anatomy of the brain, *Cerebri anatome*, was published in 1664). The significance of this is that the pressure of the blood in all four arterial systems is kept equal at all times, and that there is a potential for any area of the brain to obtain a supply from different sources if one artery becomes damaged.

Vascular lesions can occur both early and later in life. The infant can be damaged at birth following a difficult labour where the baby becomes lodged in the birth canal and is unable to receive a supply of oxygenated blood from the mother via the placenta, but yet is still unable to breathe for itself. Babies born with the umbilical cord around their neck may have the supply of oxygenated blood to the brain interrupted by the compression from the cord. The consequences of birth anoxia (sometimes called *blue baby syndrome*) are serious, resulting in serious brain damage or even death.

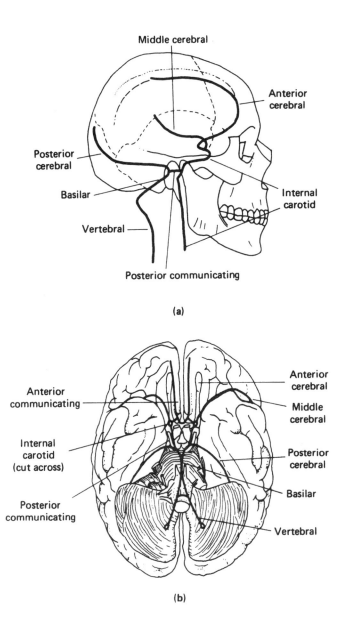

Middle cerebral

Anterior cerebral

Posterior cerebral

Basilar

Internal carotid

Vertebral

Posterior communicating

(a)

Anterior cerebral

Anterior communicating

Middle cerebral

Internal carotid (cut across)

Posterior cerebral

Basilar

Posterior communicating

Vertebral

(b)

Figure 4.7 (a) Lateral view of the arteries supplying the brain; (b) basal view of the arteries supplying the brain

Vascular lesions or *cerebrovascular accidents*[12] (CVAs) can also occur later in life, and are generally known as *strokes*. The 'accident' refers to the cell damage which takes place as a result of reduced oxygen supply. There may be several reasons for this. The most common is that due to atherosclerosis. In adult Westerners, all larger arteries tend to become 'furred up' with fatty cholesterol deposits called *atheroma* (from the Greek word for 'porridge'), particularly in the carotid arteries, the coronary arteries to the heart muscle, and the leg arteries. This is associated principally with smoking, high blood pressure, diet, and lack of exercise. The deposits cause narrowing (*stenosis*) within the arteries, and a clot of blood (*thrombus*) may form on the patches of atheroma (*thrombosis*), causing sudden complete obstruction.

A piece of a thrombus may break off from the main body and be carried away in the blood vessel. This fragment may ultimately lodge in a narrow vessel, blocking it, thus reducing or eliminating blood supply to cells distal to the blockage. The chunk of matter is known as an *embolus*, and the resulting situation is an *embolism*. Alternatively, a blood vessel may rupture (*haemorrhage*). If, for example, there is a defect in an arterial wall, the pressure of the blood passing through the artery will force the defective area outwards, forming a bubble or *aneurysm* on the artery wall. This may subsequently burst or haemorrhage. Some unfortunate people are born with small weak areas in their cerebral arteries, often near the circle of Willis, and develop 'berry aneurysms' in early adult life. The result of all these conditions is a CVA. They may potentially affect any area of the brain – the hemispheres (referred to as 'left CVA' or 'right CVA', depending on which is affected), or the subcortical areas such as the thalamus, brain stem or cerebellum.

Other disorders have a less direct effect on the cerebral hemispheres, but damage subcortical structures which are important in the control of speech. A group of degenerative conditions leads to abnormal ageing of motor and sensory components of the nervous system. In *multiple sclerosis* there is degeneration of the myelin sheath surrounding neurons, which affects the efficiency of neuronal transmission of both motor and sensory information. Abnormal rates of cell loss in regions of the basal ganglia causes disorders such as *Parkinson's disease* and *Huntingdon's chorea* (p. 110). Degeneration of cells within the cerebellum as in *Friedreich's ataxia* may cause difficulties in producing the finely controlled movements of speech. *Motor neuron disease*, a rare degenerative disease, which is slowly progressive and ultimately fatal, can attack both upper or lower motor neurons. The pattern of difficulties that the patient experiences varies with the component of the motor system that is damaged, but muscles are generally weakened and the

---

[12]The term *cerebrovascular accident* is now being replaced by *cerebrovascular event* (CVE) in some centres.

rapid movements of speech become slow and inaccurate. Difficulties in speaking may also be accompanied by difficulties in chewing and swallowing (a disorder called *dysphagia*).

A further group of disorders results from disease of the peripheral nervous system and again has consequences for the control of speech movements. *Poliomyelitis*, a viral disease, attacks lower motor neurons alone in the brain stem and spinal cord, causing paralysis and wasting of muscles. The peripheral nerves may be cut or crushed in accidents, or be damaged by tumours and infections. At the neuromuscular junction, there can be abnormalities in the neurotransmitter action, as is characteristic of *myasthenia gravis* – a disease which predominantly affects females and results in gradual loss of power of muscle contraction in prolonged exercise. Finally, the effector unit itself – the muscle – may be damaged, as in *muscular dystrophy*. These are some of the main medical conditions which language pathologists need to be aware of in order to appreciate the condition of the patient with whom they may be working. The above perspective, it should also be emphasized, is in its barest outline, and should be supplemented with specialized reading on the main issues.[13]

Motor Execution

We have reached the point in our consideration of the physical basis of the communication chain where we have discussed the brain systems involved in formulating a linguistic message, programming the motor system, and the initial stage of implementing the program – that of transmitting neuronal messages via the motor system to effector organs. What, then, are the effector systems involved in speech? The best place to start is with a view of the vocal apparatus, or vocal organs, as a whole – that is, with those parts of the body that are involved in the production of speech. This is given in Figure 4.8. Perhaps the most notable feature of this diagram is the amount of the body that has to be included. People sometimes think of the vocal organs as being solely a matter of mouth and throat, but plainly far more is involved. The vocal organs include the *lungs,* the *windpipe* (or *trachea*), the *larynx* (which contains the *vocal folds*), the *throat* (or *pharynx*), the *mouth* and the *nose.* The system of cavities above the larynx is known as the *vocal tract*, the shape of which can be altered to produce the various sounds of speech.

---

[13]For example, M.L.E. Espir and F.C. Rose, *The Basic Neurology of Speech and Language* (Oxford, Blackwell, 3rd edn, 1983), and J. Walton, *Introduction to Clinical Neuroscience* (London, Baillière Tindall, 2nd edn, 1987), both of which provide an account of neuropathology. Standard texts are J. Walton, *Brain's Diseases of the Nervous System* (Oxford, Oxford University Press, 10th edn, 1993) and K. W. Lindsay, I. Bone and R. Callander, *Neurology and Neurosurgery Illustrated* (Edinburgh, Churchill Livingstone, 2nd edn, 1991).

In discussing speech production, it is usual to divide the vocal apparatus into three component systems: respiration, phonation and articulation (p. 77). Although they are separated in this way, it is important to remember that adequate speech rests on their integrated functioning. This requires careful timing of the actions of the three components, and even minor damage to the motor control and feedback systems can impair this finely co-ordinated activity.

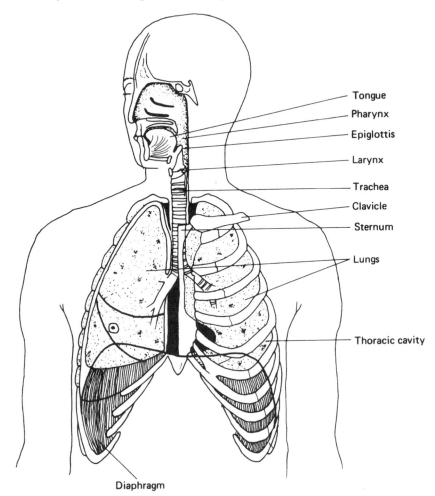

Figure 4.8 General arrangement of vocal organs

Respiration

Before any sound can be produced at all, there must be a source of energy. For speech, the energy takes the form of an airstream which has been set in motion by the lungs. The air involved in the production of the majority of speech sounds is lung air (or *pulmonic* air) flowing outwards from the lungs (the direction is *egressive*). Occasionally in speech other airstream mechanisms are used. For example, in making a *tut-tut* noise with our tongue, the sound produced is made without the help of lung air – as can be demonstrated by the fact that we can continue to breath in and out while making the noise. The source of energy in this case is within the mouth itself, arising from a sharp movement using the back of the tongue against the roof of the mouth (a *velaric* airstream mechanism). It is also possible – though not very normal – to speak while the airstream is flowing inwards towards the lungs (the direction is *ingressive*), as, for example, when we speak while out of breath. But for most practical purposes, in English, we can discuss speech production in terms of the use of pulmonic egressive air.

Speech is, then, 'superimposed' on the normal pattern of exhalation and inhalation – the *respiratory cycle*. But while speaking, this cycle changes from a pattern of equal duration for the two halves of this cycle to one where there is a rapid inhalation and a very slow exhalation. We normally breathe in about 20 times per minute, while at rest; but while speaking, our inhalations may reduce to less than 10 per minute. The respiratory cycle takes place through the action of the ribs and diaphragm, which constitute the boundaries of the *thoracic cavity*. When the volume of this cavity is increased, pressure within it drops, and air is sucked in from the mouth and nose. Conversely, when the volume of this cavity is decreased, pressure is raised and air is forced outwards. The changes in volume required are primarily the result of the movements of the ribs and sternum (or breast bone) and of the contraction of the *diaphragm*, which separates the lungs from the lower (abdominal) cavities. Several neck and shoulder muscles are involved in helping to raise the thoracic cage; several muscles of the abdomen are also involved in the corresponding lowering process.

Phonation

The airstream from the lungs is normally inaudible. It is made audible when it is interfered with on its outward journey, the molecules of air being made to vibrate rapidly. The first place where this interference takes place is in the larynx, using the vocal folds (see Figure 4.9). The larynx, or 'voice box', is a casing of muscle and cartilage, about 8 cm × 5 cm, which at the front is most noticeable in the protuberance in the neck known as the *thyroid cartilage* (or 'Adam's apple'). Its functions are both biological and linguistic. Under the former heading, the larynx acts as a valve to shut off the lungs, i.e. to aid in the process of exertion, or to prevent foreign matter entering the trachea. Under the latter heading, the larynx is involved in the production of several types of sound effect, depending on the mode of action of the vocal folds.

The larynx consists basically of nine cartilages. Figure 4.9 shows the three most noticeable cartilages: the *thyroid*, the *cricoid* and, at the top, the pear-shaped *epiglottis* (which helps to cover the trachea while swallowing). The remaining six consist of three pairs of cartilages, visible

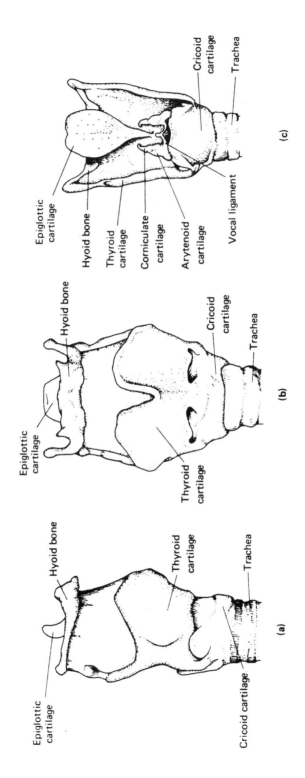

Figure 4.9 Structure of the larynx: (a) lateral view; (b) anterior view; (c) posterior view

in Figure 4.10: the *arytenoid*, the *corniculate* and the *cuneiform* carti-lages. The cartilages are connected to each other by joints, around which they move in response to the pressures from the various muscles and ligaments to which they are attached. A very wide range of movements is possible, and this permits a correspondingly wide range of sound effects. Situated above the larynx is the *hyoid* bone, which acts as a base for the tongue, and which is also connected to the larynx by various muscles.

The vocal folds (sometimes called vocal 'cords' or 'bands') are two pearly white muscular folds running posteriorly from a single point at the anterior end of the thyroid cartilage to the anterior processes of the two arytenoid cartilages (Figure 4.10). Their inner edge is about 23mm in men, and about 18 mm in women. The space between them is known as the *glottis*. It is about 12 mm wide at its widest point when fully open. The extent of the glottal opening, and also the degree and kind of tension affecting the vocal folds, is primarily due to the forces exercised by the rocking and gliding movements of the arytenoids. Just above the vocal folds is a second pair of folds, known as the *false vocal cords* (or *vestibular folds*), which seem to be uninvolved in speech.

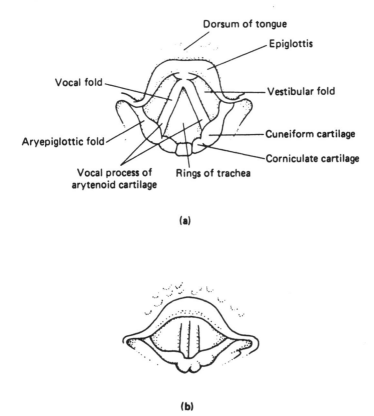

Figure 4.10 View of larynx as seen with laryngoscope: (a) glottis open; (b) glottis closed

The muscles of the larynx are divided into two types. *Extrinsic* muscles originate outside the larynx and attach to the cartilages on the outside; their primary role is to move the larynx as a whole upwards and downwards – for example, in swallowing. *Intrinsic* muscles have their origins and endings within the larynx: their function is to move the arytenoid and cricoid cartilages, and to help in the process of contraction with the vocal folds. Two types of muscles in particular should be mentioned in this connection. One type causes the vocal folds to separate from the midline, or *abduct* – the *posterior cricoarytenoid* muscle. The other type causes the vocal folds to come together, or *adduct* – the *lateral cricoarytenoid*, and the two *arytenoid* (*oblique* and *transverse*) muscles. The muscle which forms the main part of the vocal folds themselves is known as the *vocalis* muscle. All intrinsic muscles of the larynx are supplied by branches of the vagus nerve (cranial nerve X). This nerve has two such branches: the *superior laryngeal nerve* supplies the cricothyroid muscle; the other intrinsic muscles are supplied by the *recurrent laryngeal nerves* ('recurrent', because the descending nerves pass below the level of the larynx and then loop upwards again – a feature which is especially noticeable on the left side, where the nerve takes a longer course, descending into the thorax and winding round the arch of the aorta, and where it is, accordingly, more vulnerable).

The question of how precisely the vocal folds operate, from a physiological viewpoint, has been the subject of controversy, and is still not wholly understood. The most widely held theory maintains that the folds are set in vibration aerodynamically, solely by a reaction taking place between their elastic properties and the subglottal air pressure involved – the 'myoelastic' theory of voice production. This theory proposes that the vocal folds come together, or adduct, to block the passage of air through the larynx. This causes air pressure to build up below the blockage (an increase in subglottic pressure). This pressure increase reaches a point where the resistance of the vocal folds is overcome and they are blown apart, allowing a burst of air to escape upwards into the vocal tract. This escape of air results in a rapid fall of the subglottic pressure and, together with the elastic recoil of the folds, allows the vocal folds to fall back and obstruct the airflow again; thus another cycle begins. This process is known as the *Bernoulli effect*. It happens many times in a second. The average rate of vibration of the vocal folds in adult females is around 250 cycles per second, while in males the folds vibrate more slowly, because of their greater length, at around 130 cycles per second.

The vocal folds have several functions. Their main role in speech is to vibrate in such a manner as to produce *voice*, a process known as *phonation*. When the folds are not vibrating, two main alternative positions are possible. They may be tightly closed, as when the breath is held – a process which upon release can produce a sound known as a *glottal stop* (as in the Cockney pronunciation of the middle consonant in *bottle* /'bɒʔl/). Or they may remain open, so that the breath flowing through the glottis produces audible friction, as in whispering, or the [h] sound. Other 'phonation types' are possible, by varying the mode of vibration of the vocal folds in various ways: for example, if they are made to vibrate very slowly, a 'creaky' voice quality is produced; a very fast, tense mode of vibration produces a 'falsetto' voice. Lastly, by varying the rate and strength of vibration of the vocal folds, changes in pitch and loudness can be introduced into speech. Changes in the rate of vibration are caused by altering the tension of the vocal folds. Those that are tense will vibrate at a faster rate, producing a higher pitched sound, than folds that are lax (the same effect can be produced by plucking a rubber band and altering the tension within it). Increases in loudness result either from increasing the resistance of the vocal folds to the airstream, or increasing the subglottic pressure through a greater exhalatory effort. When the resistance of the vocal folds is finally overcome, larger pulses of air escape through the glottis on each vibratory cycle.

Articulation

Above the larynx, the airstream is further modified by the shapes assumed by the vocal tract. Three main cavities are involved, and these act as the main *resonators* of the sound pulses produced at the larynx: the *pharyngeal cavity*, the *oral cavity* and the *nasal cavity* (Figure 4.11). The general term used in phonetics for the physiological movements involved in modifying the airstream within these cavities is *articulation*. Sounds are classified in terms of their *place* and the *manner* of articulation within the vocal tract. Any specific part of the vocal tract involved in the production of a sound is called an *articulator*. Two kinds of articulators are distinguished: 'active' articulators are the movable parts of the vocal tract, such as the lips, tongue and lower jaw (or *mandible*); 'passive' articulators are those parts of the vocal tract which cannot move, but which provide the active articulators with points of reference, such as the upper teeth and the roof of the mouth. The whole range of articulators is illustrated in Figure 4.11. Two of these articulators, the tongue and the soft palate, are of particular importance.

Tongue

The tongue's importance lies in the fact that it is the organ of articulation most involved in the production of speech sounds – all the vowels, and the majority of the consonants (excluding only those made at the lips and in the throat). It consists of an extremely mobile set of muscles, covered with mucous membrane, or mucosa. It is divided into two areas: the anterior (oral) two-thirds is rough, being covered with tiny

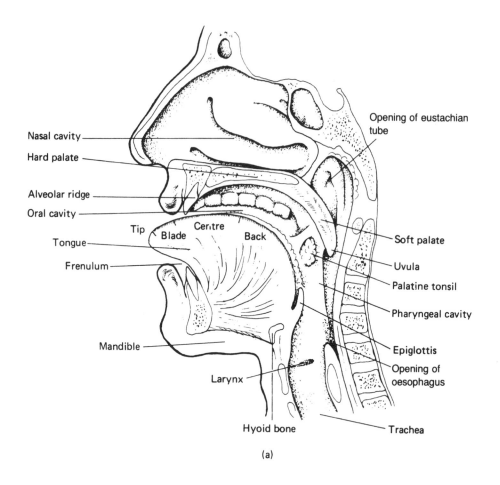

(a)

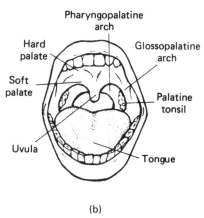

(b)

Figure 4.11 (a) Sagittal section through the vocal tract (see p. 115); (b) frontal view of oral cavity

projections (*papillae*) which can rasp and hold food (it also contains the nerve-endings for taste); the posterior (pharyngeal) third is smooth, to facilitate swallowing. The blade of the tongue is loosely attached to the floor of the mouth by a vertical fold of mucous membrane, known as the *frenum* (or *frenulum*, i.e. a small frenum) of the tongue (which can be clearly seen when the tip of the tongue is raised and pulled back). The great mobility of the tongue is due to its sophisticated system of muscular control. The *extrinsic* muscles of the tongue, originating outside the tongue in the hyoid bone, mandible and skull, alter the position of the tongue in the mouth, and work, along with the *intrinsic* tongue muscles (i.e. those internal to the tongue), to change the tongue's shape. The intrinsic tongue muscle is unique in the body in that its fibres run in all three planes – vertical, lateral and horizontal fibres all interlacing with one another. Seven basic types of tongue movement are possible, using these muscles, permitting the tip, edges and centre of the tongue a fair degree of independent movement: a horizontal anterior/posterior movement of the body of the tongue, and of its tip/blade; a vertical superior/inferior movement of the body, and of the tip/blade; a transverse concave/convex movement; a spread/tapered contrast in the front part of the tongue; and a degree of central grooving. All of these movements are involved in the articulation of speech sounds, some sounds involving only two or three of these parameters (such as the vowels), other sounds involving far more (such as [s] or [ʃ]). The lateral view of the tongue in Figure 4.11a illustrates the main functional areas that are generally recognized (*tip, blade, centre* and *back*), but it obscures the median groove.

Soft palate

The soft palate (or *velum*, or *velopharyngeal sphincter*) is the mobile, muscular posterior extension of the hard palate (the immobile bony arch forming the roof of the mouth). It culminates in the *uvula*, a muscular flap easily visible when the mouth is wide open. Three muscular forces act on the soft palate, enabling it to be raised (largely through the *levator palatini* muscle), tensed (through the *tensor palatini* muscle), and lowered (through the *palatoglossal* and *palatopharyngeal* muscles). During normal respiration the mouth is closed, and the soft palate is in its lowered position, with air travelling in and out through the nose. For most of the sounds of speech, however, the soft palate is in its raised position, closing off the nasal cavity, and thus enabling oral sounds to be produced. The soft palate is also raised during swallowing, preventing food or fluid entering the nasal cavity. A number of sounds are made by directing the airstream through the nasal cavity. English has the nasal sounds [m], [n] and [ŋ] (the last named is the sound found at the end of the word *sing*). Poor control of the soft palate due to damage to its nerve supply, or due to abnormalities in the structure of the palate (as in cleft palate – see further, p. 203), may lead to audible nasal resonance on oral sounds, and is a major cause of unintelligible or unacceptable speech.

The other active articulators in the vocal tract are, of course, important, but their effect is more localized. The lips are of particular note. They are used in facial expression, in sucking, in sealing the mouth during swallowing, and also in speech. The main muscle of the lips is the *orbicularis oris*, a muscle encircling both lips, which is important in lip-rounding and closing. It is supplied by the facial (VII) nerve, and damage to this nerve results in the condition of Bell's palsy. In this condition, the facial muscles on the affected side are weakened and the patient has difficulty in closing one eye and in moving the lips on the damaged side. The configurations of the lips of importance for speech mainly involve degrees of lip-rounding and lip-spreading (as in the vowels) and degrees of tension in their contact (as in the production of various consonants). Less important is the mandible, as far as speech is concerned: the several muscles which control its raising/lowering, protrusion/retraction and lateral movement are more involved with such processes as chewing. And lastly, there is the active role of the pharynx in speech production: recent studies of the pharynx show it to be in constant movement during speech, but it is not clear what effects this movement has.

No reference has so far been made to the teeth. Few sounds are actually formed primarily using the teeth, but many consonants and vowels use the teeth as part of their articulatory basis, and it is remarkable how much misarticulation can be the result of any misalignment or deficiency in their number. The first teeth to grow are known as the *deciduous* teeth: these are 20 in number, 10 in each jaw. There are four *incisor* teeth (the flat, cutting teeth in the front of the mouth): one on either side of the dental midline (the *central* incisors), and one on either side of these (the *lateral* incisors). Next to the lateral incisors are the *canine* teeth, one on each side; and these are followed by the *molar* teeth, two on each side. Deciduous teeth in due course are replaced by 32 permanent teeth, 16 in each jaw (4 incisors, 2 canines, 4 *premolars* and 6 molars – the most posterior pair on each side also being known as the *wisdom* teeth). The relationship between the teeth is seen in Figure 4.12. The normal alignment of the upper (maxillary) and lower (mandibular) jaw produces a complete pattern of contact between the teeth, known as *occlusion*. Various types of *malocclusion* occur, in which the misalignment of the teeth or jaw disallows this normal contact pattern (producing abnormal biting characteristics). There are also several types of teeth *malposition*, in relation to the jaw or to each other. The correction and prevention of such problems is the province of *orthodontics*.

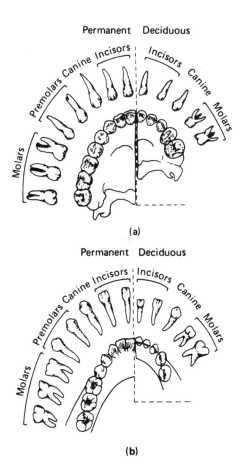

Figure 4.12 Permanent and deciduous teeth of (a) upper and (b) lower jaw

So far, we have outlined speech sound production from the point of view of where in the vocal tract the modification to the airstream takes place. On the basis of these distinctions, it is accordingly possible to classify sounds in terms of their place of articulation, and this is one of the main parameters recognized by phonetics (and usually represented horizontally on a sound classification chart, such as the one given in Figure 4.13, which is that used by the International Phonetics Association, and known as the *International Phonetic Alphabet (IPA)*). This lateral view inevitably omits some of the place variations which can be identified only transversely, such as whether only one or both sides of the tongue is involved in an articulation; but it is valuable as far as it goes. The main consonantal divisions, according to place of articulation, can be read from front to back in the mouth (left to right) as follows (illustrations are from English, unless otherwise stated):

bilabial both lips involved [p] [b] [m]
labiodental   lip against teeth [f] [v]
dental   tongue against teeth [θ] [ð]
alveolar   tongue against teeth-ridge [t] [d]
palatal   tongue against hard palate [ç] [ʝ]
velar   tongue against velum [k] [g]
uvular   tongue against uvula [q] [ɢ] (in Arabic)
pharyngeal   constriction in the pharynx [ħ] [ʕ] (in Arabic)
glottal   constriction at glottis: glottal stop [ʔ], whisper

Several other places can be recognized between these. Vowels are all articulated in the area beneath the palatal–velar region, and are classified in terms of their relative position: *front–central–back* and *high–mid–low*.

The vertical dimension of classification on the IPA chart handles the other type of factor which interferes with the airstream in the vocal tract: manner of articulation. This refers to the *kind* of articulatory process used in a sound's production. The basic distinction between consonant and vowel is one of manner of articulation (the former involving a complete closure of the articulators, or a degree of narrowing which produces audible friction; the latter being more open). Several articulatory types are in fact recognized within the consonantal type, based on the type of closure made by the active articulators. If the closure is complete, the result is a *plosive* (as in [p], [b], [t]), *affricate* (as in [ʧ] and [ʤ]) or *nasal* as in [m], [n]). If the closure is partial (along the centre of the mouth), the air is released around the sides of the closure, and the result is a *lateral* (as in [l]). If the closure is intermittent, the result is a *roll* (as in Scots [r]) or a *tap/flap* (as in the [ɾ] of *very*). And if there is narrowing without complete closure, so that audible friction is produced, the result is a *fricative* (as in [f], [v], [s], [h]). Within vowels, classification is based on the number of auditory qualities distinguishable in the sound (*pure vowels*, such as [ɪ] and [e]; *diphthongs*, such as [ei]), the position of the soft palate (whether *oral* or *nasal* vowels) and the type of lip position (whether *rounded* or *unrounded*). Some sounds are difficult to classify, sharing some of the properties of both vowels and consonants (the so-called *semi-vowels*, such as [w] and [j], and the *frictionless continuants*, such as the r [ɹ] of *red*).

This classification is an adequate basis for analysing the sound *segments* of speech, but what about those features of speech which are not capable of being analysed into segments? These, the non-segmental (or prosodic) aspects of speech have been referred to in Chapter 2 (p. 43). In terms of speech production, their origin is quite different from any of the other sounds so far described. The variables are primarily those of *pitch* (both pitch direction – the melody rising, falling, staying level etc – and pitch range – the pitch level widening, narrowing etc.) and *loudness* (the different degrees of stress that can be given to the syllables of a word, or the overall loudness of a phrase or sentence). In addition, there are *tempo* variations, mainly noticeable through changes in the duration of segments, pauses, and in the overall speed and rhythm of an utterance. And lastly, there is a large group of 'tone of voice' effects usually referred to collectively under the heading of *timbre*. The best way of explaining what is involved in timbre is by way of musical analogy: given an oboe and a clarinet, both playing the same note at the same loudness and for the same length of time, the perceived difference is one of timbre. In speech, timbre variations are the result of changes in muscular tension,

CONSONANTS

	Bilabial	Labiodental	Dental	Alveolar	Postalveolar	Retroflex	Palatal	Velar	Uvular	Pharyngeal	Glottal
Plosive	p b			t d		ʈ ɖ	c ɟ	k g	q ɢ		ʔ
Nasal	m	ɱ		n		ɳ	ɲ	ŋ	N		
Trill	ʙ			r					R		
Tap or Flap				ɾ		ɽ					
Fricative	ɸ β	f v	θ ð	s z	ʃ ʒ	ʂ ʐ	ç ʝ	x ɣ	χ ʁ	ħ ʕ	h ɦ
Lateral fricative				ɬ ɮ							
Approximant		ʋ		ɹ		ɻ	j	ɰ			
Lateral approximant				l		ɭ	ʎ	L			
Ejective stop	p'			t'		ʈ'	c'	k'	q'		
Implosive	ɓ ɓ			ɗ ɗ			ʄ ʄ	ɠ ɠ	ʛ ɢ		

Where symbols appear in pairs, the one to the right represents a voiced consonant. Shaded areas denote articulations judged impossible.

DIACRITICS

̥	Voiceless	n̥ d̥	̹	More rounded	ɔ̹	ʷ	Labialised	tʷ dʷ	˜	Nasalised	ẽ
̬	Voiced	s̬ t̬	̜	Less rounded	ɔ̜	ʲ	Palatalised	tʲ dʲ	ⁿ	Nasal release	dⁿ
ʰ	Aspirated	tʰ dʰ	̟	Advanced	u̟	ˠ	Velarised	tˠ dˠ	ˡ	Lateral release	dˡ
̤	Breathy voiced	b̤ a̤	̠	Retracted	i̠	ˤ	Pharyngealised	tˤ dˤ	̚	No audible release	d̚
̰	Creaky voiced	b̰ a̰	̈	Centralised	ë	˜	Velarised or pharyngealised	ɫ			
̼	Linguolabial	t̼ d̼	̽	Mid-centralised	ë̽	̝	Raised	e̝ (ɹ̝ = voiced alveolar fricative)			
̪	Dental	t̪ d̪	̩	Syllabic	ɹ̩	̞	Lowered	e̞ (β̞ = voiced bilabial approximant)			
̺	Apical	t̺ d̺	̯	Non-syllabic	e̯	̘	Advanced tongue root	e̘			
̻	Laminal	t̻ d̻	˞	Rhoticity	ɚ	̙	Retracted tongue root	e̙			

(contd)

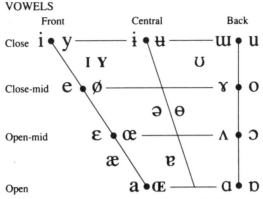

VOWELS

Where symbols appear in pairs, the one to the right represents a rounded vowel.

OTHER SYMBOLS

ʍ	Voiceless labial–velar fricative	⊙	Bilabial click
w	Voiced labial–velar approximant	|	Dental click
ɥ	Voiced labial–palatal approximant	!	(Post)alveolar click
ʜ	Voiceless epiglottal fricative	ǂ	Palatoalveolar click
ʕ	Voiced epiglottal fricative	‖	Alveolar lateral click
ʡ	Epiglottal plosive	ɺ	Alveolar lateral flap
ɕ ʑ	Alveolopalatal fricatives	ɧ	Simultaneous ʃ and x
ɜ	Additional mid-central vowel		

Affricates and double articulations can be represented by two symbols joined by a tie bar if necessary.   k͡p t͡s

SUPRASEGMENTALS

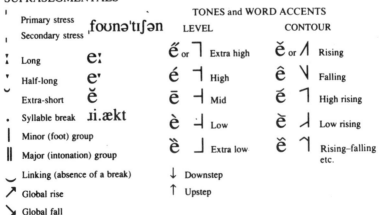

Figure 4.13 The International Phonetic Alphabet (revised to 1989). Suprasegmentals are referred to as non-segmentals in this book.

resonance and several other factors (see further, p. 194). The transcription of all these features is, as one might imagine, a much more difficult matter than with the phonetic segments above, and this aspect of phonetics has been relatively neglected in its application to speech pathology.[14]

Pathologies

We have divided this discussion of the production of speech into the three component systems of respiration, phonation and articulation. Several types of speech pathology may stem from disturbances within these subsystems, and these are described in Chapter 5. Any of the categories of pathology which were outlined with reference to the brain (p. 112) apply also to pathology of the vocal organs – for example, infections, trauma, congenital malformation or tumours. Medical investigation of such conditions would proceed in a hospital ENT department, the relevant specialisms being *otology*, the study of the ear and its diseases (see p. 137 ff. below); *rhinology*, the study of the nose and its diseases; and *laryngology*, the study of the larynx and its diseases. Some disease processes affect more than one of the component systems of speech. But it is possible to make a classification of the main pathologies in regional anatomical terms, any of which could have an effect on the intelligibility or acceptability of speech.

A range of diseases may affect the lungs and hence the patient's respiratory capacity. These include intermittent conditions such as *asthma* or permanent states such as lung tumours or *emphysema*. A common feature of such conditions is a shortness of breath. This means that the prolonged exhalation necessary for speech cannot be maintained, and patients find themselves running out of air towards the end of an utterance. This can have effects on the tempo of speech (the patient rushes to finish the utterance before the airstream runs out) and also on phonation (the tension in laryngeal muscles is increased in order to retain as much air as possible). This in turn may result in changes in voice pitch and voice quality.

A very wide range of disorders may affect the larynx. There are some rare congenital disorders, such as a child born with a *congenital vocal web*. In this condition, the vocal folds are malformed, resulting in a narrowing of the glottis. Common disorders include the infection of the upper respiratory tract, affecting the larynx and other regions of the throat, and resulting in *acute laryngitis* and *pharyngitis*. The larynx may also be affected by trauma – wounds, blows to the neck, foreign bodies

---

[14]For an introduction to general phonetics, see J. Laver, *Principles of Phonetics* (Cambridge, Cambridge University Press, 1994); P. Ladefoged, *A Course in Phonetics* (New York, Harcourt Brace, 3rd edn. 1993); M. Ball, *Phonetics for Speech Pathology* (London, Whurr, 2nd edn. 1993). For work on voice quality see J. Laver, *The Phonetic Description of Voice Quality* (Cambridge, Cambridge University Press, 1980). A detailed study of speech physiology is W. J. Hardcastle, *Physiology of Speech Production* (London, Academic Press, 1976).

etc. The nerves which control the laryngeal muscles may also be damaged: the left *recurrent laryngeal nerve* in particular is liable to damage because of its long and winding course. Such a nerve lesion causes immobility of the fold on the same side, and consequent difficulties in phonation. Various types of growth may affect the vocal folds. These can be non-malignant or benign growths such as *ulcers* ('contact ulcers') or *nodules* or *nodes* ('singers' nodules').[15] They may develop as a result of misuse of the voice – for example, singing with a poor technique or trying to project the voice incorrectly. As a result, they are common in people who use their voices professionally, such as singers, actors, teachers and lawyers. Other benign growths include *polyps*, and also firmer, more fibrous growths (*fibromas*), and tiny wart-like swellings known as *papillomas*. Some of these conditions are illustrated in Figure 4.14.

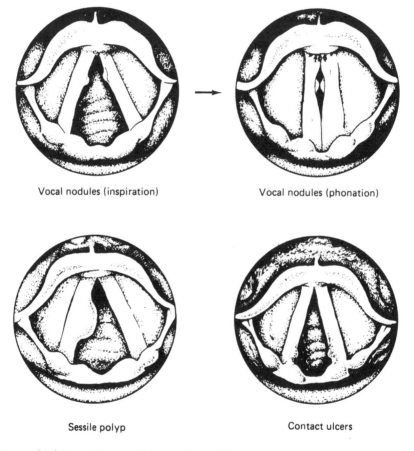

Vocal nodules (inspiration)   Vocal nodules (phonation)

Sessile polyp   Contact ulcers

Figure 4.14 Some abnormal laryngeal conditions

[15]A *malignant* tumour is one that destroys surrounding tissues, and can extend into a surrounding area often at some distance from the original site (a process known as *metastasis*). A *benign* tumour does not act in this way.

So far we have dealt with benign laryngeal tumours. Malignant neoplasms affecting the throat, and the vocal folds in particular (*carcinoma* – cancer – *of the larynx*), can be treated with radiotherapy or chemotherapy, and if this fails, with surgical removal of the larynx (*laryngectomy*). After such removal, the trachea cannot be rejoined to the pharynx, as the laryngeal valve is now gone. Without the protective function of the larynx, food and fluids would spill uncontrollably into the lungs. The connection between the pharynx and the trachea is therefore closed during the operation (Figure 4.15), and the trachea opens directly onto a hole made in the neck – a *tracheostomy*. (A tracheostomy may also be carried out, without disturbing the larynx, in a patient who has a serious respiratory blockage or insufficiency.) Great care has to be taken not to obstruct the tracheostomy, because anything entering into it will pass directly into the lungs. Consider the care that a patient would have to take in having a bath, and the virtual impossibility of taking a shower. Because patients who have undergone a laryngectomy no longer have a connection between their lungs and the oral cavity, a wholly new way of producing speech must be learned (see further p. 196). And lastly, there are the results on the larynx of the normal process of degeneration in old age – such as the stiffening of laryngeal joints and cartilages. All of these conditions will affect speech in some way: their effects are discussed further in Chapter 5 (p. 194).[16]

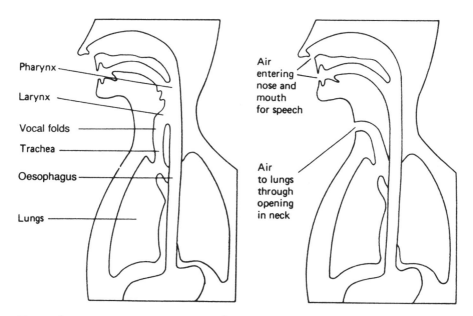

Figure 4.15 The vocal tract: (a) before and (b) after laryngectomy

---

[16]Laryngeal disease is discussed in P. D. Bull, *Lecture Notes on Diseases of the Ear, Nose and Throat* (Oxford, Blackwell, 8th edn, 1996).

The articulatory system may be affected by the same range of disorders as other components of speech production. Congenital abnormalities include cleft palate (see p. 203) or abnormalities in the structure of the nasal cavity. Infections of the upper part of the respiratory tract are common, including colds, catarrh and the various types of *sinusitis* (inflammation of the mucous membrane lining the air-filled cavities of the skull which communicate with the nose). These obstruct the nasal cavity with mucus, thus changing the balance between oral and nasal resonance in speech. Other causes of resonance abnormalities are blockages to the nasal cavity due to the introduction of foreign bodies, or the growth of tumours and polyps. A common cause of abnormal oral–nasal resonance is the *adenoids* – a mass of lymphoid (gland-like) tissue on the posterior wall of the nasopharynx; they normally atrophy (reduce naturally in size) in children by 6–7 years, but they may hypertrophy (increase in size) and need to be removed surgically. A similar development may affect the *tonsils*, found on the lateral walls of the pharynx below the soft palate, and visible on either side at the back of the mouth (see Figure 4.11b). Tumours may appear in parts of the oral cavity – for example, the tongue – resulting in surgical removal of part or all of the tongue (*glossectomy*). Despite such radical surgery, the extent to which intelligible speech can be re-established by various compensatory movements is sometimes remarkable.

Transmission

The study of the physical transmission of sound is known as *acoustics*. In this chapter, we shall be concerned only with speech sounds, and their transmission through the medium of air. From the point of view of speech pathology, the main relevance of this subject is its role in providing an alternative description of speech sounds to that provided by articulatory phonetics, which can then be used in techniques of assessment and remediation (see p. 43). It is, after all, extremely difficult to describe what sounds are like from the viewpoint of the listener: how would you describe the auditory effect on you of an [l] sound, or a [v]? All kinds of impressionistic labels have been used to try to pin down these auditory qualities, but they are extremely elusive. Words such as 'dark', 'hissy', 'sharp' (and several thousand others) can be used; but the trouble is that different people use these labels in different ways. Is there a difference between a voice that might be said to be 'hoarse', 'harsh', 'husky', or 'rasping'? Some people use these terms as synonyms; others given them subtly different senses. This is a major problem for the speech pathologist, as we shall see (p. 194). It is therefore extremely useful to have available an objective set of reference points for speech, so that sounds can be identified and discussed without the distortion imposed by differences in our hearing responses and cultural backgrounds. And this is what acoustics provides.

Any source of vibration will initiate movement in the air particles which are adjacent to it. The air particles are displaced around their position of rest, travelling backwards and forwards in a movement known as *oscillation*. The air particles do not leave their positions permanently, but oscillate around it, each particle transmitting its vibratory movement to the next, in much the same way as waves are set up in water. Two characteristics of this oscillatory movement are fundamental. The number of times the particle oscillates in a given time span (usually a second) is known as its *frequency*. The maximum extent to its oscillation is known as its *amplitude*. The relation between these two variables is shown in Figure 4.16. The whole of the movement from A to B to C and back again to A is known as a *cycle*. Frequency of a sound is thus measured in 'cycles per second', these days summarized under the label *hertz (Hz)* (after the German physicist, Heinrich Rudolf Hertz (1857–1894), who first broadcast and received radio waves). We can hear sounds whose frequency is within the range 20–20,000 Hz. The amplitude of a sound is determined partly by the energy which produced the sound in the first place, and partly by what happens to the sound as it is transmitted through the air. As its energy dies, so its oscillations become weaker (they 'decay', or are *damped*). The sound's amplitude may also be aided, if its vibratory movement causes objects in its path to vibrate in sympathy with it (*resonate*). Depending on the size, shape and texture of the object, it will have a *resonating frequency*, i.e. a 'favourite' frequency at which the maximum vibratory response will be obtained to a sound which reaches it. A buzzing sound in a room, for example, may start some objects vibrating loudly and not others: these objects thus have the resonating frequency of the buzz. From this point of view, the vocal tract can be seen as a resonating tube. The sound produced at the larynx, as we have seen, is modified in various ways by the organs of articulation. Put in acoustic terms, these organs have been made to vibrate as a consequence of the airstream passing them. By altering their shapes, we alter their resonating characteristics, and thus the quality of the sound.

The simple wave illustrated in Figure 4.16 is the sort of 'pure' waveform (a *sinusoidal* wave) that would be produced by an object such as a tuning-fork. The waveforms of speech are much more complex than this, containing many components as a result of the several vibratory sources in the vocal tract. The complete set of frequency components in a sound wave is known as its *spectrum*. The analysis and measurement of speech–sound spectra is the province of acoustic phonetics. Some sounds such as [s] and [ʃ] are composed largely of high-frequency components; others, such as the vowels, are composed largely of lower frequencies. One way of seeing these frequencies is by using a *spectrograph*, a device which analyses sounds into their component frequencies. A typical *spectrogram* is given in Figure 4.17. The time scale of an articulation of *speech pathology* is from left to right – 1.25 seconds in all.

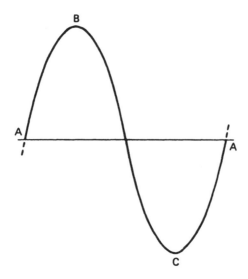

Figure 4.16 One cycle of oscillation of a pure sound wave

The frequencies of the sound go from bottom to top, and are given on the left side of the spectrogram, in Hz, from 0 to 8000 (frequencies above this cannot be represented on this type of display, but these first 8000 contain most of the information needed to understand the physics of speech). The varying strength, or amplitude, of the different frequencies is represented by the varying degree of blackness of the striations on the spectrogram. Thus, for the vowel [i:] in this spectrogram, three of the places where the acoustic energy is most concentrated (three of the *formants*) are around 280 Hz (the vowel's 'first formant'), 1900 Hz (the 'second formant') and 2900 Hz (the 'third formant'). All sounds can be acoustically characterized in this way, either by specifying their formants (as with the vowels, and with certain consonants) or by identifying other acoustic characteristics (such as the random noise in the upper part of the chart, characteristic of [s]), or the bend (*transition*) in the formants for [i:], showing the influence of the preceding [p] sound.

The other main technique of measuring the characteristics of sound is in terms of its intensity. The unit involved is the *decibel* (dB). The mathematical derivation of this unit is complex, requiring that we take into account several related concepts. We begin with the basic concept of *energy*, or power, which can be measured in various ways (by such units as watts, or horsepower). The result of energy is *pressure* being exercised against some object; this, too, can be measured, in terms of the amount of force being applied to a unit area of surface. *Bars* (millibars etc.) are a well-known way of measuring large-scale pressure variations on weather charts. For small-scale variations in pressure, the unit involved is known as the *dyne*.[17] A zero reference point for the

---

[17]The relation between bars and dynes is that one bar = 1 million (or 10^6) dynes/cm^2.

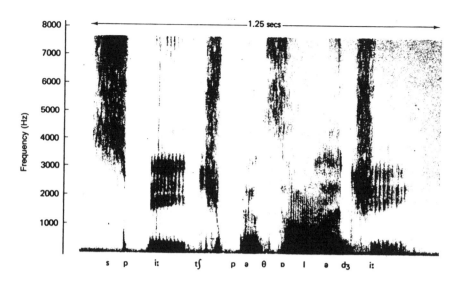

Figure 4.17 Spectrogram of the phrase *speech pathology*

measurement of differences in intensity has been established, of 0.0002 dynes/cm² (roughly equal to the smallest audible pressure increase). The intensity of a sound, relative to this reference point, is known as its *sound pressure level*, or SPL, and it is this which is measured in decibels.[18] Because of the enormous range of SPLs possible, the decibel scale has been made logarithmic, which makes it much easier to work with: this means, for example, that a sound which has been estimated as having an SPL of 20 dB is not just twice as intense as one of 10 dB – it is 100 times (10 × 10) as intense; similarly, 30 dB is 1000 times (10 × 10 × 10) as intense; and so on. The numbers get very large, it is evident, but this only reflects the reality of our sophisticated hearing mechanism. The strongest sounds that we can hear without pain are some 10 million times stronger than the minimally audible sound referred to above. Some typical decibel levels for everyday objects are:

0 dB	sound is just distinguishable from silence
20 dB	whispering at about a metre distance
60 dB	conversation at about a metre distance
100 dB	a pneumatic drill at about 5 metres distance
120 dB	jet aircraft overhead
140 dB	jet aircraft at a few metres distance

Based upon the combined scales of frequency and intensity, a graph of hearing ability has been constructed, known as an *audiogram*. An

---

[18]The underlying unit is known as a *bel* (after Alexander Graham Bell (1847–1922)). The decibel is one-tenth of a bel; it is used because of its greater convenience in handling the small variations involved.

example of an audiogram form is given in Figure 4.18. The frequency range of the sounds is given across the top of the form from left to right. Decibel loss is indicated vertically: the top of the scale is normal, and the degree of loss is indicated at 10 dB increments as one moves downwards. Thus, for example, a sound might be presented to a patient at 500 Hz, and the intensity of this sound gradually lessened until finally it would be below the threshold of that person's hearing. A theoretical normal hearing response would be a straight line at 0 on the audiogram; in practice, a certain amount of fluctuation around this line is generally encountered in normal subjects. The further away from this line the response pattern is, the more it will be considered abnormal: several such patterns are illustrated later in this book (see p. 212). The audiogram records only responses to artificially generated pure tones, as produced by an audiometer, and not to the complex tones of speech. The audiologist marks on the audiogram the hearing thresholds of the person being tested, i.e. the lowest-intensity levels capable of producing an awareness of sensation. Separate thresholds may be recorded for sound perceived through the air and through bone (see further p. 211). Standard symbols for air

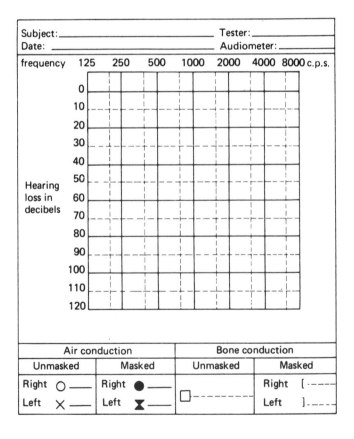

Figure 4.18 A typical audiogram form

conduction are 0 for the right ear and X for the left. Bone conduction symbols in British use are [for right ear response and] for left.[19]

One other point concerning the acoustic analysis of speech should be made, as it is a regular source of confusion, and that is to distinguish the terminology we use when describing the physical characteristics of speech from that used when describing speech in auditory terms. So far in this section, the description has been physical: sounds have been described in terms of their physical *dimensions*, of frequency, intensity (or amplitude) and time. Our *perception* of these variables is an altogether different matter, and is described in terms of sensory *attributes*, of *pitch, loudness* and *duration*. Pitch, for example, is our perception of sounds in terms of how high or low they are. It is largely, but by no means exclusively, associated with variations in frequency. To increase the frequency of a sound will generally result in our perceiving the sound as being higher in pitch; but there is no easy one-to-one correlation between these two notions. Experiments have shown that if we increase the intensity or duration of the sound, while holding the frequency steady, our judgements of pitch are affected. And a similar complexity exists for the other variables. When we have been talking of decibels, audiograms, and so on, therefore, we have been talking about some of the physical characteristics of sound, which we use as a means (the only practicable means we have) of investigating people's ability to hear (i.e. their perception of pitch and loudness). When we try to measure pitch and loudness, as perceptual responses, directly, different scales are involved (pitch being measured in units known as *mels*, loudness in units known as *sones*). There is no one-to-one relationship between these scales, and the physical scales used above. Their investigation falls within the study of auditory perception (see p. 79) – part of the final step in the communication chain.[20]

Auditory Reception

The first step in the reception component of the communication chain is when sound is received by the ear. To understand the process, the ear is usually studied under three headings, corresponding to the main anatomical/physiological structures involved: the outer ear, the middle ear and the inner ear (Figure 4.19).

---

[19]There is no international agreement concerning the symbols for bone conduction: some texts use the opposite convention to that described above: another system uses > and < for unmasked and ▷ and ◁ for masked bone conduction responses (right and left respectively). △ and □ are sometimes used for masked air conduction responses.

[20]On the acoustics of speech, see P. B. Denes and E. N. Pinson, *The Speech Chain* (New York, W. H. Freeman, 2nd edn, 1993); R. Kent and C. Read, *The Acoustic Analysis of Speech* (London, Whurr, 1992).

The outer ear

This consists of the visible part of the ear (the *auricle* or *pinna*) and the narrow passage which leads to the eardrum, known as the *external auditory canal* (or *external auditory meatus* (pron. /miːˈeɪtəs/), a term meaning an end-stopped passage). The pinna is a non-mobile structure, consisting primarily of cartilage, formed from six rounded prominences, or tubercles. It has some function as an area of erogenous stimulation, but as far as language is concerned, its role seems minor, being mainly involved in the focusing of sound waves into the ear, and assisting the process of sound localization (i.e. our ability to detect where a sound is coming from). The external auditory canal is about 2.5 cm long, and ends at the eardrum. Its outer part contains hairs and glands that secrete wax (*cerumen*). The canal acts as a small amplifier for certain sound frequencies (between 3000 and 4000 Hz), thus making weak sounds at these frequencies much more perceptible than they would otherwise be. The presence of the canal also helps to protect the sensitive eardrum to some extent from changes in temperature and humidity – and also from physical damage (though the ingenuity with which small children can insert implements right inside their ears is well attested!).

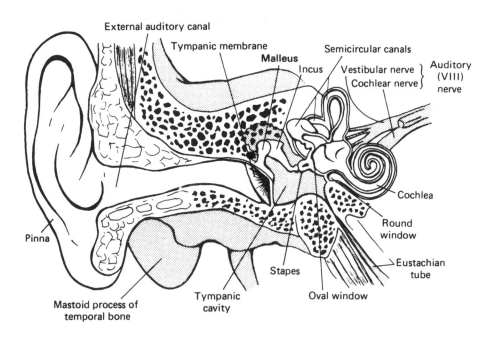

Figure 4.19 The structure of the ear: coronal section of right ear

The middle ear

The eardrum, or *tympanic membrane*, separates the outer ear from the middle ear. It lies at an angle of about 55° across the whole of the canal;

it is thus roughly circular in shape, and joined firmly to the walls of the canal. It consists primarily of a fibrous tissue with important elastic properties, enabling it to vibrate when sound waves reach it. The shape and tension of the tympanic membrane cause the vibrations to be focused at a prominence (or *umbo*) near its centre, and thus transferred to the first of the bones of the middle ear, which is firmly attached to the membrane.

The middle ear chamber is a cavity (the *tympanic cavity*) in the bones of the skull, about 15 mm long and 15 mm high. The cavity is filled with air, because there is a direct connection to the nose and throat via the Eustachian tube (after the Italian anatomist, G. E. Eustachio (1520–1574)), which enters the middle ear at its anterior end. The tube is normally closed, but such activities as yawning or swallowing open it (often making a clicking sound in the ear). The need for this opening is to maintain the pressure level of the middle ear with that on the other side of the eardrum. If the pressure outside were greater than that inside, the eardrum would become deformed and function less efficiently. By allowing air into the middle ear, this possibility is lessened.

The primary function of the middle ear is to turn the sound vibrations which reach the eardrum into mechanical movement – movement that will then be transmitted to the inner ear. It does this by using a system of three tiny bones, known as the auditory *ossicles*. These bones are the smallest in the body; they are suspended from the walls of the tympanic cavity by ligaments, and are delicately hinged together, so that vibrations can be passed smoothly between them. The three bones have been given their names because of their physical resemblance to items from the blacksmith's forge. The most lateral ossicle is the *malleus*, or hammer: this is attached to the inner side of the eardrum by its handle, whence it picks up sound vibrations. These are then transmitted to the *incus*, or anvil, which in turn joins with the head of the third ossicle, the *stapes*, or stirrup. The base, or *footplate*, of the stapes fits into an opening in the bony wall which forms the boundary between middle and inner ear: this opening, known as the *oval window*, is the means of transferring the vibrations into the fluid-filled inner ear.

This system of bony connections may seem a complicated way of getting vibrations from point A to point B, but it has several advantages. Chief among these is that the process acts as a kind of leverage system, which enables these vibrations to be greatly amplified (by a factor of about 35) by the time they reach the inner ear. As the inner ear is filled with fluid (see below), vibrations would very readily get lost without this amplification; the system thus allows the inner ear to pick up more sound than would otherwise be possible. A second function of the bony network of the middle ear is that it helps to protect the inner ear from sudden, very loud sounds. The muscles which control the movement of the eardrum and the stapes function in such a way that they lessen the chances of massive vibrations hitting the inner ear and causing damage. Unfortunately, the time it takes for these muscles to come into operation is not so rapid that the inner ear can be protected from all such sounds; and in fact damage to the eardrum or the inner ear does occur.

The inner ear

This is a system of small interconnecting cavities and passageways within the bones of the skull, sometimes referred to as the *labyrinth* or *aural labyrinth*. The system has two main parts. The *semicircular canals* (or *vestibular canals*) are a series of passages organized into three loops set at angles to each other (anterior, posterior and lateral). The canals control our sense of balance. They are filled with fluid, and contain many tiny hairs, attached to nerve endings: the movement of the head and body causes the fluid to move in the canal; this moves the hairs and causes impulses in the associated nerves. The other main part of the inner ear, and the part with which we are primarily concerned, is the *cochlea*, a cavity which is coiled, resembling a snail's shell. It is about 35 mm in length, and coils $2^3/_4$ times. The primary function of the cochlea is to turn the mechanical vibrations produced by the middle ear into nerve impulses, capable of being transmitted to the brain.

The cochlea is divided along most of its length into an upper chamber (the *scala vestibuli*) and a lower chamber (the *scala tympani*) (Figure 4.20). Separating these chambers is the *cochlear duct*, which has a complex internal structure of its own (see below). Both chambers are filled with a clear, viscous (i.e. sticky, slow-moving) fluid known as *perilymph*. Vibrations enter this fluid in the scala vestibuli from the middle ear, via the oval window (compare above); they are then transmitted all the way around the cochlea, passing from upper to lower chamber through an opening in the cochlea partition at the end, or *apex* of the cochlea (the *helicotrema*), and finishing at a second opening in the wall of the middle ear, sealed with a membrane, called the *round window*. This permits fluid vibrations to travel freely in the perilymph, the round window yielding outwards when the footplate in the oval window moves inward, and vice versa (since perilymph, like all fluids, is incompressible).

The *cochlear duct* is separated from the upper and lower chambers of the cochlea by membranes, and filled with a potassium-rich clear fluid, known as *endolymph*. The membrane which separates the cochlear duct from the scala vestibuli is known as *Reissner's membrane* (after the German anatomist, E. Reissner (1824–1878)); the membrane which separates the duct from the scala tympani is known as the *basilar membrane*. One end of the basilar membrane is attached to a bony process, or shelf; the other to a ligament (the *spiral ligament*) on the outside wall of the cochlea. This membrane is very narrow at the cochlea's basal end (about 0.04 mm) and gradually becomes thicker as it approaches the apical end (where it is about 0.5 mm). The importance of this is that the basilar membrane is thus able to respond differentially to different vibratory pressures: high frequencies in vibration primarily affect its narrow end; certain lower frequencies the thicker end; and other low frequencies activate the entire membrane.[21] An analogy is often drawn here with the strings of a piano: the thin, taut strings respond best to high frequencies, whereas the heavy and looser strings respond best to low frequencies. Indeed, the uncoiled basilar membrane has been compared to a kind of piano keyboard – though the analogy is not a particularly good one, and enormously underestimates the complex characteristics of this system's properties in responding to sound.

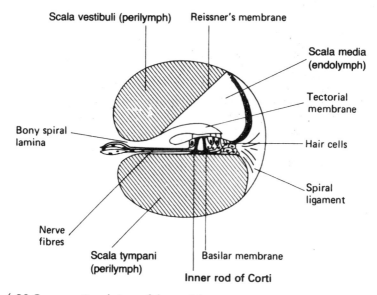

Figure 4.20 Cross-sectional view of the cochlea

Resting on the basilar membrane is the highly sensitive organ of hearing, called the *organ of Corti* (discovered by the Italian anatomist, Alfonso Corti (1822–1876) in 1836). Its task is to translate the mechanical movements of the membrane into nerve impulses. It contains a systematic arrangement of cells covered with very fine hairs, distributed in rows and layers along the membrane: these *hair cells* act as sensory receptors, picking up the pressure movements in the endolymph. The cells synapse with fibres from the cranial VIII (auditory) nerve; their movement is turned electrochemically into nerve impulses along this nerve, and thus are sent to the brain.

---

[21]This is the so-called 'place' theory of pitch perception. There is also a 'frequency' or 'temporal' theory of pitch perception, in which the cochlea is viewed rather like a microphone, transmitting impulses to the auditory nerve: pitch is then determined by the frequency of the impulses along the nerve.

Anything that interferes with the normal structure and function of the ear is likely to promote a degree of hearing loss. The outer ear may be affected, e.g. if it contains abnormal amounts of wax, is penetrated by foreign bodies, or is inflamed as the result of infection (*otitis externa*). The tympanic membrane can be damaged, and perhaps ruptured ('perforated'), by trauma such as a foreign body, a blow or an explosion. The majority of ear complaints, however, affect the middle ear. Particularly common is acute bacterial inflammation of the middle ear (*acute otitis media*), the infection having travelled into the ear along the Eustachian tube from the upper respiratory tract. If the infection persists (*chronic otitis media*) the risk of damage is much increased, and surgical intervention may be necessary. Obstruction to the Eustachian tube (e.g. by overgrown adenoids) may lead to an infection causing the middle ear to be filled with fluid; this fluid becomes increasingly viscous, and results in the condition of *secretory otitis media* (popularly known as 'glue ear'). To drain the ear, a tube can be inserted through the tympanic membrane (in a procedure known as *myringotomy*). *Otosclerosis* is a further common problem affecting the middle ear; it refers to a condition where new bone develops in the region of the base (or footplate) of the stapes, markedly reducing its mobility and thus its ability to transmit vibrations to the inner ear. In the operation of *stapedectomy*, the stapes is removed and replaced by a prosthesis (i.e. an artificial substitute), in the form of a small piston, which is placed so as to join the incus to the oval window.

The inner ear, and particularly the cochlea, is very susceptible to damage, from a variety of sources. Diseases such as rubella (German measles), mumps and meningitis can have a direct effect on the cochlea, as can the excessive use of certain drugs (such as aspirin). The efficiency of the cochlea may also deteriorate if the ear is exposed to very loud noises over long periods (as in some factories and some discos); and there are in fact laws governing the ear protection of workers in noisy conditions (though not yet in discos!). There are also some congenital malformations which affect the inner ear. In none of these cases is it possible to repair the damage done to the inner ear. Too little is known about this structure for clear procedures to have developed. One recent line of research has been into *cochlear implanting*. Cochlear implants are tiny wires, implanted in the cochlea, which pick up signals from a transmitter placed within a hearing aid. They can produce a sensation of sound, but it takes a while for patients to learn how to decode the sound they hear, as the effects this technique produces are at some remove from the normal. As a technique, also, it is used only for those patients who are profoundly deaf, as the operation is a *complete* substitute for normal hearing.

The branch of medicine which deals with diseases of the ear is known as *otology*; the specialists are *otologists*. Their role, and that of audiologists, is discussed further in the section on deafness in Chapter 5.[22]

---

[22]Further reading: P. B. Denes and E. N. Pinson, *The Speech Chain* (New York, W. H. Freeman, 2nd edn, 1993); J. Katz, *Handbook of Clinical Audiology* (Baltimore, Williams & Wilkins, 4th edn, 1994).

Perception and Recognition

Once an auditory input, converted into mechanical vibrations, has been received by the cochlea, this information is relayed to the brain via the acoustic (VIII) nerve. The pathway from the ear to the auditory cortex is a crossed one – that is, fibres from the right ear cross to the left cerebral hemisphere, and vice versa – but there are also fibres which do not cross, so that each hemisphere receives inputs from both ears. This means that whereas a lesion in the visual cortex can result in loss of information from one visual field (see p. 106), lesions in the auditory cortex do not cause a unilateral deafness. Regions within the temporal lobe are described as the *primary auditory cortex*, and are responsible for the first-stage reception and analysis of incoming auditory information. Surrounding the primary cortex is the *secondary auditory cortex*, which is involved in a second-stage analysis of incoming information. Electrical stimulation of the primary auditory cortex results in subjects reporting simple auditory sensations – for example, hums of a set frequency. Stimulation of the secondary auditory cortex results in more complex auditory perceptions, such as sounds of changing pitch.

Our knowledge of the processes which operate within the temporal cortex and which result in auditory information being perceived, recognized and categorized is, however, elementary. The various steps in the transmission process are fairly well established, from an anatomical and physiological point of view, but from a psychoacoustic angle much less is known. *Psychoacoustics* studies the way in which the brain responds to sound, and investigates the nature of our sensations when we listen to auditory stimuli (*auditory perception*). It must be stressed that the psychoacoustic answer to the question 'What do we hear?' is very different from the articulatory and physical answers provided above. Two people may both be presented with the same sound, but 'hear' it in very different ways – as can be demonstrated by getting subjects to react to known sound stimuli, and observing the differences in their behaviour (e.g. whether they judge two sounds as being the same in pitch, loudness or duration).

The study of brain lesions gives some insight into the complex processes involved in the perception and recognition of incoming sensory information, although precise localization of cortical areas responsible for the different stages of perceptual processing is not possible. Lesions in and around the region of the left temporal lobe may cause difficulties in the processing of auditory stimuli. These disorders are varied and are bewildering in their complexity, and include conditions such as auditory agnosia (see p. 219). Some patients may have difficulties in making discriminations between all sounds, whereas others appear to have difficulties in making differentiations within the phonemic information of speech. Within this second category of patients, some individuals may have difficulties in discriminating differences between sounds which are markedly different – for example, deciding that [pi] and

[ha] are different – whereas others may have difficulties discriminating sounds which are only minimally different from each other – for example, [pi] and [ti]. All these patients are going to have some degree of difficulty in decoding speech because of these perceptual deficits.

Language Decoding and Message Interpretation

Once the incoming message has been received and its perceptual characteristics established, its meaning has to be interpreted. This process of decoding involves establishing the linguistic identity of the input and then integrating the linguistic meaning with other sources of information available to the recipient of the message – including contextual information and non-verbal information. This decoding process is highly complex and so, not surprisingly, involves large areas of the left hemisphere. Brain scans which measure the metabolic activity of the cortex during different types of processing, such as PET scans (p. 103), reveal that large areas of the left hemisphere are active while the subject is listening to words, with the locus of activity being in and around the left temporal lobe. Lesions within this area of the cortex are therefore likely to cause difficulties in understanding linguistic messages. Brain scans also reveal that the parallel areas of the right hemisphere show increased activity when linguistic messages are being decoded; and similarly, detailed study of patients with right-hemisphere lesions have detected subtle impairments of language understanding. These impairments are not as obvious as those that occur following damage to the left side of the brain. Whereas patients with left-hemisphere damage might have difficulty in understanding the meaning of a simple word such as *table* – for example, being unable to point to a picture of a table on hearing the word – patients with a right-hemisphere lesion might have difficulties in understanding humour, or perhaps might interpret metaphors in a very literal way. For example, on hearing the expression *she had a heart of gold*, this might be interpreted as referring to an individual who possessed a heart made of gold, rather than an individual who was good-natured. The process of understanding linguistic messages is complex, and involves linking the message with other sources of information available to the recipient. This is why large areas of the cortex are likely to be involved in the decoding process, and why damage to the cerebrum may cause very varied patterns of comprehension failure. These points are discussed further in Chapter 5.

In this chapter, we have reviewed what is known about the physical basis of the communication chain. The normal function of these physical systems is essential for normal communicative functioning, and many communicative impairments can be traced to abnormalities in the structure or functioning of these systems, as in the case of brain damage, cleft palate and hearing impairment. The language pathologist may, however, also meet disorders in which there is no apparent physical abnormality. We therefore now need to review the whole range of communication disorders, and discuss the basis of their classification.

Revision Question

Write out the stages in the model of the communication chain and then write down the body system which underpins each stage. Be as specific as possible; for example, 'motor cortex of the left hemisphere' is preferable to 'the brain'.

Tutorial Activities

1. In much of this chapter we have been concerned with the brain and its importance in the process of communication. What communicative behaviours *might* be impaired following a lesion of the left hemisphere in the region of the temporal–parietal–frontal junction?
2. In this chapter we have emphasized the complexity of the control and execution of speech. Consider the following motor activities and evaluate which you feel to be the most complex, giving reasons for your answer:
   (a) touch typing/keyboarding
   (b) a golf swing
   (c) movements involved in driving a car
   (d) knitting and sewing
   (e) speech.
3. Isolate the first sound of the following words:
   *sh*oe *ch*ew cue *z*oo
   (a) place your fingers lightly around your larynx and decide whether or not each sound is produced with vibration (i.e. voiced), or without vibration (i.e. voiceless)
   (b) focus on the articulatory movements involved in producing the sound and decide:
   (i) is the sound oral or nasal?
   (ii) how do the sounds differ in terms of their active and passive articulators, and also in the type of stricture created by the articulators?

Chapter 5
The Classification of Linguistic Pathologies

Earlier chapters have described the main variables which need to be taken into account when commencing the investigation of linguistic disability. We can now use this information, and specifically the framework provided by the communication chain, to help construct a classificatory system in which the different kinds of abnormal language behaviour can be incorporated. But where to start? There can, it seems, be breakdowns at any point along the communication chain. The solution we have adopted is to follow the sequence of the communication chain, from message encoding through to message decoding and interpretation, and identify failures at each step of processing. But this solution is by no means perfect because, as we shall see, some patients who have difficulties in formulating linguistic messages also have corresponding difficulties in decoding messages.

Before we proceed to a description of the various pathologies, it is useful to consider some of the general principles guiding our approach. The main aim is to classify abnormal linguistic behaviour into categories that make medical and behavioural sense. But this is not a straightforward task. Several attempts have been made to define two or three very broad types of pathology, as a preliminary to more detailed investigation, and several of these initial classifications have been influential in shaping the present-day conception of the field. None of them is without criticism, however.

Production Disorders versus Reception Disorders

This classification would seem to follow on nicely from the communication chain model presented in Chapter 3. But it should be plain, following our discussion of feedback (p. 74), that such a classification is very much a simplification. A purely auditory deficit can, and invariably does, lead to major problems of production, as we shall see in our discussion of deafness (p. 209). A purely production problem, such as stuttering, can raise difficulties of listening (see p. 192). And when we deal with disorders of the central nervous system, such as aphasia, or the psychopathological syndromes, it proves extremely difficult to disentangle the two. Aphasic patients are sometimes described as 'receptive' or 'expressive' (i.e. of production), as we shall see (p. 167); but the majority of aphasic patients have problems in both domains. Likewise, in children who have failed to develop language normally (see p. 172), the issue of whether there is primarily a production or reception problem may be unresolvable. The impairment of the brain systems responsible for the processing of language may result in such children experiencing difficulties in identifying the regularities in the language they hear around them, with consequences for both comprehension and production. The distinction between disorders of production and disorders of reception, then, is best seen as a rudimentary means of guiding, but never constraining, research and classification.

Organic Disorders versus Functional Disorders

This distinction is also commonly encountered in language pathology. It is a consequence of the priority given to the medical approach to analysis (compare Chapter 2) whereby disorders are divided into two broad types: those where there is a clear organic (anatomical, physiological, neurological) cause and those where there is not. Various terms are used to refer to the latter category (e.g. psychogenic, psychological), but the most widespread term is 'functional'. So, for example, if a person loses the ability to make the vocal folds vibrate, and there is plainly a neurological cause for this (for example, damage to a recurrent laryngeal nerve), the voice disorder would be classified as organic (see further p. 197). On the other hand, if an ENT examination could establish no cause, it would be concluded that there were psychological reasons for the problem, and the diagnosis would be functional. Other disorders – for example, in articulation and fluency – can also be classified in this way. However, the apparently clear-cut nature of this division is misleading. Many disorders represent a combination of organic and psychological factors. A person who has suffered a stroke has a neurological cause of subsequent communicative difficulties, but if embarrassment at changed physical appearance and communication abilities leads to avoidance of social contacts, there is also a psychological element to the disorder. And this is so often the case; either it is plain that both types of factor are involved or it is unclear which of the two types is involved. Long and often acrimonious debate has taken place in the field of psychopathological disorders such as schizophrenia, autism and depressive illness regarding the weight that should be given to organic, as opposed to functional, components of disorders. There are also cases where we may classify a disorder as functional but by default. It may simply be that modern science does not yet possess the techniques by which organic causes to disorders can be identified. Some fluency disorders provide an example of this: it might be that some stutterers have deficits in neurophysiological functioning which remain, as yet, undetected.

Speech Disorders versus Language Disorders

This classical distinction is still in widespread use, though with the application of ideas from linguistics its applicability has increasingly been questioned. The origins of the distinction lie in the difference between 'symbolic' and 'non-symbolic' aspects of communication. Certain aspects of communication have as their primary role the communication of meaning: they have a symbolic function. By contrast, other aspects of communication have no direct involvement with meaning; their presence is an incidental result of the choice of communicative medium; they do not affect the meaning at all (are 'non-symbolic'). Grammar and vocabulary were considered to be the main symbolic factors in communication; and when speech was the medium of communication involved, it was the phonetic characteristics of speech which were considered to be non-symbolic. The former factors were grouped under the heading of *language*; the latter were grouped under the heading of *speech*. The position can be represented as follows:

Speech	*Language*
Phonetics	Grammar
	Semantics

Under the heading of speech disorders, in its broadest sense, then, were placed any disturbances arising out of damage to the motor functions of the vocal organs – disorders in the anatomy, physiology or neurology of the systems concerned. In this general sense, disorders of voice production (see p. 194), fluency (see p. 188) and articulation (see p. 200) could all be subsumed as 'speech disorders', as in no case was the formulation of meaning affected, but only its transmission through the medium of sound.[1] Under the heading of language disorders were grouped those disturbances which affected the formulation and comprehension of meaning – aphasia in particular (see p. 165), and also a wide range of developmental and psychological disorders.

There are several things wrong with this distinction. First, it gives exclusive emphasis to sound as a medium of communication, as opposed to the visual or tactile media – an understandable emphasis, of course (see p. 2),

---

[1]Sometimes a more restricted definition would be given to the notion of 'speech disorder', excluding, for example, the range of voice disorders: in this tradition, one would thus talk of 'voice, speech and language'. There is also a much broader definition: see later.

but a theoretically restricting one. Second, it apparently gives priority to the motor disorders of communication, as opposed to the sensory ones. Why is not hearing mentioned, being a category of disability comparable in generality to speech, in the above sense?[2] Third, there is a confusion because of the everyday meaning of the term 'speech' to mean 'spoken language' – in which, inevitably, meaning is involved. Some textbooks on disability in fact use the term in this general sense, and thus constitute a quite different tradition from that referred to above. Fourth, there is considerable uncertainty over how to apply the model in several clinical conditions. This happens especially when the disorders in question involve the phonological component of language. Phonology is 'mid-way' between phonetics and the other levels of language organization (see p. 42). It has in fact often been called a 'bridge level' or 'interlevel'. Because it constitutes the sound system of the language, it is intimately connected with the transmission of meaning: the fact that *pin* and *bin* are different in meaning is a consequence of the phonological opposition that distinguishes the words; and a similar point can be made about the non-segmental aspects of phonology (though here the relationship between sound and meaning is at times even more direct, as when we talk of the emotional role of intonation in speech). On the other hand, this level is intimately connected with phonetics, i.e. with the physical realization of sound through the use of the vocal organs. There are, as we have seen (p. 35), a wide range of possible realizations for a given phonological contrast, depending on the vagaries of our individual pronunciation habits. So the question is: how are we to classify disorders of the phonological system, whether segmental or non-segmental? Are they disorders of speech or of language?

The obvious answer would seem to be 'both', or 'don't know'. But whenever a question is unanswerable in this way, it is usually because the terms in which the question has been put are in some way irrelevant. Phonological disorders form a unique class in linguistic pathology; they should not be identified with the meaning-generating levels of language, nor should they be identified with the phonetic manifestations of language. A disorder of intonation, for example, being primarily a phonological problem, does not fit easily under the original headings of speech or language. A more satisfactory model of linguistic pathology will therefore be more along the lines of Figure 2.1, as re-presented in Table 5.1. The term 'spoken language', in this respect, is far more illuminating than 'speech', and preserves a useful parallelism with other media (compare 'written language', 'signed language').

---

[2]The answer, of course, lies in the professional boundaries between speech therapist and teacher of the deaf, which have forced a division between the two sides of communication that has no theoretical justification. A teacher of the deaf has to be concerned with production, and a speech therapist with hearing. Any model of language pathology has to reflect these interdependencies, and might (it is to be hoped) suggest ways in which a measure of integration between the professions might be achieved.

Table 5.1. Main categories of linguistic pathology

Spoken language	Phonetic disorders	Phonological disorders	⎡ Grammatical disorders	Semantic disorders ⎤
Written language	Graphetic disorders	Graphological disorders	⎣	⎦

Acquired Disorders versus Developmental Disorders

This classification is pervasive through much of language pathology. Its influence can be seen in the literature, the organization of clinical services, the structuring of language pathology courses and the development of clinical specialisms. Acquired disorders are those in which previously learned speech or language ability becomes impaired. A developmental disorder is one in which the acquisition of speech or language ability is impaired. The distinction rests on the loss of already acquired knowledge, in contrast to difficulties in acquiring this knowledge. An adult who suffers brain damage following a stroke or head injury, and who subsequently has difficulties in speech or language, demonstrates an acquired disorder. The child who is slow to learn language illustrates a developmental disorder.

The distinction is important in classifying disorders and it does have clinical implications. The language pathologist who works with a patient with a developmental disorder will be attempting to facilitate the patient's learning of linguistic knowledge. The clinician who treats clients with acquired disorders may also be working in this way, but as these patients may not necessarily have lost all of their previously stored linguistic knowledge – rather, it is temporarily inaccessible – the clinician may be working to help patients re-access this knowledge. The evidence for temporary inaccessibility of knowledge comes from observations of variability in the performance of adults with brain lesions. The extent of this variability can at times be marked. One aphasic patient, whose speech usually consisted of unintelligible phonemic jargon (his output consisted of syllables which were not words of English – ['boʊ iː 'boʊ], for example), entered the clinic one day and asked his therapist 'Can I have a new book please?' – much to his own and the clinician's astonishment. On being asked to repeat this same utterance, his output reverted to the more usual jargon, to the frustration of both parties.

Despite the clinical importance of the distinction between acquired and developmental disorders, the consequences of this classification are at times too pervasive. The language pathology literature – beyond the level of an introductory text such as this – is divided into books and research papers dealing with acquired disorders and those addressing issues in developmental disorders. Training courses for language pathology students are typically divided into developmental disorders and acquired disorders. Often the two types of disorders might be covered in different years of an academic programme, thus emphasizing the split and discontinuity between the two. Clinical services are organized into those dealing with developmental disorders (often termed a 'paediatric' service) and those working with acquired disorders (termed the 'adult' service).[3] But we can question the value of this divide. It would suggest that the knowledge base and skills required of the different specialists are distinct; but is this really so? Both groups of clinicians need knowledge of normal language functioning – how language is organized and how it is processed. The physical basis of communication is common to both categories of disability, as are many of the general aspects of assessment and treatment – for example, the importance of holism. There are specialized techniques and knowledge which separate the two fields, but these are in danger of being over-emphasized and the commonalities of being ignored. There are advantages if each of the developmental and acquired fields keeps a watch on changes in its fellow, thus permitting cross-fertilization of ideas and opportunities for theoretical and practical advances.

Language Deviance versus Language Delay

This is a classification of a rather different order, because it is generally applied only to cases of disorders in the acquisition of language by children. The term 'deviant' is here being used in a much narrower sense from that commonly encountered in language pathology. In its broadest sense, 'deviant' can be applied to *any* pathology, by definition – i.e. it means no more than 'abnormal'. In the present context, however, it has a more restricted application, referring to the child's use of structures, pronunciations, words etc. which are outside the normal patterns of development in children (and, we might add, which are also outside the normal range of adult possibilities for the dialect). For example, a child who said or wrote *man the* would be illustrating linguistic deviance, because this is not a possible or expected structure in the contexts just described. Similarly, a child who pronounced /h/ sounds as /k/ sounds would again be considered as showing deviant behaviour, as this is not one of the normal substitution processes involved in language acquisition (compare p. 202). Or again, a child who passed through the various stages of increasing complexity of language acquisition, but in the wrong order, would also be classed as displaying

---

[3]The conversion of the acquired–developmental distinction into an 'adult–child' one is not always accurate. It is possible to find child patients with acquired disorders (e.g. following a road traffic accident) and adult patients with developmental disorder (e.g. a developmental disorder which, due to severity or lack of treatment, persists into adulthood).

deviant behaviour. Against this, there is the notion of language 'delay', where the suggestion is that everything the child says is a normal developmental feature of language; it is simply that a time-lapse has taken place – the child should have been at that stage of development several months or years before. The delay may be in pronunciation, grammar, semantics, or in some combination of these three. An alternative way of putting it is that the language is still 'immature' for the child's age.

This is quite a useful distinction but, as with the others reviewed in this chapter, it must not be adopted uncritically. Let us consider the notion of deviance. This is not a homogenous notion: there are many degrees and kinds of deviance, as we move from the area designated as 'normal'. Let us take, for example, a child's use of the /t/ phoneme in English. In a group of patients, a whole range of sounds might be substituted for the [t] which we would normally expect. A fairly predictable type of substitution is [k] – the child says /kɪn/ for /tɪn/, and so on. Rather less predictable is [p], but we can at least see some possible reasons for the confusion (they are both voiceless plosives). Less predictable still is [s], [w], and [h] – but at least these are all sounds from the same dialect. Quite inexplicable would be a sound from outside the child's dialect and apparently having nothing in common with [t] – such as the uvular trilled r (as in French). There are evidently degrees of deviance between these substitutions, though it is not always possible to give reasons as to why one sound should be more or less deviant than another. And a similar argument applies to a child's deviant use of grammar or vocabulary. Which of the following two deviant sentences would you say was the more deviant (compare the examples on p. 219)?

cat the on be mat
going to the boy play

It is extremely difficult to decide; and deviant sentences, therefore, often have to remain unanalysed in a grammatical analysis of language disorders.

There are also complications within the notion of delay. If you take this notion literally, then the category probably does not exist. A 'delayed' child of 7 years of age would be interpreted to mean that *exactly* the range of linguistic habits is being displayed as we would expect to see in a younger child. This would mean that not only the qualitative range of the language reflected this less mature norm, but also the quantity of language would be that characteristic of the younger group. This rarely, if ever, happens. What we find is several different kinds of 'unbalanced' language delay – a delay which is mainly located under the heading of pronunciation, or of grammar, or of vocabulary – and if, say, grammar, then affecting certain aspects of grammar more than others (see further, p. 175). If such children were developing normally in all other domains they would also be wanting to 'do' several things with their language which younger children would not be doing, and this would add further differences. In diagnosing such children, therefore, an important step is the drawing up of as complete a profile of their linguistic abilities as possible, to establish to what extent and in what areas of language there are genuine delays. And in the course of doing this, we may well encounter deviance as well as delay – a 'mixed' category of patient, once again.

Abnormal versus Normal

Underlying much of this discussion is an assumption which itself is not immune from criticism – the idea that it is possible to draw a clear dividing line between the concepts of normality and abnormality. Of course, this is a distinction with which everyone attempts to work, despite the unhappy overtones which the term 'abnormal' carries. (But notice that 'abnormality' means 'significantly different from normal or from the average', a definition which encompasses idiosyncrasy, eccentricity or brilliance.) There is likely to be a gradient between the two (as already seen, in the notion of deviance), and the decision as to whether a behaviour is normal or abnormal will often be very difficult to make. But there are certain useful guidelines to be obtained from a consideration of this distinction.

The concept of abnormal is plainly dependent on some kind of prior recognition being given to the notion of normal (compare p. 7). One would not teach ENT pathology on a speech pathology course, for instance, until a basic understanding of the normal anatomy and physiology had been established. But this point is not quite as obvious as it sounds, when it comes to linguistic studies. Let us imagine a child who has been identified as having 'abnormal' language behaviour turning up at a clinic. An assessment must be carried out, and the nature of the abnormality pinpointed. But with what norm should the child be compared? How should the child be speaking? The language pathologist will need to know the dialect that the child's family and peers use, in case there are differences between the way the clinician speaks and the way the child will be expected to speak by parents and peers. It will be important to know how much language the child should have acquired for his or her age. The child's sex will also be a factor here (in some areas of language, the rate of acquisition in girls is faster than that in boys), as will social background (there are differences in the expectations parents have about their children's language, and this may relate to differences in social class).[4] It will also be necessary to know how rapidly children of the patient's age (sex, etc.) generally pick up new language, in order to evaluate whether the child's response to language treatment is normal.

---

[4]See J. R. Edwards, *Language and Disadvantage* (London, Whurr, 1989)

If only we were all in the position of having fully mastered knowledge about these norms! Unfortunately, the real world is a long way away from the ideals of the previous paragraph. Some norms are fairly well established (e.g. grammatical norms of development up to age 4 or so), but others have received little scientific study (e.g. the detailed difference between rates of development for boys and girls). And the more 'exceptional' the patient, the less likely there will be information about norms. As soon as we consider the special problems of immigrants, bilinguals, physically disabled, and other 'exceptional' groups, the size of the problem should be apparent.

Before we leave these terminological issues, there is one further area that needs to be addressed. The choice of terms to refer to certain disabilities – such as *mental handicap* or *deafness* – is always a sensitive issue. The problem is one of what is commonly called 'political correctness', or the use of language in an ideologically correct way – that is, an ideology which suggests that the disabled should not be excluded from society or construed in negative or stigmatizing ways. Over the past two decades there has been a mushrooming of pressure groups whose aims are to raise the profile of individuals with disabilities and to counter the marginalization of these individuals from society. A concern of these groups has been with the terms society uses to refer to individuals with disabilities, some of which are claimed to be demeaning. These concerns are illustrated by a debate which has been taking place in Great Britain within the charity 'MENCAP', which represents the interests of the mentally handicapped. MENCAP's name is derived from the term 'mentally handicapped' – a label which some people have come to regard as unsatisfactory. The suggestion is to replace it by 'learning disability' or even 'intellectually challenged'. Changes of this kind present authors of introductory textbooks on disability with huge problems. Failure to use the current term may disappoint readers who are knowledgeable in a particular area; but use of fashionable neologisms may leave the novice reader confused.

An additional problem with changes in terminology is that this is a perpetual process. The term 'mental handicap' was once an approved term, replacing labels such as 'educationally subnormal'. 'Educationally subnormal' was also once an approved term, replacing the labels which emerged from the early days of intelligence testing, such as 'idiot'. What we are seeing here is a process of euphemism. Some topics in a society are viewed by a large number of individuals as taboo – people do not like to talk about them – and the negative connotations which are attached to the subject transfer to the words that are used to refer to them. In a situation where the issue has to be addressed, therefore, a polite form of euphemism is used. The problem is that the negative connotations eventually attach to the euphemism, thus spurring the creation of a new term. This process is aptly illustrated by the observation that 'LD', the acronym for learning disability, has emerged as an insult in the playgrounds of Britain. In the following sections, in which we describe how the communication chain may be disrupted, we shall try to present terms that are familiar to the student new to the field, but also point out variations in terminology of this kind.

Disruptions of the Communication Chain

The remainder of this chapter reviews the chief characteristics of the major categories of linguistic pathology. We shall follow the direction of the communication chain, beginning with disorders of message encoding. The communication chain is presented again in Table 5.2, but this time the labels of disorders representing impairments at each level are also included. Presenting a review of disorders in this way does have its dangers: the reader may come to view each disorder as isolatable at a single level of the communication chain. It is therefore necessary to remember that a disruption at one point in the chain may lead to difficulties in others. A hearing impairment will lead to impaired efficiency in receiving acoustic messages, but this will also reduce the efficiency of auditory feedback mechanisms in speech – potentially causing speech production difficulties – as well as difficulties in receiving spoken messages. This can in turn lead to comprehension failures and, if the hearing-impaired individual is a young child, to difficulty in receiving sufficient auditory input to permit easy language learning. Similarly, a group of disorders which we have linked together as language disorders commonly display difficulties in learning or using a language system both to encode and to decode linguistic messages. Any patient with such a disorder will have difficulties at both ends of the communication chain – in sending and receiving linguistic messages. With this qualification in mind, we can proceed to the first of our categories of communicative pathology.

Pre-linguistic pathologies

Disorders which represent disruptions of the pre-linguistic stage are grouped together under the heading of 'cognitive disorders'. This title is not entirely adequate for two reasons. First, although many of the disorders included within this category – for example, dementia – do represent very serious disabilities in the processing of information, they also result in much broader impairments of personality, emotion and social competence. Second, it suggests that cognition is in some way entirely separable from language, and that disorders grouped under this heading represent a failure solely at the pre-linguistic level. Neither point is entirely valid, as we shall see. However, the grouping is still of value, because it emphasizes that individuals suffering from these disorders are likely to have difficulties in a broad range of abilities; that is, their difficulties will extend beyond language.

Table 5.2. Disruptions of the communication chain

Stage	Disorder

Pre-linguistic	*Cognitive disorders*
	    Thought disorders
	    Autism
	    Learning difficulties

Language encoding	*Language disorders*
	    Aphasia
	    Developmental language disorders

Motor programming	Apraxia

Motor execution	Dysarthria
	Disorders of voice
	    e.g. vocal misuse, laryngectomy
	Disorders of fluency
	    e.g. stuttering, cluttering
	Disorders of articulation
	    e.g. cleft palate, glossectomy

Reception	Hearing impairment
Perception/recognition	Agnosia

Language decoding	*Language disorders*
	    Aphasia
	    Developmental language disorders

Message decoding	*Cognitive disorders*
	    Thought disorders
	    Autism
	    Learning difficulties

Problems of this kind are grouped under the heading of psychopathology – the study of mental illness. This notion covers a wide range of disturbances, ranging from mild emotional problems to the severest forms of mental abnormality. It is a highly complex and controversial field, containing several competing systems of classification and terminologies in addition to conflicting theories of aetiology and modes of intervention. The effect of a psychopathology on communication is also variable. Some disorders, such as schizophrenia, autism and dementia, have profound communicative consequences; others, such as phobias and obsessive-compulsive disorders, have few communicative effects.

In the classification of mental illness, one of the most traditional distinctions is that drawn between *neurosis* and *psychosis*. Under the heading of neurosis is included a broad range of moods, fears, preoccupations and exaggerated traits about which a person is to some degree defensive or anxious. For example, a person may have an irrational fear of heights, or spiders, the fear being out of all proportion to the stimulus (what is known as a *phobia*). They may have an exaggerated concern over their health or bodily functions (*hypochondria*), or find that they act in obsessive or compulsive ways (as in compulsive washing, stealing, fire-lighting). Anxiety disorders are also included under the heading of neurosis, together with *hysterical* or *conversion* reactions, where aspects of a person's physiology fail to work normally, although there is nothing wrong organically. For example, stress might lead to sexual impotency, poor vision, or (compare p. 199) loss of voice. All these neuroses have two things in common: patients cannot readily control their reactions through their own efforts; and they are only minimally out of contact with reality – they generally recognize the inappropriateness of their feelings and behaviour, and will often seek advice and help, especially from psychotherapy.

In this respect, neurotic reactions are said to differ from the second main category of mental illness: *psychotic reactions* or *psychoses*. These are major psychiatric disturbances, which often have serious communicative consequences. They differ from neuroses in that there is a fundamental disintegration of personality, with patients no longer being aware of the abnormal nature of their condition, and accepting their behaviour as a normal way of living. A distinction is generally made between *organic* and *functional* types. Organic psychoses, as the name suggests, are disorders where there is a demonstrable physical abnormality in the brain. Examples include the abnormal brain degeneration that may accompany ageing, known as *senile dementia*: the most common form is *Alzheimer's disease*. In Alzheimer's disease there is a loss of neurons throughout the brain, with regions of the pre-frontal and temporal cortex and the limbic system (areas important for planning, abstract thought, language and memory) particularly subject to cell loss. Individuals with Alzheimer's disease have progressively little or no insight into their problems, and make no effect to care for themselves. Sufferers experience a broad spectrum of cognitive deficits and gradually become detached from reality and disoriented as to who they are, and where they are. The linguistic impairments begin with difficulties in word-finding (or *lexical retrieval*) and changes at the level of discourse structure and pragmatics. The speaker may repeat the same topics again and again and have difficulty making contributions to the conversation when a new topic is introduced by another speaker. As the condition progresses, the vocabulary and pragmatic difficulties become more marked, and all levels of language processing become impaired, both in comprehension and production. In the late stages, the sufferer may have little understanding of spoken or written language and may be mute, with output restricted to repetition of others' utterances (a behaviour called *echolalia*) or a small stock of stereotyped phrases and sentences (*perseverations*).

Functional psychoses, by contrast, are disorders where no underlying physical abnormality can be established (which is not, of course, to say that this does not exist – merely that none has been found, using present day techniques (p. 147)). This is in fact currently a controversial issue in the main category of functional psychosis, *schizophrenia*. It is possible that excessive levels of the neurotransmitter dopamine may be responsible for the symptoms observed, in which case we should be dealing with an organic disturbance. Dopamine affects regions of the brain important in mediating emotion, thought and personality; these include the amygdala, and the temporal and frontal lobes. Evidence of genetic factors in the disorder also point to an organic cause; but the point is disputed, and some argue that the neurochemical and structural abnormalities in the brains of schizophrenic patients are due to the effects of antipsychotic medication. The chief symptoms of the disorder are major abnormalities and fluctuations in mood, unexpected (inappropriate, dramatic) reactions to normal situations, social withdrawal, delusions and hallucinations. The communicative signs are most marked at a pragmatic level. During psychotic episodes, the patient may be unwilling to communicate, or output may be chaotic with constant shifts in topic, incoherence between sentences, perseverations and inappropriate emotional expression (e.g. in intonation and tone of voice). Comprehension may also be disrupted, for instance an innocuous utterance might be interpreted as a threat. Several of these features can be seen in the following sample, taken from a conversation with a female schizophrenic, in her mid-50s, with a long history of anxiety problems and institutionalization.[5]

T   you're in 'ward thirtèen now/
P   yès/
    yès/
    was –
    been –
    I've been
    I'm – in – in
    I'm in 'ward thirtèen/.
T   how 'long have you been in 'ward thirtèen/
P   gòod 'while/
    a 'few 'years I thínk/
    'two or three 'years I thínk/
    I'm not –
    yès/
T   do you líke it on 'there/
P   not bád/ – ùsual/
T   have you 'got any frìends 'Mary/
P   from the sỳna – er –
    'Anytown sỳnagogue/.
    'please Gòd/.
    I'll be gòing on the 'ninth of Jánuary/

[5]For transcription conventions, see p. 167.

T   you've got frìends 'there háve you/
P   yès/.
    yès/.
    fróm/ –
    'used to be with me ín/ –
    gòod while 'back/
    er –'May in –
    'used to be 'with me gòod while 'back/
T   tèll me Máry/. 'what 'things do you 'like dòing/
P   I 'used to be 'in the 'laun –
    I was.
    I don't knów/
    they 'carried òn a bit/.
    but I 'don't knów/
    I mìght be going báck/ – –
    'Monday the sècond/.
    I 'don't knów/
    it'll be 'bank hòliday hére/.
    I 'don't knów/
    the fòllowing week/ –
    Sùnday/ –
    'Monday 'week I thínk/

This patient would tend not to speak at all, unless directly questioned. Most of her sentences are short; many are unfinished; and there is much disjointedness between one sentence and the next. Her tendency to split up a meaning into smaller chunks, giving each a separate intonation unit, is clearly illustrated by the transcription, where the units are put on new lines. Her tendency to repeat, or partly repeat, what she has said is also noticeable. What does not appear in the transcript is an indication of her general behaviour throughout the conversation – in particular, the way in which she avoided eye contact, and generally left the therapist with no sense of 'rapport'.

A pre-linguistic pathology for which there is a clear organic basis is the cognitive disorder that follows damage to the pre-frontal cortex, as illustrated by the case of Phineas Gage (p. 105). This brain region is responsible for executive functions, and by extension, disorders of this type are sometimes called 'dysexecutive' or 'frontal lobe' syndromes. These disorders can occur following head injuries caused by road traffic accidents, blows and falls. The pattern of brain injury is generally diffuse, with delicate brain tissues being subject to impact and rotational forces which cause crushing of tissue against the skull and twisting and tearing of axons and blood vessels. The pre-frontal cortex is particularly vulnerable to injury because of its juxtaposition to a shelf of bone which separates the cranial cavity from the nose and eye cavities. The communicative component of frontal lobe syndrome is again distinguished by difficulties at the level of pragmatic and discourse structure – a recurring pattern of deficit in the pre-linguistic pathologies.

In addition to acquired disorders, there are a series of developmental conditions which operate at the pre-linguistic stage of the communication chain. Mental handicap (or learning difficulty) is a major category of psychopathological disorder which is of particular concern to the language pathologist. Individuals who fall within this category are likely to have cognitive, emotional or social skills which place them significantly below the level of the rest of their age group. A range of disorders are associated with the condition, including the genetic abnormality of Down's syndrome, metabolic disturbances such as *phenylketonuria* (a disorder in which the child is born without the enzymes necessary to metabolize certain proteins, leading to a build up of toxic substances within the brain), and disabilities caused by infections such as meningitis or serious brain trauma, including birth anoxia in early life.

It is impossible to generalize about either the cognitive abilities or language skills in the context of learning disability. There is no straight-forward correlation between any of the many syndromes and the language produced. Children with Down's syndrome, for example (compare p. 27), will show a wide range of individual differences in their cognitive profiles and linguistic abilities. Perhaps the only safe claim that can be made is that when learning disabilities become really severe, there will be no language – which is hardly a brilliant insight. And yet, even here there is great scope for research. Even in the minimally purposive behaviour of the most severely handicapped, there may be signs of pattern, or desire to communicate, which might be made the basis of a teaching programme. What, upon first encounter, might seem to be random grunts may on analysis turn out to be a systematic use of a very limited vocal apparatus. Everything depends, it would seem, on the investigator and teacher finding the right mode of input to the child, and to keep trying, if early attempts to make contact fail. It is an easy, and a natural, reaction to give up with such children, and conclude that 'they just won't learn'. Such comments, properly interpreted, can only mean: 'so far, I have not been able to find a way to enable them to learn'. Whether it is practical or economical to keep trying, of course, given the pressing demands of others for attention, is a difficult and often emotional decision. But theoretically, at least, the answer is plain: of course one keeps trying. And from the analytical point of view what this means, usually, is careful analysis – not only of the children's language (if any) but of the language of their environment, from which they are attempting to learn. How carefully has this been structured, to enable them to make best sense of it? One of the general problems with mentally handicapped children or adults is the difficulties they have in resolving a large number of competing stimuli. They cannot cope with too many inputs at once, but get confused. Using this guideline, then, we can look at the language inputs to children, to see whether they are too complex for them. It is very easy for complexity to creep in, unnoticed. One child's small teddy was being referred to as 'teddy', 'cuddly', 'Fred' and other names, by the people who came into contact with him; no-one had bothered to check whether they were all using the same language to the child, and as a result they unwittingly complicated his world in this small but crucial respect. Standardizing the learning environment, and yet not making it so stereotyped that there is no potential for growth and creativity: this is one of the main methodological issues facing those who work in learning disability.

Autism is a further developmental psychopathology which has profound consequences for communicative ability. It is usually identified in the second or third year of life and is a disorder for which, at present, no definite organic cause has been identified, although there is much debate about possible neuropathological mechanisms behind the disorder. Autism represents a complex pattern of abnormal behaviour in which three core behavioural deficits are identified: bizarre interpersonal relationships (such as avoidance of eye contact, lack of response to others, no attempt to initiate contacts, preference for objects rather than people), obsessive and ritualistic behaviour, and communication difficulties. The following extract illustrates the tendency of the autistic child not to respond directly to conversational stimuli, but to keep up a monologue of his own:

T: 'what are you going to 'do with 'that car nòw/
P   I like my cár (*pushing it on floor*)
T   lòok/. I've got 'one like thát/
P   in hère it 'goes (*pushing car into garage*)
T   'don't for'get to 'shut the dóors/
P   'find the màn nów/ (*looking about*) . . .

In each case the child ignored, or seemed to ignore, the therapist's stimulus sentence, and yet by keeping up a flow of language an 'apparent' conversation was obtained.

In the discussion of the *holistic approach* (p. 18), it was suggested that it is important to consider an individual's communicative impairments in the context of the total cognitive profile. This is particularly true in cases of pre-linguistic pathology, where much of the communicative impairment follows directly from cognitive impairments. The management of pre-linguistic pathologies, in particular, requires full consideration of a range of cognitive functions, and language pathologists working with these conditions often work in tandem with psychologists. The word-retrieval difficulties of the person with Alzheimer's disease need to be viewed against the backdrop of general difficulties with storage and retrieval of information from memory. The failure of a child with autism to show usual patterns of eye contact in an interaction has to be evaluated against more general impairments in social relationships. The communicative impairments of individuals with pre-linguistic pathologies are often some of the most evident signs of the disability. The chaotic thought of the schizophrenic patient is not available to observation, but the incoherent encoding of these same thoughts into language is clearly apparent. Communication, by its essential nature, is a very public function and, rather like an iceberg, it is possible to see the communicative manifestations which appear at the surface, but to neglect the underlying mass of other cognitive abilities which underpin and inter-link with language. The proper management of the pre-linguistic conditions must necessarily adopt a broad perspective on behaviour.

Language Disorders

The essential characteristic of the previous category of communicative disability – the pre-linguistic or cognitive disorders – is that they represent a very broad deficit across a range of cognitive and other abilities. In the second broad category of communicative deficits – language disorders – we are dealing with disabilities which feature more specific impairment of language, and these disabilities are often referred to as *specific language disorders*. This is not to say, however, that they are purely linguistic impairments. It may be that they are underpinned by a cognitive deficit, but one which has much more discrete consequences than the cognitive failures of dementia, schizophrenia and the like. It is also important not to lose sight of the fact that a language disorder may have effects on other cognitive functions, such as memory or concept development. Whereas the model of the communication chain represents pre-linguistic and linguistic deficits as discrete entities, in reality we are dealing with closely interrelated functions.

The distinction between specific language disorders and more global cognitive disorders is important in the diagnosis and management of conditions. Whereas teaching specific vocabulary items or grammatical structures might be an important component in the treatment of specific language difficulties, communicative impairments linked to more general cognitive deficits might first benefit from intervention directed at underlying cognitive deficits. For this reason, the initial evaluation of an individual, particularly a child, with a language disorder may consider a range of abilities in both a linguistic and a non-linguistic sphere. Psychological assessments such as the *Wechsler Intelligence Scale for Children* are divided into verbal (language) and performance scales.[6] Assessment of a child with a specific language disorder may result in unequal scores across verbal and performance scales, with a performance score which may be within the normal range expected for a child of that chronological age, but a verbal score significantly below the expected range. A child with a language disorder which is a component

---

[6]D. Wechsler, *Wechsler Intelligence Scale for Children – Third UK Edition* (London, The Psychological Corporation, 1992).

of a more general developmental delay might show a more balanced profile of verbal and performance scores, although both scores would be significantly below those expected for a child of a particular chronological age.

An important characteristic of language disorders is that their effects may appear at different points in the communication chain, and in any of the modalities of language use. The disorder may affect both language encoding and decoding – that is, the patient could have difficulties both in formulating linguistic messages and in understanding them. It is possible, however, that language encoding alone may be affected, with the ability to understand language being relatively normal; and, more rarely, that language decoding may be affected, with the ability to produce language appearing normal. In both cases, there needs to be careful assessment by the language pathologist, because comprehension disorders may go unnoticed – the patient perhaps using other sources of information to decode messages, such as the contextual or the non-verbal (see p. 82). In addition to affecting performance across input and output, language disorders may disrupt performances across both auditory and visual channels of language use – that is, speech/listening and reading/writing. Thus a child with a language disorder may have difficulties in creating grammatical sentences in speech, and problems of a similar order may also be observed in writing. Pre-school children with language disorders may also go on to have difficulties in learning to read and write.

Different degrees of involvement of the four channels of language use result in one patient potentially being very different from another. Language disorder is not a homogenous category. Not only are there differences in performance across modalities; patients may also differ in the type of difficulty they have within modalities, such as when formulating a spoken message. One patient may have particular difficulty in producing a grammatical sentence, whereas another may have problems in finding the appropriate words for use in a sentence. The language pathologist might describe the first patient's difficulty as one of grammatical encoding, and the second as one of semantic or lexical encoding. Any of the levels of language organization that were identified in Chapter 2 – grammar, semantics, phonology and pragmatics – may be affected, and to varying degrees. The language pathologist must therefore have considerable skill in performing linguistic analyses in order to be able to pinpoint areas of deficit in the patient's linguistic knowledge and performance. During the 1970s, several important developments in the analytical study of language disability took place within the range of disciplines categorized as 'behavioural' (p. 30). The application of ideas from the fields of psychology and linguistics have, as a result, shaped present-day perceptions of language disability.

From this account, it will be clear that the proper explanation of a patient's linguistic symptoms is a complex and time-consuming process. A language sample has to be analysed into its various levels of organization, the interactions determined, and the rules governing the competence of the impaired speaker deduced. To engage in clinical linguistic diagnosis is a truly professional task, and to be successful it requires a degree of training, time, resources, status and pay for its practitioners which one would associate with any complex area of enquiry. Unfortunately, as language clinicians and teachers know only too well, it is rare to find all these elements being satisfactorily recognized, and thus it is routine to encounter teaching and therapy taking place where it has been possible to engage in only a minimum of analysis. It is not surprising, then, to hear complaints from professionals that they do not have the time to practise the techniques associated with the behavioural model of investigation, apart from a few special settings, such as residential speech and language schools or university language pathology clinics.

The solution to this problem goes well beyond the brief of the present book, involving a wide range of political and professional issues. But it is important to stress that no solution will be found if it ignores the clinical realities of the nature of language disability. Given the demonstrable enormous complexity of human language, it should be no surprise to discover that language disabilities are also complex, and require correspondingly complex intervention procedures. A full clinical linguistic enquiry is thus a major enterprise, involving the description and analysis of the patient's language at several points in time, and also of the kind of language being used to the patient by the people who have a caring role. The complexity is no greater, in principle, that that which is encountered in medical diagnosis. In practice, however, the two domains are worlds apart. If behavioural studies of language disability had the range of resources corresponding to the hospital pathological laboratory and the medical hierarchy (from general practitioner to hospital consultant), the situation would be drastically different.[7]

Let us now move to the more specific discussion of language disorders. They may occur in two broad forms: acquired and developmental. The chief acquired language disorder, *aphasia*, results from damage to the central nervous system and, in particular, the cerebrum. Previously established language knowledge is lost or disturbed by the brain injury. Conversely, a developmental language disorder represents acquisition of language knowledge at an abnormally slow rate, with the consequence that children are significantly different from their peers in language performance.

---

[7]The argument of this section is developed at length in D. Crystal, *Linguistic Encounters with Language Handicap* (Oxford, Blackwell, 1984).

Aphasia

Aphasia (sometimes also called *dysphasia*) is an acquired language disorder.[8] Established language knowledge is disrupted by damage to (usually) the left hemisphere of the cerebrum. Damage to the temporal, frontal, and parietal lobes can especially disturb language functions. Controversies abound within the field of *aphasiology* – terminological, theoretical, and methodological. We may begin with an uncertainty of definition. Is aphasia a *specific* language disorder – does it affect language and only language – or does it represent an impairment of language together with broader cognitive or intellectual deficits? According to the British neurologist, Henry Head, for example, aphasia was a disorder of 'symbolic formulation and expression'.[9] Language, being the main means of symbolic expression, would be centrally affected; but so would other forms of behaviour involving symbols, e.g. the ability to understand traffic signs, play cards, interpret gestures, produce drawings. There would also be changes in the intellectual capacities of the person with aphasia, such as an inability to retrieve and store information in memory, draw logical conclusions, perform arithmetical operations or pay attention. There would be a general reduction in efficiency of information processing, e.g. the aphasic person would respond more slowly, and tire more quickly. An individual might show personality changes, perhaps becoming more irritable, emotional or depressive. Given these characteristics, seen in many patients, it was difficult to see aphasia as constituting a purely linguistic disorder. At the very least, it seemed to involve a more deep-rooted incapacity to use symbols (*asymbolia*), and cognitive and personality changes as well.

A more specific conception of aphasia defines it solely as a linguistic pathology. Advocates of such a view might point to evidence of people with aphasia who manage to live independently, coping with activities of daily living without help, and who are able to manage their finances and drive a car. These individuals appear to have clear communicative intentions which they struggle to realize either through language, or via gesture, drawing or attempting to cue in the listener to the intended message. Individuals with aphasia may show changes in personality such as depression or anxiety, but these changes may be a reaction to the frustration of communicative difficulties and the changes in social roles that result from a stroke or other brain injury. On this account, therefore, we are exclusively within the area of language, and we will allow for the possibility that aphasic people will be very much the same as they were

---

[8]In the past, the change of prefix carried with it a difference in meaning: *a-* 'total lack of'; *dys-* 'partial lack of'. There are trends in the use of the terms, and currently in the UK *dysphasia* is widely used. *Aphasia* is in international use and for this reason we will use this term.

[9]H. Head, *Aphasia and Kindred Disorders of Speech* (Cambridge, Cambridge University Press, 1926).

before – in all respects – bar their reduced ability in speaking, comprehending, reading or writing.

In the final analysis, the difference between the two approaches may
rest on how one interprets the *association* of deficits following brain
damage. An individual patient may show a variety of impaired abilities
following brain injury, and this may be because the lesion may have
damaged a variety of neuronal groups which are involved in different
functions. The larger the amount of brain tissue that is damaged, the
greater the likelihood that the patient will experience impairments
across a wide range of functions. Conversely, a patient with a small
lesion, perhaps centred in the auditory processing areas of the temporal
cortex, may have difficulties restricted to the domain of language and
would show few signs of intellectual or personality changes in domains
largely independent of language. Many of the differences between the
several theoretical positions taken concerning aphasia are the result of
sampling and methodological differences on the part of the analysts. It is
wise, accordingly, for the clinician to adopt a fairly flexible position at
the outset – expecting linguistic problems to be the primary symptoms,
but not excluding the possibilities of significant deficiencies in other
areas of cognition.

The main impression that hits anyone entering the field of aphasiology for the first time is the bewildering variety of pathological behaviours that are presented by people who have suffered from brain
damage. No two patients seem identical, as far as their linguistic and
cognitive faculties are concerned. And this turns out to be more than
just a first impression because detailed analysis of patient samples show
the differences to be considerable. This leads to a second major controversy within aphasiology – whether similarities in behaviour between
some aphasic people permit the disorder to be divided into subtypes or
different syndromes, or whether individual differences in behaviour
should be emphasized, with any subtypes that might be identified being
regarded as abstract categories which cannot account for the behaviour
of the individual aphasic. In practice, a number of classificatory
schemes are often used to categorize patients for research purposes
and to assist communication between clinicians. Most of these schemes
stem from a binary classificatory system, some of the pairs of terms
being as follows:[10]

---

[10]A widely used classificatory system for aphasia can be found in H. Goodglass and E.
Kaplan, *Boston Diagnostic Aphasia Examination* (Philadelphia, Lea & Febiger, 1972).
This system is based on the work of the nineteenth-century neurologist Karl Wernicke
(p. 107), and is often labelled the Wernicke–Lichtheim model. It first divides the
aphasias into fluent and non-fluent types, and then subdivides the fluent syndromes
into Wernicke's, anomic, conduction and transcortical sensory aphasia. The non-fluent
syndromes divide into Broca's and transcortical motor aphasia. The seventh syndrome,
global aphasia, represents a profound impairment of all language functions.

fluent	non-fluent
receptive	expressive
sensory	motor
Wernicke's	Broca's
posterior	anterior

The terms in each column are often used synonymously, and the differences in terminology stem from the different disciplines from which researchers into aphasia are drawn. Labels such as motor/sensory, anterior/posterior, and Broca's/Wernicke's are based upon distinctions in neurology. Lesions anterior to the central sulcus, in the region of the motor cortex and Broca's area, are believed to result in forms of aphasia which are distinctively different from those caused by lesions posterior to this boundary. The fluent/non-fluent and receptive/expressive dichotomies are based to a greater extent on description of the most evident impairments displayed by the aphasic patient, such as hesitant and laboured speech output in non-fluent aphasia. We have already said that individuals with aphasia present with a bewildering variety of pathological behaviour. The reduction of this diversity to a binary classificatory scheme inevitably entails that there will be considerable variety within each category and such schemes can be seen only as a preliminary way of subdividing the spectrum of aphasic impairments.

How can we characterize a non-fluent or expressive aphasic patient? Here is one sample, taken from a man aged 51, who two years previously had suffered a left-hemisphere CVA (see p. 114). The therapist (T) and the patient (P) are discussing the activities the patient undertakes at a day centre that he attends.[11]

T   'they do all sorts of áctivities/ . wòodwork * and
P   * nò/ 'me còok/
T   you cóok/ grèat/
P   àye/ . once a wèek/
T   yĕah/ . 'that's todày/ Thùrsday/
P   àye/ . and thèn/ - 'night-tìme/ sèven o"clock swímming/
T   rêally/
P   yès/ . smàshing/
T   'how do you 'manage one hànded/
P   oh it's alrìght/ àye/ . màte/ . 'mate . 'Jack 'comes and àll/ but – er/ . oh dèar/. 'Jack - er . òld/ er - sèventy/ . 'no . sìxty 'eight/ . Jàck/ - but swìm/ . 'me . 'me 'like thìs/ - swìmming - er/ - 'I 'can't sày it/ - but Jâck/ - er - 'swimming on frònt/. er - bàck/
T   so he cán * do -

---

[11]Transcription conventions: increasing pause length marked by . (short). – . – – (long); each unit of intonation (compare p. 43) is marked by /; the main pitch movement in this unit is indicated by an accent (` falling, ´ rising, ‾ level, ˇ falling-rising, ^ rising-falling); stress on other syllables is marked by '; * indicates that the participants were speaking at the same time; T = therapist; P = patient.

P   * àye/ but 'one hànd
T   'one-'handed 'back-strȯke/ . I 'can't i'magine what it's lȉke . 'swimming
     one-hànded/ . 'doesn't one side 'keep sȉnking/
P   àye/ . it's àlright though/

The first characteristic of the extract we would note is that the two
interactants are working together to construct this dialogue. Unlike
the example transcripts given for the pre-linguistic pathologies of
schizophrenia (p. 158) and autism (p. 161), there is no evidence of
pragmatic disability or interactional failure. The patient responds
promptly to the therapist's questions and provides relevant information in his answers, which in turn suggests that the patient's comprehension is not grossly impaired. But there are abnormalities in the
patient's language output. Aphasiologists often make preliminary
observations about a patient's language under two headings: grammatical or sentence processing, and lexical-semantic processing.
Observations of grammar would include the patient's ability to understand and produce elements of clause and phrase structure (p. 45).
Lexical-semantic observations would concern vocabulary choice: is the
patient able to select words which convey the intended meaning, and
is the patient able to locate word forms with ease? The extract illustrates features of both grammatical and lexical-semantic disturbance,
with the disruptions of the former being most marked. Under the
heading of grammar, we would note the reduced and incomplete
sentence structure (what is often referred to as *agrammatic* speech).
The intonation units are also short, and pausing is frequent – features
which are particularly important in the categorization of the extract as
an instance of non-fluent aphasic speech. There is one sentence within
the aphasic person's output that is a complete sentence (*I can't say it*).
This sentence is atypical of the rest of the data, both for its completeness and also for the correct use of the first person pronoun. Notice
that in all other instances in the extract *I* is replaced by *me* – an
unusual feature of adult language although one which is characteristic
of early child language. This suggests that the sentence is a *stereotype*:
a linguistic unit which has been stored as a complete chunk and is
used at specific points in the interaction, namely when the patient has
difficulties in formulating his message. In terms of maintaining the
interaction, the stereotype is useful as it signals to the other participant
that the next part of the message may contain an error, or that help or
patience may be needed from the non-aphasic participant in order to
convey this part of the message. Under the heading of lexical semantics, there are two instances of mis-selection of vocabulary in the
extract (*seventy/sixty-eight; front/back*), but in each instance the
patient rapidly self-corrects his errors, which suggests that the degree
of lexical-semantic impairment is mild. The mis-selected words are

semantically linked to the intended target, and this error type is labelled *semantic paraphasia*.[12]

The second extract is taken from a conversation with a man with a diagnosis of fluent aphasia. The patient is aged 67, and experienced a left-hemisphere CVA three months earlier. The therapist and patient are discussing the patient's war-time military service.

T   so you were at Dùnkirk/

P   yès/

T   'what do you re'member of thát/

P   [nə nə] not very 'far because they 'kicked us òut/

T   do/ did you have to get a 'boat from the béach/

P   yès/ but 'then we had to 'come bàck because they were/ - [sə psə psə psə] (+ *gesture*) they were 'sending 'things dòwn/ you knòw/ so we 'came bàck/. we 'came bàck/ and we 'came up from – / rîght up/ then we 'got òut/ – ònce/ – er er a gùn/ er nò/ . 'what do they cáll 'them/ the vèry 'little/ – the smàll men/. the smàll –

T   the smáll 'men/

P   nò/ 'small sòldiers/. nò/ the òther 'one/ . say . 'not sòldier/ . 'not sòldier – /

T   are they the Gúrkhas/

P   nò/ . nò/ . 'what's the 'opposite to a sóldier/

T   sàilor/

P   thàt's it/

The degree of collaboration between the participants is a remarkable feature of this transcript. The patient has marked word-finding or lexical retrieval difficulties in the latter part of the extract. In order to circumvent this linguistic difficulty, the patient cues the therapist to the intended word through asking her questions and giving feedback on the accuracy of her guesses at the intended target. The accuracy with which the patient monitors the therapist's guesses suggests that his comprehension abilities are relatively unimpaired. There is considerable pausing within the patient's turns, but interspersed between these there were also complete and often lengthy intonational units. It is this latter characteristic that leads to the categorization of the speaker as a fluent aphasic. In terms of grammatical structure, many sentences are incomplete but there are also examples of full sentences. The incomplete sentences may be a product of the marked lexical-semantic disruption evident in the extract. The patient tries to talk around a subject (*circumlocution*), for example, *sending things down* for 'bombing'; specific items of vocabulary are replaced by general words, such as *things* for 'bombs', and *small men* for 'sailors'.

---

[12]The term *paraphasia* is a general term, which refers in its broadest sense to any error involving the unintentional substitution, transposition or addition of a basic unit of language – whether a sound, syllable, morpheme or word – in speech. Errors which show a phonological relation between the intended target and the word actually produced are termed *phonemic paraphasias*. The equivalent term to describe errors in writing is *paragraphia*, and in reading aloud, *paralexia*.

Let us turn now to another example of a fluent aphasia, but in this instance where the patient also shows comprehension or receptive problems. The following sample is taken from a 66-year-old male patient, six months after a left CVA, with associated right hemiplegia. He spoke rapidly and loudly, producing several stretches of fluent but unintelligible speech (*jargon*, indicated below by the number of syllables), and paying little attention to many of the therapist's efforts to intervene. There were also major problems in his reading and writing. In this extract, the therapist is trying to establish whether the patient can identify various objects in the room. The sample shows some echolalia – repetition with minimal change of what has just been said to him, in a context which suggests that comprehension is absent. There is also some *perseveration* on words – a tendency to repeat a behaviour, in this instance a word, even though it is no longer appropriate to continue.

T 'show me a pìcture/ on the wàll/
P 'picture on the wàll/ òh by [*2 syllables*] / thère/ [*looks in wrong direction*] in the . [*2 syllables*] look at the er . whàt do they cáll them/ 'knights . of the chùrch/ and there [*1 syllable*] we can 'go no [*syllable*] and . of . over [*syllable*] . and [*2 syllables*] . there's pàrt of [*2 syllables*]
T yès/ 'show me the pìcture/ of the mòuse/
P the móuse/
T 'where's the pìcture/ of the mòuse/
P òh/ 'picture of a môuse/ . pìcture/ . mòuse/
T it's 'up on the wàll/ it's 'next to the càlendar/ . sée/ . hère/
P thére/ . 'this one hère/
T thàt one/
P oh/ . you've 'got to 'move .
T the 'calendar is 'next to thāt/ .
P thàt's right/ . it's 'next to the 'person .
T ÒK/
P 'that where . and 'there . and 'there something here as wèll/ somewhere 'other 'end of . [*4 syllables*] 'there's....

In this sequence, the lack of comprehension is very much in evidence: the patient echoes the therapist's sentences, but does not relate them to the objects in question; several of his own sentences are unrelated to the theme being discussed; several are relatively 'empty' of meaning (e.g. *what do they call them; this one here*); several grammatical structures are begun, but they lead nowhere, and it is unclear what, if any, meaning they have for the patient. Overall, there is a confident, definite intonation, which in fact is no guide to the patient's ability.

There are certain important issues in the aphasia literature which the above samples do not illustrate. The first concerns the extent to which all modalities of communication have been affected by the brain damage. The above discussion focuses on speech and listening comprehension; but what about reading and writing? Inability to read (*alexia*) and write (*agraphia*), along with their less severe forms (*dyslexia* and *dysgraphia* – though these terms are sometimes used to include the former, regardless of severity) may also be apparent, but in some patients reading and writing remain largely unaffected. It is also possible to have the one without the other (i.e. 'pure alexia', or 'alexia without agraphia'), or to have the disorder focused *solely* on reading/writing ability, speech/auditory comprehension being largely unaffected. Because of the several possibilities for disturbance, full assessments of aphasia always include, as part of their battery of tests, components in which all four modalities of language are investigated. The possibility of independent impairment of the different modalities of language use indicates that the mental processing routes for the different input and output channels of language use – and presumably also their neurological substrate – are distinct. Where dissociations between performances across different modalities occur, brain damage has disrupted one processing route, but selectively spared others.

A second big issue concerns the extent to which the notion of aphasia can be applied to children as well as to adults. This is not a major issue if a stroke or other brain damage affects young children after they have acquired language: as with the adult, an aphasic condition can result.[13] But the term has also been used to apply to children who, for some reason, have failed to develop language at all, or who have done so only partially or deviantly. The term *developmental aphasia/dysphasia* (occasionally *childhood* or *infantile aphasia/dysphasia*) is sometimes used in such cases, where the 'obvious' causes of underdeveloped language can be ruled out (i.e. there is no evidence of deafness, other learning disabilities, motor disability, or severe emotional or personality problems). This is a kind of diagnosis by exclusion: in the absence of known alternatives, one concludes that there must be some minimal brain damage present, and it is this which justifies the extension of the term. Against this, it has been argued that, if aphasia means basically 'loss of acquired language', then it is hardly right to use this label to apply to children who are slow to acquire language knowledge. Such children present very different problems of assessment and treatment, particularly with regard to the discussion of the issue of intermittent access to language knowledge in cases of acquired aphasia (p. 150). Whereas patients with acquired aphasia may show considerable variability in language performances, these same degrees of variation in behaviour are not observed in developmental conditions.

---

[13]Even here though, there are major differences. The young brain is more 'plastic' than the adult brain and capable of compensating for damage, hence recovery is likely to be more rapid and more complete. There is, however, evidence that children who have made an apparently good recovery from aphasia have long-lasting subtle language impairments and also difficulties in subsequent literacy and arithmetic learning. See D. Bishop, 'Language development after focal brain damage'. In D. Bishop and K. Mogford (eds) *Language Development in Exceptional Circumstances* (Hove, Psychology Press, 1993).

It should be plain, both from the terminological confusion which exists within this subject, and also from the uncertainty with which different aphasic syndromes are postulated, that this is an area of language pathology which provides enormous scope for research – perhaps more than any other. The importance of aphasia research is undenied – not only for clinical reasons (i.e. to help sufferers from the disorder) but also for theoretical reasons (to obtain a clearer understanding of the structure and function of the brain). Aphasia research has in fact been one of the main means of discovery about how the human mind processes language (compare p. 101). This is the only syndrome where the various levels of language (grammar, vocabulary etc.) can be seen functioning separately from each other. By examining what can go wrong, and whereabouts in the language system that something goes wrong, suggestions can be made about 'how language works', which might be useful in other contexts than the clinical. Aphasia, it has been said (though not without controversy), is a key to our understanding of language as a whole.[14]

Developmental language disorders

Most of the children who are noticeably behind their chronological peers in their ability to produce or comprehend speech fall into one of two categories: they are learning disabled (or mentally handicapped), to some degree; or they suffer from a degree of hearing loss. A significant number of children, however, manifest neither of these problems, and yet are still well behind their peers in language ability. These are the children who have been referred to in the past as *developmentally aphasic*, but in more recent usage, as having *specific language disorder*. Their diagnosis is classically one of exclusion (compare p. 24): there is no deafness or other sensory-perceptual deficit, no motor disorder, no evidence of global learning difficulties, and no psychiatric difficulty (such as maladjustment, or severe emotional problems). Their learning environments appear adequate, and parenting practices are not in any way unusual. On the other hand, they do display psychological, social and educational problems – although whether these are the cause or the result of the linguistic difficulty remains an imponderable. There is no gross neurological impairment, although advances in methods of brain imaging (p. 102) have shown indications of subtle abnormalities in brain structure.[15]

---

[14]Further reading in aphasia, M. T. Sarno, *Acquired Aphasia* (New York, Academic Press, 1981); A. Ellis and A. Young, *Human Cognitive Neuropsychology* (Hove, Psychology Press, 1996). A review, stressing the linguistic angle, is R. Lesser, *Linguistic Investigations of Aphasia* (London, Whurr, 2nd edn, 1989). See also D. Caplan, *Language: Structure, Processing and Disorders* (Cambridge, Mass, MIT Press, 1992).
[15]See, for example, E. Plante, L. Swisher, R. Vance and S. Rapcsak, 'MRI findings in boys with specific language impairment', *Brain and Language*, 41, 52–66, 1991.

In recent years a great deal of progress has been made in our understanding of the bases of these disorders, through a range of psychological and linguistic studies which have investigated the problem from several interrelated points of view. Two broad hypotheses have been advanced: first, that the disorders are a consequence of a more fundamental deficit of a cognitive nature; second, that the disorders are a result of a deficit in the linguistic processing system alone. There is evidence to suggest that both hypotheses are right, some of the time. There is clear evidence that some of these children have deficits in their auditory perception ability (compare p. 143); some have problems in their auditory storage capacity (a very poor auditory short-term memory); some have difficulty in processing the information perceived through the auditory channel (requiring slowly presented inputs); and some have difficulty in attending to sequences of items presented auditorily (a 'reduced auditory attention span'). An interesting feature is that the rhythmical abilities of many of these children are poor, both in non-verbal as well as prosodic ways (e.g. in dancing, movement, or tapping rhythms out). Some have poor awareness of symbolic behaviour generally, showing poor appreciation of what is involved in play, or gesture (particularly the case with children displaying autistic tendencies, compare p. 161). Some are highly distractible and disorganized in all aspects of their behaviour (*hyperkinetic* or *hyperactive* children). All of this adds up to a view that many of these children have definite cognitive problems, especially in relation to auditory imperception and attention control. If they do have these problems, then naturally their speech processing abilities will be affected. The disorder is not primarily one of language, on this view; and treatment would proceed primarily on the basis of attacking the underlying cognitive difficulty, e.g. by working on attention, space/time relationships, symbolic play or rhythmic skills.

By contrast, there are some children (as many as a third, according to some estimates) who display the same kind of marked language delay, but who seem to have few difficulties with any of the tasks referred to in the previous paragraph. On general sensory processing and auditory processing tasks, their performance is within normal limits, or only slightly abnormal. The analysis of their language brings to light a range of abnormal patterns which it is difficult to associate with any cognitive explanation, and we are forced to conclude that the problem is restricted to the linguistic processing system as such. These difficulties may be primarily phonological, i.e. the children have particular difficulty in learning the sound system of their language. Difficulties quite commonly lie in the development of the system of sound contrasts, resulting in speech which is not easily intelligible; and delay in acquiring the suprasegmental aspects of phonology (see p. 43) is possible, although less widely reported. Developmental disorders of grammar and semantics can also be identified. In the former, children might be significantly behind their peers in their morphological development or in their ability to combine linguistic units to form phrases, clauses and strings of sentences. In the latter, children might demonstrate a limited vocabulary, errors in word use, or particular difficulties in retrieving appropriate words. Difficulties in understanding may be present, as well as the more evident difficulties in speech. 'Pure' disorders – that is, disorders which can be observed in one level of language organization alone – are less common than disorders in which the child has difficulties across a range of levels of linguistic organization. In the pre-literate child, difficulties will be restricted to speech and the understanding of speech. But when the child subsequently is taught to read and write, problems of a similar order may be observed in written language.

Here is an example of a child who was diagnosed as having an expressive language problem. His comprehension of speech, using one of the standard tests, was normal for his age; hearing was within normal limits – indeed, everything that could be tested was within normal limits. The only trouble was that he was producing language such as the following, and he was 4 years of age:

T   nòw/ 'here's the bóok/ – 'this is the 'book we were 'looking at befòre/ ìsn't it/
P   tèddy bear/
T   there's a tèddy bear/ yès/
P   'teddy a hòme/
T   you've 'got one at hŏme/
P   yèah/
T   'what do you càll him/ – –
P   a tèddy bear/
T   has he 'got a náme/
P   yèah/ – he nàme/
T   what ìs it/
P   er
T   'what's his nàme/ –
P   tèddy bear/
T   tèddy bear/
P   yèah/
T   does he – do you 'keep him in your bédroom/
P   yèah/ –
T   whère in your 'bedroom does he 'live/
P   don't knòw/
T   you don't knòw/ – – 'let's have a 'look at this pìcture/ – 'what's thàt/
P   a bàth/
T   yès/ – and 'what's thàt/
P   dùck/
T   yès/ – there's anòther 'duck like thát one/
P   sàme/
T   sàme/ 'that's rìght/ 'good bòy/ – and 'whàt's thàt/ – – – do you knów/
     [*points to towel in the picture*]
P   swìmming/ –
T   it's a tòwel/

P tòwel/
T that's rìght/ yès/ – I 'wonder who's 'going to gò in that 'bath/
P mè/

Three kinds of information are necessary before we can carry out a linguistic assessment of children with developmental language disorders. First, we must have descriptive information, so as to be able to identify and label every feature of the language being used or responded to by the patient. This will basically take the form of a phonological and a grammatical description (see Chapter 2). What we must remember is that to be really useful the description must be systematic and comprehensive: it is not enough to collect a few examples of abnormal structures or sounds that happen to have caught your attention. Only a systematic description, supported if necessary by statistical analysis, can provide a solid foundation for assessment conclusions to be drawn. Second, we need information about the strategies of linguistic interaction being used between therapist and child: what means are being used to elicit language, and how far does the child initiate conversation? Is the child being involved in a free-moving conversation, or are tasks being linguistically structured in some way (for example, is the child being asked to imitate, to complete a sentence, to choose between alternatives)? Differences in the sampling situation, and in task difficulty, need to be carefully watched in carrying out assessment (compare p. 34).

Third, it is necessary to grade the sounds and structures encountered in order to provide a yardstick for carrying out assessment and treatment. It is this last point on which most attention has been focused. The usual (some would say the only) way of grading linguistic features is to arrange them in terms of their expected order of appearance as found in studies of normal language acquisition (compare p. 153). Scales of language acquisition are established, on which are placed in sequence those sounds/structures which appear first in normal children, which appear next, and so on. Not everything is known about the acquisition of language, of course, and so there will be many gaps in these scales; but enough information is available these days to enable the task to be carried out, at least in outline, in the form of general assessments and profiles of individual children. The following sentences illustrate some aspects of this developmental progress in the area of grammar: on the left is an indication of age; on the right are given some sentences that might be expected to be in use at that time:

16 months	dàddy/ gòne/ mòre/ thère/ nò/ tèddy/
21 months	'daddy thère/ 'see dàddy/ 'want bòok/ nò 'potty/ 'big càr/ 'in bòx/ whère téddy
24 months	'want that càr/ my dàddy 'gone/ bòx in thére/
27 months	'daddy 'kick bàll/ 'teddy gòne nów/ 'where 'that tèddy 'gone/ 'want more mìlk in thére/

30 months	'daddy gone 'town in càr/ 'me 'want mòre thóse/ that 'man do 'kick that bàll/ 'where you 'put that 'big càr/
36 months	'daddy 'gone in the gàrden/ and he did 'fall òver/ you 'pick that bàll up/ 'cos it's prètty/

Even if no further information is given about the types of structures that characterize each age range, it should now be possible to make informed guesses about the likely level of developmental delay involved in the child illustrated above – or with the following set of sentences, taken from a conversation with another 4-year-old:

the 'cat had kìtten/	'Mummy 'house 'be in thère/
it blàck/	it 'have a 'nice bèd/
yès/	'what it 'doing nòw/
it 'play 'lots and lòts/	it 'fall òver/[16]
'mother cat lìke it/	
it crỳing/	

A similar kind of progression could be established for the development of phonology (see further p. 202).

No mention has so far been made of semantic development. Undoubtedly, the more we learn about the normal processes of semantic development in children, the more we will be able to understand what is taking place in developmental disorders. But, as pointed out in Chapter 2 (p. 47), work in semantics lags far behind the other domains. All we can do in this book is express caution about the use of oversimplified measures, such as the idea of vocabulary counting. It would seem to be an obvious thing to do – to estimate a child's developing linguistic capacity by working out the size of the vocabulary – and estimates are often given, for children at different ages. The trouble is that these estimates vary enormously. One pair of estimates for 5-year-olds varied from 2000 words to 10000 words. Why is this? One reason is the difficulty in identifying what is to count as a word in spoken language (compare *it's, shan't* etc. – one word or two?). Another is that everything depends on what kind of vocabulary we are thinking of: is it *active* vocabulary (i.e. words actively used) or *passive* vocabulary (i.e. words known and understood, but not necessarily used)? The latter will be a much larger figure. Then there is the problem of how to be sure that the child does indeed *know* the vocabulary we are counting. A child who uses such words as *reptile* or *dinosaur* may be getting them only half right – as one child did who pointed at a picture of *Tyrannosaurus rex* and called it a lion. The problem for vocabulary counters is this: do they include this word in their estimates of that child's knowledge, or exclude

---

[16]Most of these sentences have three main clause elements, but there is plainly some uncertainty, especially about verbs. In terms of the above progression, a level of 24–27 months is suggested.

it? There are arguments both ways. Last, there is the problem of different senses of the same word: should we count *top* (meaning 'summit') and *top* (meaning 'toy') as the same or different words? If that seems an easy decision, then what about the various meanings of most of the common verbs in the language – *take, give, get* etc.? It is for such reasons that vocabulary development is a field which it is difficult to make firm decisions about, and thus difficult to use in clinical language studies. We can make rough estimates, but little more. Of far greater importance is to see how the vocabulary is used by the child – or, in other words, how the child puts the vocabulary into sentences and differing situations (which is what a grammatical analysis is basically trying to do).

We have mentioned disorders at all levels of language structure – grammar, phonology and semantics – but what of language use or pragmatics? It is a truism that many patients have difficulty in using language appropriately; what is less obvious is why this happens. Typically, children who have a good command of language but a poor command of language use are given a wide range of impressionistic and often misleading descriptions: we have heard them called 'confused', 'awkward' and 'obstinate'; one was described critically with the words, 'he's always trying to be funny'; another with 'he just won't co-operate'. Now although there are undoubtedly many children for whom these words would be an apt description, there are also many for whom they miss the point entirely. It is so easy to assume that those who use language inappropriately are displaying a perverse attitude, especially if they have an excellent command of language structure. But it is gradually becoming apparent that there are many children whose behaviour is not under conscious control, and who are genuinely handicapped by an inability to understand and control the way in which language is used in everyday interaction. These are the children who have been referred to as having a 'pragmatic disorder', or, when seen in the context of an accompanying difficulty of vocabulary and comprehension, a 'semantic–pragmatic disorder'. A similar functional inadequacy can also be seen in some adult patients, notably in the more 'fluent' kinds of aphasia, the conversational deficits seen following right-hemisphere damage, and in certain psychopathological conditions (such as schizophrenia).

It is important to appreciate that these children display a wide range of symptoms, and that at present it is not possible to generalize about the condition. There are many anecdotes about how the children behave, but few detailed case-studies.[17] Plainly there exists a continuum of pragmatic handicap, ranging from children who say little or nothing to those who talk normally. At one end of this continuum, there are

---

[17]But see M. McTear and G. Conti-Ramsden, *Pragmatic Disability in Children* (London, Whurr, 1992).

those who are completely unwilling to engage in conversation, and who are totally unresponsive to the demands of normal social interaction. They may, to all intents and purposes, appear mute. Somewhat less extreme are children who are responsive, in a limited way, but not very assertive; they will talk when spoken to, but will not initiate a conversation themselves. Then, further along the continuum, there are those who are willing to engage in conversation, but who introduce their own rules, such as bringing in bizarre or irrelevant topics, answering their own questions, echoing what has just been said, not listening to what has just been said, talking too much, or changing the subject in unexpected ways. And last, at the near-normal end of the continuum, there are children who carry on a generally normal conversation, but who occasionally introduce a remark which is 'odd' (e.g. asking 'why?' at the wrong place), sounding rather stereotyped, or failing to cope when someone uses language in a special way (e.g. when people are 'kidding' or being sarcastic).

The following examples illustrate just a few pragmatically abnormal interactions. (It is important to emphasize that some of these examples could occur in normal children or adults – for example, when they are not paying attention, or are temporarily confused. A diagnosis of pragmatic disorder would be appropriate only when an accumulation of similar instances presented a general picture of inappropriate language use.) In the first, P does not answer the question, and keeps straying from the point:

T   'where do you 'go to schòol/
P   Tòmmy 'goes to mý 'school/ be'cause I 'see him in the 'hall everydày/ but
we   have 'different tèachers/ and 'he has a 'new bìcycle/

In the next case P seems unable to see the point of T's question:

T   thàt's a 'nice pícture/ – can you téll me a'bout it/
P   yès/ *silence*
T   well 'go ón then/ tèll me a'bout it/

In the next, P says something which he couldn't really know, because T hasn't told him what the games are yet:

T   will you 'play some gámes 'with me/
P   yès/
T   they're 'very èasy gámes/
P   they 'are indèed/

In the following case, P imitates T, inappropriately:

T   [*greeting the headteacher*] good mòrning 'John/
P   good mòrning 'John/

Here, P takes T literally:

T　'take this 'note to Mr Smìth's 'room/
P　*obediently goes to Mr Smith's room and returns still carrying the note*

In the following sequence, things get really confused:

T　which ràce would you 'like to be 'in/
P　I 'like to be in Blànktown at the spórts day/
T　in Blànktown/
P　yès/
T　what do you mèan/
P　I mèan sómething/
T　'is there a spòrts day in 'Blankschool/
P　there is nòt/
　　there is a 'sports day in Dàshschool/
T　then what's Blànktown 'got to 'do with it/
P　nòthing/
T　then whý did you mèntion it/
P　in'deed I dìd 'mention it/
T　whỳ did you 'mention it/
P　I don't knòw/

And, as a last example, a further piece of inappropriateness:[18]

P　[*meeting the first author as he arrives at P's school*]
　　helló/ are 'you Pro'fessor Crỳstal/
A　yès/
P　mỳ name is 'J– 'K–/ I have to 'take you to 'see the headmàster/
A　thànk you/ 'which way ìs it/
P　'down hère/ [*they begin to walk*]
　　do you lìke being márried/

The interaction between levels

Although it is possible to find patients whose ability to control linguistic structure is excellent and whose problems are solely pragmatic in character, it is far more usual for them to display a mixture of difficulties. Most patients who present with pragmatic symptoms have linguistic problems too, such as a poor command of the way verbs are used, or a difficulty in stringing sentences together in a narrative. The structural and pragmatic aspects of the handicap, one would now say, *interact* in various ways. This emphasis on the interaction between the different aspects of linguistic disability is something which came very much to the fore in the 1980s. The language model on p. 41ff, however, does not

---

[18]Several of the above examples are taken from published studies; some are from our own files. See further, M. McTear, *Children's Conversation* (Oxford, Blackwell, 1985), Chap. 9; T. M. Gallagher and C. A. Prutting (eds), *Pragmatic Assessment and Intervention Issues in Language* (San Diego, College-Hill Press, 1983).

reflect this: rather, it shows the way clinical linguistics was developing in the 1970s, where a great deal of attention was devoted to a detailed analysis of individual levels of language. An account would be given of the patient's phonological ability, with no reference being made to other (grammatical, semantic, pragmatic) domains; or a patient's grammar would be studied independently of phonology and semantics; and so on.

In cases where it is plain that only one level is affected (as in a simple kind of articulation problem), this focus would not be misleading; but in the majority of cases, such simplicity does not obtain. The language of most children with developmental disorders or of most adult aphasics is a mixture of symptoms that can be located at different linguistic levels; and the question of how they interact thus immediately arises. We can elect to examine the grammatical aspect of the problem alone, or the phonological aspect, in just the same way as a doctor can investigate one part of the body while temporarily ignoring other parts; but before arriving at a linguistic diagnosis, the language clinician would be wise to bear the medical approach in mind, with its proper emphasis on the ultimate need to consider the way the body functions in an integrated, balanced manner. In language, as in the body as a whole, what happens in one domain may affect the functioning of another domain. The linguistic evidence is slowly accumulating, both in normal child language studies and in clinical studies, that a great deal of interaction between levels of language organization is routine, and may be an important element in the diagnosis of language disability.

As an example, we may consider the following dialogue between a therapist and a child patient aged $4\frac{1}{2}$, whose grammar was close to that of a 2-year-old. Therapy had been proceeding on building up Subject–Verb (e.g. *the boy is eating*) and Verb–Object (*kick a ball*) sentences, and had been succeeding. The child's vocabulary was also limited, for his age, but he was known to have about 200 words, and the therapist decided to elicit a three-element sentence of Subject–Verb–Object (such as *the boy is kicking a ball*), and part of the dialogue went like this:

    T   'what's the 'boy dòing/
    P   'kicking a bàll/
    T   that's rìght/ he's 'kicking a bàll/ the 'boy's 'kicking a bàll/ – whát's 'happening/
    P   'kicking a bàll/
    T   whò is/
    P   a bòy/
    T   yês/ 'can you 'say the 'whole thíng/
    P   'him kìcking/
    T   whò's 'kicking/
    P   the bòy/
    T   'what's the 'boy dòing/
    P   'kicking the bàll/ ... ...

This kind of conversation proceeded for some time, with P 'evading' the complete form of the sentence which T was trying to get him to say. Finally, he tried it, with the following result:

P   he – 'him 'boy ki – 'kicking a bàll/
T   góod bòy/ 'say it agáin/ whát's he 'doing/
P   [dum] 'boy bi – 'bicking a a bàll/

What is of note here is the way P's pronunciation deteriorates as he tries for the more complex sentence: the word *kicking* is affected by the surrounding [b] sounds; a nonsense word comes in ([dum] may be a blend of *the* and *him*); and the child becomes really quite non-fluent. In some cases, attempting a complex sentence can cause a noticeable stutter – something which has often been heard in normal children as they pass through certain grammatical stages (p. 190). The dialogue thus illustrates the existence of an interaction between phonology and grammar, and incidentally indicates how careful a clinician has to be in pacing language training.

It is not yet clear what is happening when patients display effects of this kind, whether between phonology and grammar, phonology and semantics, grammar and semantics, or any other combination. There may be a general constraint which limits the amount of linguistic complexity it is possible for the brain to process at any moment; or perhaps some components of language are more central than others, or more easily disrupted. One of the most important current developments in psycholinguistics is the construction of models of mental function which interrelate the linguistic components in different ways. Using these models, it is then possible to suggest hypotheses about the form language should take when one component is impaired, and to test these hypotheses in experiments or by analysing language samples. Commonly, these models also incorporate the elements thought to be involved in the process of reading and writing.[19, 20]

---

[19]There is a review of the literature on the interaction between levels in D. Crystal (1987), 'Towards a 'bucket' theory of language disability: taking account of interaction between linguistic levels.' *Clinical Linguistics and Phonetics* 1, 7–22. For the psychological issues involved, see M. Harris and M. Coltheart, *Language Processing in Children and Adults: An Introduction* (London, Routledge & Kegan Paul, 1986).
[20]For reviews of literature on developmental language disorders see W. Yule and M. Rutter (eds), *Language Development and Disorders* (London, MacKeith Press, 1987); S. Gathercole and A. Baddeley, *Working Memory and Language* (Hove, Lawrence Erlbaum, 1993); D. Bishop, *Uncommon Understanding: Development and Disorders of Language Comprehension in Children* (Hove, Psychology Press, 1997); D. Bishop and K. Mogford, *Language Development in Exceptional Circumstances* (Hove, Psychology Press, 1993).

Motor programming disorders

The model of the communication chain proposes that once the linguistic encoding phase is complete, the message-sender has 'decided' which meaning to convey, and has chosen a grammatical construction and the relevant vocabulary. All that remains is to give this abstract structure a phonological-phonetic 'shape'. The evidence that a model of this kind has some psychological reality comes from the disorder known as *apraxia*, or *dyspraxia*.[21] In its most general sense, apraxia refers to the disruption of the ability to produce an intentional motor response – that is, patients know what they want to do, but are unable to retrieve movement programmes and command the motor system to implement the plan. This inability to perform muscular activities cannot be explained by any weakness or paralysis of muscles, or difficulties in co-ordinating movements, or by deficits in sensory feedback systems. A defining feature of an apraxic disorder is a disparity between automatic and volitional behaviour. Involuntary activities, using the same muscles, are not affected. We might observe a patient's tongue moving rapidly and with normal power and range of movement to remove a biscuit crumb from the lips, but when the same patient is asked to stick out the tongue, we might observe a delay in initiating any movement, then numerous false starts and groping attempts to protrude the tongue. In severe cases, where patients are unable to comply with the command, they may show that they know what is required of them by reaching with their fingers into their mouth and pulling out their tongue. In the same way, we might ask a patient to perform a particular speech activity (such as to repeat the phase *Good morning*), and he or she will be unable to do it. A little while later, however, we might notice that the same patient had said the phrase automatically, while passing someone on the way out of the clinic. The more an activity is automatic and embedded in a context, the more cues are provided to aid retrieval of an appropriate motor plan. Highly volitional activities, which are less supported by context, are more difficult to organize, and it is within these activities that the effect of an apraxia will be most evident.

These difficulties in performing simply voluntary acts are by no means restricted to linguistic tasks, and indeed the neurological and neuropsychological classifications of apraxia are mainly concerned with non-linguistic abilities. A number of forms of apraxia can be traced to disturbances of perceptual systems, and tend to follow lesions in the

---

[21]As with the aphasia/dysphasia distinction above, usage varies: *apraxia* implies a complete disruption of the motor activity involved; *dyspraxia* implies a partial disruption. In discussion of acquired forms of the disorder, however, the term *apraxia* is more usual – prefixed by *mild*, *moderate* or *severe* to indicate the severity of the disorder. Developmental forms of the disorder are usually referred to as *dyspraxia*.

right parietal lobe. *Constructional apraxia*, for example, refers to a specific difficulty with visuospatial tasks, such as drawing, or arranging bricks in a certain order. In *apraxia for dressing*, patients are unable to relate the forms of their clothes to that of their bodies. A vest, for example, has four holes into which particular body parts have to be placed in a specific order, and it represents a complex visuospatial puzzle for the patient with a dressing apraxia (and also for the young child learning to dress). The more specific movement-related apraxias can be found in any movement system that is capable of finely controlled volitional movement. It is not surprising, therefore, that apraxias are described in the movements of the hand and arm (*limb apraxia*) and the oral musculature (p. 121). Limb apraxia interferes with volitional hand and arm movements, and can cause disturbances of writing and signed communicative systems. When speech is affected, the syndrome may be specified as *apraxia of speech, verbal* or *articulatory apraxia* (or *dyspraxia*): it then refers to a disruption in the ability to control the position of the muscles for speech, and the sequence in which they are used. Putting it briefly, the patient aims to say one sequence of sounds, and another comes out. *Oral apraxia* represents an impairment of both speech and non-speech oral movements, and is generally seen as a more severe variant of apraxia of speech.

The movement apraxias may occur in both acquired and developmental forms. The acquired form results from lesions in the language-dominant cerebral hemisphere – usually the left. It often co-occurs with aphasia, and so careful assessment is required in order to make a differential diagnosis. In the developmental form of the disorder, no clear pattern of brain pathology has been demonstrated. The theoretical problems over using the phrase *developmental dyspraxia* are the same as those involved in using *developmental dysphasia* (see p. 171).

Here is an example of some adult apraxic speech. It is part of a conversation with a severely apraxic woman of 60, who had had a left CVA two years previously. It would seem from later in the extract that underlying the opening utterances is an attempt to produce the word *mill* or *milling*.[22]

    T   you 'used to 'live on a fàrm/ dìdn't you/
    P   yés/ yés/ . yés/
    T   what 'sort of 'farm was thìs/
    P   də . də . 'mɛnɛ . ədə . yes . there
    T   did you have cóws on it/
    P   yés/ . yés/ . də – əm – mɛː . əm.

---

[22]It is difficult to be sure what the patient's target is, in spontaneous conversation of this kind. In order to analyse apraxic language, a structured test of articulation is always essential, in which the therapist knows in advance what word the patient is attempting to say.

T   or 'was it cròps only/
P   yés/ . yés/ . əm . bə . pə . tʃ . ə:m – –
T   where wàs your 'farm/
P   jɛ – dɛ:
T   'was it around hére/
P   nó/ . nó/
T   'was it in Èngland/
P   tɪ . sjɔ:s – də – təs . sɔ:'tə/
T   Yòrkshire/
P   yés/ yés/
T   ahà/ whereabòuts in 'Yorkshire/
P   ə:m . ə:m – 'bɑ:nz . tìn/
T   oh wèll/ gòod/ did you lìke it up 'there/
P   yês/ . yês/ . yês/
T   was it a bíg 'farm/
P   nó/ – there was – də – ə:m . ə:m – mə̀nɪsp/
    – òh/ whàt/ – – wɒ'ræntən/ yès/ – ə:m
T   can you wrìte it 'for me/
P   yès/ (writes) mìn/
T   a mìll/
P   yès/ yès/ . yès/ . yès/
T   I sèe/ - for pùmping/
P   nó/
T   was it for grìnding/
P   yés/ yés/ yés/
T   'grinding whàt/
P   kɔ̀:rs/
T   còrn/
P   yès/

Theoretically, the difference between aphasia and apraxia is clear enough. There is normal (or less disordered) use of language in other modalities, and normal awareness of vocabulary, grammar, etc. within the speech modality. But as soon as patients attempt to construct connected speech, other than for the most automatic of phrases, they encounter major difficulties of expression. Their ability to repeat a sequence of the same sounds is also much reduced. The errors that are made are very inconsistent: a /p/ phoneme may emerge as a [p], [t], [f] etc. in a relatively short space of time; some sounds may perseverate (compare p. 170) throughout a word or phrase, as in the following example from an apraxic child of 4½, who had a tendency to perseverate on bilabials: *Christmas tree* was produced as /'pɪ'bɪ'pi:/ and /'bɪ'mɪ'pri:/; *elephant* as /hɛpɪpɪmp/. In the more severe cases, even vowels may be affected. Speech rhythm will tend to be slow and erratic, as the patient tries to obtain some measure of control. Difficulty in starting words may produce an effect which resembles stuttering (see p. 188).

This set of characteristics permits a potentially clear contrast to be made with aphasic symptomatology. The linguistic problems in apraxia are primarily identifiable at the phonetic–phonological level, and do not affect other modalities; as a result, remediation involves a quite different kind of therapy. However, the fact that apraxia involves phonological as well as phonetic difficulties means that there must be some overlap with aphasia.

It is possible to make a theoretical distinction between apraxia and an aphasic disorder in which access to and the structure of phonological forms has been affected; in the former case, the phonological system is intact, but patients are unable to control their use of it. In the aphasic disorder, speech output is often distorted by numerous phonemic paraphasias (p. 169), but in comparison to an apraxic disorder the prosodic structure of speech is relatively undisturbed and the paraphasic errors are found within stretches of fluent speech. In contrast, apraxia of speech is accompanied by a marked prosodic disturbance, and speech output often sounds forced or effortful. Despite these theoretical and behavioural distinctions, the clinical situation is a fairly confused one, and the term 'apraxia' has sometimes been used to identify the phonological abnormalities of aphasia. The qualitative differences between aphasia and apraxia, however, are sufficiently great to warrant the two being seen as distinct syndromes, and this is the view represented in the model of the communication chain (see Figures 3.2, 5.2). On this basis, we may have a patient displaying (a) aphasic symptoms, with no apraxia, (b) apraxic symptoms, with no aphasia (i.e. grammatical and semantic construction is correct (for the patient's age), but phonology is wrong), and (c) a mixture of both apraxia and aphasia – which is perhaps the most common of the three possibilities in adults. Category (b) is particularly common in children, involving a range of symptoms which may run from mild to severe.[23]

Motor execution disorders

In the model of the communication chain, a general distinction was made between (1) the formulation of meaningful expressions and their organization in phonological terms (language encoding), (2) the retrieval and implementation of an articulatory programme (motor programming), and (3) the subsequent action of the speech production system to give linguistic units phonetic reality (motor execution). Disorders at the first stage were discussed under the headings of psychopathological disorders, aphasia and developmental language disorders, and of the second stage under the heading of apraxia. It remains now to consider the range of disorders which interfere with the process of phonetic realization. There are numerous disorders within this category, and a number of ways in which these disorders of speech

[23]Further reading: R. Lesser, *Linguistic Investigations of Aphasia* (London, Whurr, 2nd edn, 1989), P. Square-Storer, *Acquired Apraxia of Speech in Adults* (London, Taylor & Francis, 1989).

production could be classified (for example, organic versus functional disorders, developmental versus acquired disorders). But the system we shall adopt is one which is commonly encountered in the speech pathology literature. The following types of interference are recognized:

1. Interference with the sequencing of linguistic units in connected speech; this raises problems of *fluency*.
2. Phonetic interference with the source of phonation; this raises problems of *voice*.
3. Interference with the phonetic realization of the phonemes of a language; this raises problems of *articulation*.

Before we work our way through this classification, however, we will discuss a disorder which cuts across it. This is dysarthria – a disorder that may have consequences for fluency, voice and articulation.

Dysarthria

Dysarthria is the name given to a series of motor speech disorders which result from damage to the movement control systems of the central or peripheral nervous systems.[24] Any component of the system can be damaged – the upper motor neuron, lower motor neuron, cerebellum, extrapyramidal or sensory feedback systems. The disorder results in clear neuromuscular disability. Unlike apraxia, there is evidence of muscular weakness or inco-ordination. Any aspect of speech production might be affected, depending on where in the central or peripheral nervous system the lesions occur; there may be problems of respiration, phonation, articulation or prosody; and other activities involving the vocal organs, such as chewing and swallowing,[25] facial expression, coughing or sneezing may be affected. A second characteristic which differentiates the dysarthric from the apraxic patient is that dysarthric errors will be fairly consistent, reflecting the fact that the effector system or a group of muscles is affected, and many of them will be outside the normal patterns of the language. If there is poor muscular control of the soft palate, for example, then abnormal nasalization will be a noticeable feature; if tongue movement is badly affected, vowels will be indistinct, and only rough approximations to many oral consonants will be heard; and so on. In short, the difference between apraxia and dysarthria is often very clear, but it must not be forgotten that the two types of production disorder can combine – the patient having problems both with the organizational ability for sounds and also with the ability to

---

[24]The *a-/dys-* distinction does hold here. *Dysarthria* is an impairment of speech, whilst *anarthria* is a total loss of articulate speech. The latter is uncommon, compared with the varying degrees of partial insufficiency, ranging from mild to severe.

[25]Where this occurs the disorder of *dysphagia* is identified, the assessment and treatment of which is often part of the responsibilities of a speech-language pathologist.

implement them. It will not always be obvious, without considerable investigation, which factor is predominant in accounting for a patient's difficulties with a particular type of sound.

Within the broad category of dysarthria, several specific syndromes have been established, relating to the level at which the motor system is damaged. *Ataxic dysarthria* refers to the behavioural consequences of damage to the cerebellar system: it is characterized by a slowed, erratically stressed utterance, with abnormally flat prosody, harsh voice quality, and considerable difficulty co-ordinating the fine movements required in articulation. Bilateral damage to the upper motor neurons can produce *spastic dysarthria*, a condition in which increased tone in the muscles of the larynx results in a very distinct strained voice quality and prosodic changes, together with articulatory errors. Damage to the lower motor neurons can result in *flaccid dysarthria*. In this condition, muscle tone is reduced, resulting in a breathy voice, and difficulties in the control of the muscles of the palate, tongue and lips. A number of dysarthric syndromes result from damage to the extrapyramidal system. Parkinson's disease (identified in 1817 by the British surgeon, James Parkinson (1755–1824)), a degenerative disease of the basal ganglia, is characterized by rigidity of muscles, coarse tremor, and slowness and poverty of voluntary movement, with a typical mask-like face. Other extrapyramidal conditions, such as Huntingdon's disease, a rare degenerative disease resulting in a movement disorder and ultimately dementia, show an increase in involuntary movements. These involuntary movements can affect all components of the speech production system, resulting in sudden forced exhalation, dramatic changes in voice quality, and interference with tongue, lip and palatal movement. In addition to these specific syndromes, mixed forms of dysarthria can occur. In such cases, the motor and sensory systems are damaged at various points. Disorders such as multiple sclerosis and motor neuron disease are characteristically associated with mixed dysarthrias.

Dysarthrias may occur in both acquired and developmental forms. The acquired dysarthrias may result from many causes. Many of the categories of pathology listed in Chapter 4 (trauma, infection, tumour, degenerative, vascular, metabolic) may have consequences for motor function. Developmental dysarthria is commonly found in *cerebral palsy*, a disability which results from very early damage to the infant brain, perhaps due to anoxia or trauma during birth. A variety of forms occur. *Spastic* cerebral palsy shows an increase in muscle tone, whilst the *flaccid* or floppy form is marked by very weak muscle tone. *Athetoid* cerebral palsy is characterized by slow, writhing, involuntary movements.[26]

---

[26]Further reading on dysarthria, see L. Cogher, E. Savage and M. Smith (eds), *Cerebral Palsy: The Child and Young Person* (London, Chapman & Hall, 1992); J. Duffy, *Motor Speech Disorders: Substrates, Differential Diagnosis and Management* (St. Louis, Mosby, 1995).

Disorders of fluency

The popular sense of fluency refers to the degree of proficiency someone has developed in performing a motor activity. In relation to language, the term implies ease and rapidity of speaking, a continuous flow with little hesitation, and a good command of grammar and vocabulary. In speech pathology, these implications are also present, but when the notion of *non-fluency* is discussed, it is usually with reference to specific disturbances in the rhythm and timing of speech, and not to such notions as size of vocabulary. The terms *arhythmia* and *dysrhythmia* are sometimes used to refer to phonetic interference with the normal rhythms of speech – one might be 'mildly' or 'severely' dysrhythmic, for instance, or (wholly) arhythmic. But the usual terms to describe the main non-fluency syndromes are *stuttering*[27] and *cluttering*; and it is in relation to the first of these that most investigation has been carried out.

Stuttering seems a very obvious category of speech disorder; but it is in fact one of the most complex to describe and define precisely. The trouble is (as we have seen elsewhere in this book) that stutterers are hardly ever exactly alike. It is as if there is a pool of characteristics of dysfluent (or disfluent) speech, and any one stutterer picks out of this pool some of these characteristics. These characteristics can be grouped into seven main types:

1. An abnormal amount of segment, syllable, word or phrase *repetition*, as in *p-p-p – please, the pol- pol- policeman, I think he's got a – got a – got a –*.
2. Obstructions to the airflow, due to the inability to release the tension that has built up in preparing to articulate a sound: on a tape, the result is a long pause; but face-to-face there may be many signs of the struggle that is going on within for control – facial spasms and grimaces, sudden movements of the head, or of the whole body, and awkward gestures. This phenomenon is referred to as *blocking*, and the individual sounds affected as *blocks* or *hard contacts*.
3. Abnormal prolongations of sound segments, as in *f-f-f-feels*, where the initial *f* is being produced as a single lengthened sound, and not with brief pauses between (compare (1) above).
4. The introduction of extra words or sounds with a solely emotional force at points of difficulty, e.g. *gosh, oh, tut*.
5. Erratic stress patterns in words, and abnormal intonation and tempo patterns in sentences, mainly because of the very hesitant speech, and the accompanying irregular breathing.
6. Words being left unfinished.

---

[27]The term *stammering* is also used, especially in the UK, to refer to exactly the same set of behaviours.

7. Awkward circumlocutions: stutterers may know very well which types of sound cause them particular problems, and will therefore go out of their way (linguistically) to avoid saying them – sometimes to quite surprising lengths: one stutterer, in the middle of a story, said '. . . and lying in the road was one of those – animals that meow . . .'.

To illustrate some of the effects encountered in stuttering, here is an extract from a conversation with a fairly severe adult male stutterer.[28]

> T　and do you 'have any hòbbies/
> P　yès/– òne . 'of – my . 'hob – – bies/. is 'mus – sìc/. and the óther – – 'one/
>　　is erm – 'playing – – hòckey/– –
> T　'when you say músic/ do you 'mean do you 'like lìstening tó it/ or 'do you
>　　plày 'anything/
> P　I – – I 'actually – – plày in/– – 'two erm – bànds/ 'and 'I 'als . so . 'like lìst . e . ning
> –　　– to 'mus . 'sic/– –
> T　'what do you plày/
> P　I – – erm – well – – my – –
> T　I 'mean what ìnstrument/
> P　yès/ quìte/– – 'my máin 'instru – ment is the/– erm – (h h) is the – – 'bass . gui –
>　　tàr/– – but 'I 'also 'play – – the erm bán – – jo/ and òrdinary – gui – 'tar/

This extract shows the way the 'transition smoothness' between sounds, syllables, words, phrases and larger units can be interfered with. Non-fluency, it should be plain, is a much larger phenomenon than is suggested by the traditional view – that stutterers have problems with sounds. It is *not* just a matter of sounds: it is a problem of the entire rhythmic organization of speech.

There is a second reason why a watertight definition of stuttering is so difficult to achieve, and that is the problem of distinguishing it from what is called *normal non-fluency*. For example, it is perfectly normal to hesitate in our speech: indeed, it has been estimated that two-thirds of our spoken language comes out in chunks of six words or less. About 30 per cent of an average conversation consists of – silence. And if we listen carefully to an ongoing conversation, we will be able to hear other non-fluencies also – changes of direction in mid-sentence, prolongations of sounds, and several types of sound or syllable repetition. Some clinicians have in fact argued, on the basis of this, that *no* boundary line can be drawn between stuttering and normal speech. Nor is it simply a matter of degree, with a single continuum from the one state to the other: some experiments have shown that at certain linguistic tasks (such as word repetition in controlled settings) there is always a

---

[28]These excerpts are based on transcripts in P. Dalton and W. J. Hardcastle, *Disorders of Fluency* (London, Whurr, 2nd edn, 1989). Several phonetic details have been omitted, e.g. the first occurrence of *guitar* was pronounced /skwi:?–tɑ:/, *and* was pronounced /ən/, *the erm* was pronounced /ðəm/.

proportion of stutterers who are in fact *more* fluent than the population of non-stutterers brought in as controls! On the other hand, it is not the case that the frequency of these errors, taken all together, is to be found in normal speech, and there are certain characteristics of stuttering which are hardly ever to be found there – the blocking phenomenon being a case in point.

The distinction becomes particularly sensitive when we observe young children, at certain points in their language development. It has been said that 'all kids stutter' – by which is meant that young children (say, between 2 and 5 years old) have an abnormally high amount of word repetition in their speech, compared with adults, and from time to time become noticeably non-fluent in their production of initial segments too. Take the following extract from a 3-year old:

> and – and – my 'daddy did – did 'fall off the làdder/ and he – he – he did 'hurted his knèe/ and it was – it was 'all sòre . . .

Although this might sound like stuttering – and many parents do indeed refer to it as such – it can be argued that it should not really be interpreted in this way, as the non-fluency is probably only a consequence of the language acquisition process. A child's expanding linguistic resources, both grammatical and lexical–semantic, result in attempts to produce novel and more complex utterances involving integration of all levels of language processing (p. 179). Such utterances may involve more planning time, which translates into more hesitations, and vocal behaviours (such as *er*) which allow the child to hold on to the conversational turn in the face of competition from other speakers and other demands on the listener's attention.

A helpful characterization of factors which contribute to non-fluency emphasizes the multifactorial nature of fluency disruption. The *demands and capacities* model fits well with the concepts drawn from information theory upon which the model of the communication chain is based (p. 62).[29] One component of information theory is the issue of the amount of information a channel can process. The demands and capacities theory suggests that when the demands on a speaker's cognitive, linguistic, motoric and/or emotional resources exceeds capacities, speech fluency will break down. This is a useful notion in understanding the non-fluencies of normal speakers and of young children whose existing capacities may well be overstretched in attempts to tackle a range of cognitively, linguistically and socially novel tasks.[30] It also provides an account of the observation that other types of speech

---

[29]See M. Adams 'The demands and capacities model I: theoretical elaborations', *Journal of Fluency Disorders*, 15, 135–41, 1990. See also footnote 19 above.

[30]Several factors can cause the fluency of normal speakers to break down: cognitive demands (well rehearsed versus novel arguments); linguistic demands (speaking a native language versus a second language); motor demands (saying a 'tongue twister' at speed); emotional demands (speech when excited versus in a state of low arousal).

pathology evidence abnormal fluency as a part of behaviour. Patients with dysarthria, apraxia and aphasia will all illustrate non-fluencies, ranging from mild to severe, due to very real constraints operating on various language and speech encoding capabilities.

But what of fluency disruptions which are not classified as normal non-fluency and are of sufficient severity, or involve such qualitatively different patterns of behaviour, as to be classed as stuttering? There are many classifications and theories of stuttering behaviour, and one reason for their number, and for the controversy that exists within the literature on stuttering, is the different emphases that clinicians place on different components of the problem. For example, many theories make a distinction between various elements of stuttering behaviour. The core or *primary* behaviours are the various forms of speech non-fluencies such as prolongations, hesitations and repetitions. At an early stage in the development of a fluency problem, there is no anxiety, struggle or self-awareness regarding speech; there are no defensive reactions about the stutter and, indeed, the dysfluent person may not even refer to his or her speech difficulties as such. A gradient of increasing severity is then postulated, with the stutter becoming more chronic and the person more self-aware (*transitional* stuttering), until the phenomenon could be called *secondary* stuttering. At this stage, there is full awareness of the existence of the problem, and major attempts are made to modify or avoid the stutter, leading to the uncontrolled, tense and irregular characteristics of speech referred to above. Many of the most evident behaviours displayed by the individual with a stutter may not be speech characteristics at all, but a range of grimaces, hand movements and eye blinks which began as attempts to control non-fluencies, perhaps through trying to impose some external rhythmic pattern upon dysfluent speech. These *secondary* features then become incorporated into the stuttering behaviour and move the total pattern of communicative behaviour displayed by the stuttering individual from the range of normal non-fluency into something qualitatively different. In addition to overt communicative behaviours, the individual with a stutter acquires a set of beliefs about speaking, which often leads to extreme anxiety and attempts to avoid both moments of stuttering and situations requiring speech.

It is when we investigate the attitudes of stutterers towards their own communicative abilities, and towards their stutter in particular, that we encounter a peculiar problem: how they rate their fluency may be quite different from how it is rated by other people. You may be struck by someone's stutter, and may have some mild difficulty in attending to that person (until you adapt), but you may not feel that the problem is particularly serious, and you may actually say this (if, for instance, the person apologized for the stutter). But this attitude of the listener is probably vastly different from the feelings stutterers privately hold about their inarticulateness. At one London clinic, a group of adult stutterers were asked about their feelings about their own stutters. Many of them were greatly preoccupied with their speech, whatever the level of severity of their stutter. Some of them were very anxious about it; others were simply alert to the prospective difficulties involved in speaking – always scanning ahead to see if any problem words were coming up. An interesting consequence of this is that several said they thought this made them poor *listeners*, because they were concentrating too much on what they themselves were saying. Many of the more severe cases complained of the amount of physical and mental energy taken up by this activity, amounting at times to exhaustion.

> Several spoke of cutting down any explanation needed to the bare minimum, simplifying an argument to the points they felt they could make easily. Some gave up argument altogether, agreeing with another speaker rather than getting involved in complicated disagreement. Others even spoke of saying the opposite of what they felt, because it happened to be easier . . .
>
> The therapists were under the impression for several weeks that a member of the group was engaged to be married, because, when asked if he was married he replied, 'Pending'. What he meant to say was that he was divorced, but he was having great trouble with 'd' at that time.
>
> (Dalton and Hardcastle, p. 98)[31]

Many clinicians advocate the view that, before lasting change can occur in stuttering behaviour, the beliefs that the stuttering individual holds about communication must be altered, and psychotherapeutic techniques are accordingly a component of many management regimes. Intervention which focuses only on speaking behaviour may have a transient effect on fluency, but the underlying learned fear, anxiety and avoidance of speaking will result in relapse if they too are not addressed.

Stuttering behaviour may therefore involve a series of components, and many of the disagreements which abound over the main theoretical questions may stem from different theorists addressing different components of the stuttering-complex. The multifactorial demands and capacities model, with its emphasis on cognitive, linguistic, motor and emotional factors in disruptions of speech fluency, may be useful in directing research to the potential variety of causes of the disorder. Psychoneurotic theories of stuttering, for example, attempt to relate the disorder to factors in the personality of the stutterer. One group of theories tries to identify the personality types of people who stutter – perhaps over-anxious or over-hostile individuals. These accounts may be useful in describing the emotional consequences and beliefs that develop with chronic stuttering, but may be less relevant to addressing the mechanisms in the genesis of the stuttering disorder. There are also

---

[31]This account is given in P. Dalton and W. J. Hardcastle, *Disorders of Fluency* (London, Whurr, 2nd edn, 1989), pp. 97–9.

several organic theories of stuttering which may address cognitive and motor mechanisms implicated in the disorder. One view tries to relate stuttering to abnormal patterns of dominance between the cerebral hemispheres. An alternative neurological theory proposes a defect in brain structure so that there is a predisposition to perseverate when using language, the result being a stutter. Biochemical reasons have also been advanced: a defect in myelination which interferes with the way impulses are transmitted along neurons or across synapses. And a further theory argues that there are defects in the auditory feedback mechanism between vocal organs, ear and brain (compare p. 75), so that split-second delays in sensory feedback disturb speech encoding, and stuttering is the result.

Other theories seek explanations not in the intrinsic capacities of the speaker, but in the demands placed on young speakers by those around them. Anxiety theories of stuttering suggest that stuttering begins because the speaker believes that speech is a problem, that he or she has failed, or will fail. The stuttering person may have been told this directly, as when children are corrected by their parents for normal non-fluency (compare above): the feelings of impatience generated by anxious parents who disapprove of non-fluency produce insecurity and anxiety in the child, and a worsening of the behaviour. This 'diagnosogenic' theory was proposed by the American speech pathologist Wendell Johnson, who argued that stuttering begins not in the child's mouth, but in the listener's ear! There is some evidence in support of the theory, in that the incidence of stuttering is greater in cultures which prize early oracy skills, and many early intervention programmes for stuttering focus primarily on parental attitudes to the problem.

Stuttering is likely to be a disorder with many different causes, and once stuttering has become established there are many components to the disorder. The latter is also true of chronic disorders of communication, such as aphasia and developmental conditions which have not resolved. In addition to the linguistic impairment, the patient may develop beliefs and anxieties about communication which lead to the avoidance of social and communicative situations. In the field of stuttering, the *psychosocial* issues linked to a communicative disorder have been the subject of a large amount of theory, research and intervention, with the recognition that failure to address these issues in the management of a disorder leads to only a transient change in behaviour. Clinicians in other subfields of language pathology might therefore be wise to address issues such as patient's beliefs in order to manage chronic communicative disabilities effectively.[32]

---

[32]See further, P. Dalton and W. J. Hardcastle, *Disorders of Fluency* (London, Whurr, 2nd edn, 1989); M. E. Wingate, *The Structure of Stuttering: A Psycholinguistic Analysis* (New York, Springer-Verlag, 1988); E. Boberg (ed), *Neuropsychology of Stuttering* (Edmonton, University of Alberta Press, 1993).

Although the bulk of this section has to do with stuttering, it would be wrong to conclude that disorders of fluency are solely a function of that disorder. A further major category of non-fluency exists, known as *cluttering*. The primary characteristic here is the rapidity of the utterance: patients attempt to talk too quickly, and as a result they introduce distortions into their rhythm and articulation. Sounds become displaced, misarticulated or omitted; words and partial words get repeated; syllables telescope into each other; the utterance comes out in relatively short bursts, often interfering with syntax; the speed may increase as utterance proceeds (a phenomenon known as *festination*). The description and theoretical study of cluttering is, however, less advanced even than that of stuttering. Once again, there is the need to take into account organic, personality, situational and other variables. The overlap between the categories of stuttering and cluttering should also be borne in mind: some patients present a mixture of both behaviours. It is possible that brain damage accounts for a greater proportion of clutterers (often, EEG recordings show significant abnormalities), but the evidence is by no means conclusive.[33]

Voice disorders

The concept of 'voice', in popular usage, is a fairly general one, carrying a wide range of associations, such as when we interpret the variations in our voices as conveying emotions ('angry voice', 'sarcastic voice' etc.) or projecting our personalities ('young voice', 'depressed voice' etc.). Often the notion of voice relates to its aesthetic properties, and to someone's desire to improve his or her speech habits, by taking lessons in voice training (elocution). In speech pathology, however, a much more restricted sense is involved. Voice, and its associated disorders, refers to one of two variables, which have been labelled *phonation* and *resonance* (compare p. 77). Phonation refers to the source of sound vibration in the vocal tract – primarily, therefore, the larynx. Resonance refers to the gross modifications of this vibration in the cavities contiguous to the larynx (i.e. excluding the fine modifications involved in articulation: see p. 116). Disorders of phonation thus arise when something interferes with the normal functioning of the larynx, so that instead of the expected range of vocal effects (in pitch, voicing of consonants and vowels, and so on) noticeable distortions occur (such as hoarseness or excessive breathiness). Disorders of resonance arise when something interferes with the functioning of the adjoining cavities (both beneath the glottis and above) so that abnormal timbres are introduced into the voice quality as a whole (as in excessively nasal voice).

---

[33]On cluttering, P. Dalton and W. F. Hardcastle, *Disorders of Fluency* (London, Whurr, 2nd edn, 1989), Chapter 7; and F. I. Myers and K. O. St Louis (eds), *Cluttering: A Clinical Perspective* (London, Whurr, 1992).

The language pathologist will be interested in the implications of vocal abnormality for the way speech is affected. What are the main auditory effects likely to be produced by these abnormalities, therefore? Based upon our phonetic understanding of the variables involved (compare p. 120), these effects can be grouped into three main types: abnormalities of pitch, of loudness and of timbre. Under the heading of *pitch* would be included voices which were excessively high or low in pitch range, or involved excessively widened or narrowed range (with the maximum narrowing being reached with so-called 'monotone' voices). The vibratory level of pitch might also be affected – producing, for instance, tremulous or over-vibrant qualities. There may also be an abnormal use of a pitch register (e.g. talking persistently in falsetto or excessively deep voices).[34] Under the heading of *loudness* would be included voices which were excessively loud or weak, or erratic in their control of loudness. Also included would be the effects of abnormally intense voice production on articulation – any general effects which characterized the whole of the patient's articulatory ability (such as a tendency for voicing to start too sharply at the beginnings of words, or to die away at the ends). Under the heading of *timbre* would be included the whole range of 'other' abnormal effects that affect the quality (as opposed to the pitch and loudness) of the tone (compare p. 127). It is thus a very broad category, and it is usual to distinguish four types of vocal effect within it.

1. First, we must note the abnormal timbre that accompanies variations of the direction of the airflow – if we speak while breathing in (compare p. 117). Sometimes, noise is produced simply while breathing, with no attempt being made to speak; such noise is known as *stridor*, and is a feature of many laryngeal conditions.

2. Second, there is a range of specific phonation timbres produced at the larynx: the voice may emerge as a whisper, lacking any vocal fold vibration; or vocal fold vibration may be present to some degree, but accompanied by excessive airflow (a 'breathy' voice); or, there may be structural interference with the airflow (e.g. due to the growth of abnormal tissue on the vocal folds) which will produce a 'hoarse' quality – a quality that will vary in its auditory effect, depending on the extent of the interference, and where in the vocal tract it takes place (e.g. whether parts of the lower pharynx are also affected). This group of timbre effects is collectively referred to under the heading of *dysphonia* or *aphonia* (the latter being used when there is no vocal fold vibration present at all). Voices may be consistently or intermittently dysphonic or aphonic.

---

[34]It should be noted that we are here talking about the *phonetic* use of pitch, and not its phonological use, as in intonation. A patient may be speaking in an abnormally low pitch range, for example, but still making all the intonation contrasts of the language, e.g. distinguishing between questions and statements.

3. Third, there is a range of abnormal resonance timbres, which may originate infraglottally (for instance, if the vital capacity of the lungs is reduced, as in lung or heart disease), or (more commonly) supraglottally: in this latter case, the main effects encountered are those that increase or decrease the amount of nasality present in the voice (an abnormally nasal, or 'twangy' voice (*hypernasality*); or a denasal voice (*hyponasality*) – common, for instance, in the sound of a blocked nose during a cold).

4. Fourth, there are the abnormal timbres which result from alternative sources of phonation than the larynx. The most important ones to know about here are the result of the substitute voice-producing mechanisms which have to be learned as a result of laryngectomy (compare p. 131). Laryngectomy patients may be able to learn to use the upper part of their pharynx and oesophagus to initiate vibration, and the resulting 'oesophageal' and 'pharyngeal' voices are distinctive in their timbre. Alternatively, they may use an *artificial larynx* to provide them with a source of vibration – for instance, a buzzing device which they place against the outside of the neck beneath the chin, while mouthing speech. Again, a distinctive timbre is the result.

These are just the broad categories involved in the study of the voice disorders. Each can be subclassified: for instance, several types of hoarseness and nasality have been proposed. The difficulty here, of course, is how to label them. Descriptive terminology for voice qualities is notorious for its ambiguity and vagueness. Take some of the terms for the description of hoarseness, for example: 'wet', 'dry', 'rough', 'guttural', 'strident', 'metallic' and other such terms have been used in an attempt to characterize the auditory effects. At present, there is no consistent terminology, though several research projects have attempted to impose some order on the field.[35]

A useful strategy to adopt when investigating the aetiology of a voice condition is to ask three related questions: is the condition the result of abnormality in the normal course of physiological development? If not, is it the result of some organic damage to the vocal organs? If not, is it the result of functional factors? In other words, we are here once again dealing with a process of diagnosis by exclusion. We can apply this reasoning to the range of auditory variables described above.

Developmental disorders
There are several congenital disorders which will produce abnormal birth, hunger etc. cries in the infant (abnormally formed vocal folds, for

---

[35]The background to the voice quality research is given in J. Laver, *The Phonetic Description of Voice Quality* (Cambridge, Cambridge University Press, 1980), and an account of the clinical voice profile in the University of Edinburgh Department of Linguistics Working Papers, Vol. 14 (1981).

example (compare p. 129), or disorders of chromosomal origin – a particularly dramatic example being the disorder known as *cri-du-chat syndrome* ('cat-cry syndrome'), so called because of the high whining sound the baby produces when it is crying).[36] At puberty, several abnormal things may happen to the voice during the period of adolescent change. In boys, instead of the normal process of *voice mutation* taking place, in which the voice becomes gradually lower, the prepubertal voice may stay, to produce an apparently falsetto effect known as *puberphonia*. In girls, the opposite effect may be found – an abnormally low or husky voice, which has been labelled *androphonia*. There could be a variety of causes for both disorders: the reasons may be organic (e.g. hormone imbalance, which in its extreme forms can result in gigantism, obesity, dwarfism etc.) or psychological (e.g. a subconscious desire to 'sound' child-like, female, male etc., or a belief that the abnormal voice is pleasant, trendy etc. – one recalls the low husky voices of several female film stars, for instance). And there are other possible causes – for instance, early cigarette smoking can produce an abnormally husky voice at this time in the female.

Later developmental stages in adult life can also produce voice problems, particularly in the female, where menstrual function, climacteric (menopause) and pregnancy can all affect pitch, loudness and timbre, producing lower, weaker and harsher voice qualities in many women. Senescence is also a time when marked changes in voice characteristics occur, due to the normal degeneration of the vocal folds, and associated physiological and psychological changes. The laryngeal cartilages often stiffen, and the vocal folds become less elastic: reduced pitch range results, along with reduced loudness variation, tremulousness, variations in timbre and a generally reduced length of vocal performance.

Organic disorders
Voice disorders of organic origin can be related to the conventional medical categories referred to in Chapter 4. These include organic damage resulting from direct trauma to the larynx following a blow or a road traffic accident; disturbances in the endocrine or hormonal system (in the thyroid and pituitary glands, for instance); and inflammations that may effect the larynx as a result of upper respiratory tract infections. Such infections are one of the most common causes of hoarseness and, in addition to any inflammation of tissues, the extra mucus which is produced by the respiratory tract during a cold coats the vocal folds and prevents normal vibratory action. Neurological damage to the motor control system can also disturb laryngeal function, and many forms of dysarthria involve phonatory disruptions.

---

[36]The condition is the result of a partial or complete deletion of the short arms of chromosome number 5. Apart from the cry, infants are mentally handicapped and display abnormal physical signs (such as abnormally small jaws or low-set ears).

There may be structural abnormalities in the vocal tract, in particular affecting the vocal folds. Abnormal cell growth can occur on the vocal folds, including carcinoma of the larynx. Chronic hoarseness may be an early sign of carcinoma in the laryngeal region, and is an important presenting symptom, as it can lead to early intervention with treatment such as radiotherapy (which may remove, or delay, the need for subsequent surgery). If a tumour cannot be controlled through other means, surgery can remove parts or all of the laryngeal structures (*laryngectomy*, p. 131).

There is also a group of benign vocal cord growths which, unlike malignant carcinoma, do not infiltrate surrounding tissues. Severe hoarseness may result from the development of papillomas (compare p. 130), which are caused by viral infection and are especially encountered in children in the first five years of life, and rare after the 30s. An important class of vocal fold pathology includes *vocal nodules* (or *nodes*), *polyps* and *contact ulcers*. These organic pathologies result from prolonged or severe vocal misuse and abuse (or vocal *hyperfunction*) and are an important example of how a functional problem can lead ultimately to organic disturbance. Misuse of the voice includes excessive shouting, as when trying to project the voice over large distances or above background noise (many people are familiar with the hoarse voice which follows trying to hold conversations at noisy clubs or at parties). Phonation with excessive tension in laryngeal muscles results in tremor and pitch abnormalities – phenomena which are very evident when listening to a nervous speaker. Short-term vocal misuse results in swelling (*oedema*) of the vocal folds, small haemorrhages in tissues, and an increase in mucus production. These changes are exacerbated by the presence of laryngeal irritants such as cigarette smoke and alcohol. Prolonged misuse results in structural changes in the delicate tissues of the vocal folds. Vocal nodules are tiny beads of fibrous tissues on the margins of the vocal folds (p. 130). They are the result of excessive friction between the vocal folds – an irritative reaction to the mechanical trauma of over-using the voice. For this reason, they have been variously called 'singer's nodes', 'teacher's nodes' and 'screamer's nodes'. The nodes prevent the vocal folds coming together normally; their potential for vibration is thus affected; and the result is a marked hoarseness and erratic voicing. In order to compensate for the loss of phonatory efficiency, the sufferer may over-adduct the vocal cords, with this excess tension in the folds resulting in further damage. Vocal nodes occur in both children and adults, and the condition is about four times as likely to occur in women as in men. The usual treatment is voice rest, along with a period of voice therapy in order to promote healthier patterns of voice use. Therapy can be very effective in reducing and eliminating nodules, although surgical removal is also possible. If, however, vocal hyperfunction is not reduced, new nodes will re-emerge in due course. Polyps and contact ulcers also result from vocal misuse; the former are softer forms of growth than the more fibrous nodes, while the latter result from ulceration of the surface of the vocal folds. Contact ulcers may form as a result of the over-forceful adduction of the vocal folds, producing a very tense, low-pitched, hoarse or breathy voice, with an explosive quality. This condition, by contrast with vocal nodules, predominantly affects males, especially in middle age.

Functional disorders

The concentration on developmental and organic voice disorders is to some extent an unreal emphasis. It has been estimated that over 70% of the disorders which turn up in a voice clinic are due to causes other than these, i.e. functional conditions. Two major types of functional aetiology have been proposed. First, there is the pattern of excessive use (vocal abuse), already described above, which ultimately can produce nodules, polyps and contact ulcers, and in which emotional and personality factors can be evident. Common in this category of patients are the 'voice professionals' – individuals for whom the voice is fundamental to their occupation – such as teachers, singers, actors and traders. These individuals often have to produce supra-normal vocal performances, in far from ideal conditions, and often when they are in a state of high physiological arousal, which in turn leads to high degrees of muscular tension.

The second main category of functional voice disorders – psychogenic conditions – involves a degree of overlap with the first grouping. Individuals who experience high degrees of stress and who are therefore in a constant state of high arousal and muscular tension are at risk of phonatory problems. The most common of these conditions is referred to as *conversion aphonia*, in which in its extreme form the patient is able to speak only in a barely audible whisper. The larynx is held rigidly, and speaking is abrupt and spasmodic; the voice is at times weak, at times harsh. It occurs more frequently in females than males, in a ratio of 7:1. ENT examination may reveal no significant laryngeal pathology, and non-speech phonation, such as in a cough, laugh or cry, is surprisingly normal, showing that it is *speech* that is being primarily affected. This is perhaps highly significant: what seems to be happening is that patients have lost control over their (healthy) musculature because of underlying emotional stress; the voice is symbolic of this stress (often a personal conflict in which communication difficulties between the patient and others have played a prominent part). It is argued that patients are using their voice complaint as a means of not facing up to emotional problems directly, and will usually deny that they have these problems, preferring to focus on the possibility that there is an organic cause for the complaint. These examples suggest that, in managing disorders of voice, the speech pathologist needs to work closely with the ENT specialist. An individual presenting with a hoarse voice may have no observable pathology, as in the case of a conversion aphonia or, at the other extreme, may have an invasive carcinoma which requires urgent medical intervention.[37]

Disorders of articulation

This is the traditional centre of the speech pathologist's enquiry, involving the phonetic and phonological description and analysis of the patient's pronunciation. The notion of an articulation disorder is, however, a very wide-ranging one: at one extreme, it can refer to a completely misarticulated sound system, so that the person is largely unintelligible; at the other extreme, it can refer to a difficulty in a single sound or group of sounds (as with 'lisping', or 'weak' *r*). Classification of these problems is made, in the first instance, in terms of the normal parameters of phonetic description (compare p. 126). From an anatomical (or 'structural') point of view, abnormal articulations can be identified at each of the possible 'places of articulation':

- at the *lips,* e.g. the result of cleft lip (compare p. 203), paralysis or scar tissue
- at the *teeth*, e.g. the result of absent or misaligned teeth, or a deformity of the alveolar ridge
- at the *hard palate*, especially if cleft palate is involved
- at the *velum*, especially if poor contact is made with the pharyngeal wall
- using the *tongue*, e.g. the result of abnormality in its size or shape (after surgery, for instance, including the possibility of its partial or total removal – the operation known as *glossectomy*)
- in the *pharynx* and *larynx*, insofar as the articulation of sounds is concerned (as opposed to the phonation and resonance of voice, compare p. 117).

It is not so much an abnormal anatomical structure which is the cause of misarticulation, however; indeed, it is often possible for the human vocal apparatus to compensate greatly for absent or malformed structures, and produce speech that is difficult to distinguish from normal speech. A more important factor is physiological inco-ordination, which can produce a general oral inaccuracy in sound production that may or may not be capable of being traced to neurological causes in encoding (apraxia, compare p. 182) or transmission (dysarthria, compare p. 186).

---

[37]For a general introduction to the field of voice, the classic reference is M. C. L. Greene and L. Mathieson, *The Voice and Its Disorders* (London, Whurr, 5th edn, 1989); R. H. Colton and J. K. Casper, *Understanding Voice Problems: a Physiological Perspective for Diagnosis and Treatment* (Baltimore, Williams & Wilkins, 2nd edn, 1995).

Physiological factors are more pervasive because so many articulatory variables are involved: to get a sound right, the active articulator must be moved *in the right direction* towards the passive articulator, *at the right speed*, maintaining the *right shape*, making the *right amount of surface contact* and maintaining the *right pressure*. If any of these variables is uncontrolled, the result will be a misarticulation, e.g. a fricative 'overshoots' and becomes a plosive; a plosive is delayed in its release phase and becomes an affricate; there is inadequate pressure to maintain an articulation, and the sound becomes erratic or weak. A particularly common cause is when one articulator fails to be released before the next articulation begins, as a result of which the auditory effect of the first articulation carries on through the rest of the syllable or word – as when the soft palate does not raise itself sufficiently quickly and the remaining articulations all become nasalized. Hearing loss is another factor that can disturb the ability to co-ordinate, discriminate and produce sounds.

We have already seen the amount of phonetic detail in which it is possible to specify the articulatory and acoustic identity of a sound. A great deal of articulatory skill is involved in producing, say, a [d] sound: the correct part of the tongue (the blade) must be placed against the alveolar ridge (further back will produce auditory confusion, e.g. with [g]), along its whole horizontal extent (otherwise air would be released during the articulation and a hissy or breathy articulation would result); it must be placed there with a fair amount of muscular tension, in order to allow pressure of air to build up behind it in preparation for its release as a plosive sound (inadequacy here will produce a weak, indistinct articulation); the soft palate must be kept raised throughout the articulation (otherwise nasality will interfere and the [d] will become [n]-like); there must be accurately-timed vocal fold vibration – not too little (otherwise the sound will emerge as more [t]-like), and not too much (otherwise it will be 'over-voiced', emerging as a 'duh'). It should be plain from this brief description that there are several possible ways in which a [d] sound can 'go wrong' – and these are only some of the possibilities (we have not referred to the effects of simultaneously occurring articulations elsewhere in the vocal tract). There are also several variations in the 'preferred' articulation of /d/ in a given dialect, and this will need to be considered before an articulation can be considered as abnormal.

But in all this, an important point emerges: the approach as so far described is concerned to get the [d] sound *phonetically* correct; it is not directly concerned with the *phonological* status of the sound. In recent years, far more attention has come to be paid to the phonological implications of articulation problems. The change in emphasis can be summarized in this way. A phonological distinction, as we have seen (p. 42), is one where two sounds (or groups of phonetically similar sounds) have the role of distinguishing meanings in a language – for example, /p/ vs /b/ vs /d/ vs /s/ etc., as in *pin, bin, din, sin*. These are the phonemes of the language. Let us take one of these – say /d/. There is in fact no single phonetic articulation of this phoneme in normal speech: how /d/ is actually pronounced depends on what sort of word it appears in, and where in the word it appears – a /d/ at the beginning of a word is phonetically somewhat different from a /d/ at the end of a word (it is more voiced in initial position, for example). These phonetic differences do not affect the status of the phoneme: the sounds are all recognized as variants of /d/ – and would continue to be so recognized, even if they were somehow mixed up (if you gave full voicing to /d/ in final position, for instance, it would still be recognized as a /d/, though as a very carefully articulated and emphasized one). Now, this principle carries through into articulation disorders. There are many distortions which can be given to the /d/ phoneme, as we have seen, but as long as they remain within certain limits, they will be perceived as just that – /d/ distortions. If they go over certain limits, however, then a different problem arises: if loss of voicing becomes too great, the /d/ will emerge as a voiceless [t], and will thus be confused by the listener with the /t/ phoneme; /din/ will now sound like *tin*, and not just like a distorted version of *din*. For listeners, one phoneme is now being confused with another; the meaning of words is being directly affected; and we have a phonological problem on our hands.

A purely phonetic articulatory problem is common enough; variations in the articulation of /r/, /l/ and above all /s/ are cases in point. It is not uncommon for the child, in acquiring the phonetic realizations of these phonemes, to learn a faulty articulatory posture. The gesture learned for /r/ normally involves the approximation of the tongue tip to the alveolar region, although there is no contact between the two structures. There is a variant realization of the /r/ phoneme in British English, with the tongue tip/alveolar approximation being replaced by a labiodental approximant [ʋ]. This faulty or variant realization of /r/, or various realizations of /s/, rarely raises phonological problems: English makes no contrast between alveolar and labiodental approximants, and there is no likelihood of listeners confusing the defective sound with some other consonant or vowel phoneme. Such problems, moreover, may never reach the speech clinic, being left to sort themselves out as the child grows up. The labiodental variant of /r/ is particularly interesting, because it is used by a number of people with high-profile and high-prestige positions in society, such as politicians and journalists, and because of the association with high-status individuals it may become more prevalent in future years.

A more serious problem is when there is a limitation in the patient's ability to express all the contrasts in a language's phonological system. Either the patient's phonetic inadequacy is so great that it has blurred the distinctions between the phonemes; or there is something wrong with the underlying ability to organize speech phonemically, and phonetic confusion is one of the results. From the perspective of the listener, both types of condition will lead to confusion of phonemic contrasts and difficulty understanding the speaker; but from the speaker's viewpoint, and in terms of planning intervention, the two possibilities are rather different.[38] In the case where the underlying phonological system is normal, but phonetic realizations are aberrant, the speaker needs assistance to develop more normal phonetic realizations. Where the phonological system is aberrant, the patient may benefit from different techniques, such as learning to discriminate the phonemic contrasts of a language in order to establish a normal phonological system before accurate phonetic realizations can be developed. Instrumental analyses of disordered speech using techniques such as electropalatography and spectrography (p. 134) have proved particularly useful in understanding the nature of speech impairments where the phonological system is intact. These techniques have revealed cases where the speaker is signalling phonemic contrasts, but due to the limitations of the articulatory system, the distinction is realized in unusual or subtle ways to which listeners are not particularly sensitive. For example, a vowel tends to be longer before a voiced final consonant than a voiceless one (compare *board* and *bought*). Spectrographic analysis of one patient who was unable to signal the voiced/voiceless contrast, due to difficulty in controlling laryngeal action, revealed a distinction in vowel length, with words ending in a final voiceless sound displaying shorter vowel durations than those ending with a corresponding voiced sound. The instrumental analysis here provides an important tool in diagnosis and planning the management of an articulatory disorder.

Cleft palate

There are several syndromes which involve a combination of production/reception problems, and thus cut across the conventional classification of linguistic pathologies outlined in this chapter. This is particularly true of language disorders, which often involve a combination of reception and production impairments, but cleft palate is also a particularly distinctive example of a disorder which has surprisingly wide ramifications for linguistic performances.

Cleft palate is a congenital fissure in the midline of the palate which may extend throughout the whole of the palate, or affect only the uvula

---

[38]See N. Hewlett, 'Phonological versus phonetic disorders: some suggested modifications to the current use of the distinction', *British Journal of Disorders of Communication*, 20, 155–64, 1985, on discussion of the difference between speaker and listener perspectives in phonological disruptions.

and/or soft palate in varying degrees. *Cleft lip* is the name given to the associated condition in which the upper lip is split in varying degrees – ranging from the slightest notch to a complete division, and often including the whole of the alveolar process behind.[39] From an embryological point of view, the two deformities are part of the same basic process of development. During the second month of intra-uterine life the development of the anatomical processes begins which will ultimately form the structure of the lower part of the face. First, the mandibular processes come together and fuse, to provide the basis for the jaw and lower lip; then the distinction appears between median and lateral nasal processes (Figure 5.1). The maxillary process (the bone which will form the upper part of the jaw) then moves upwards and forwards to separate the eyes from the mouth, fuses with the lateral nasal processes (i.e. the nose and cheek are now continuous), and then with the median nasal process (i.e. the upper lip and floor of the nose are now continuous, thus producing an oral versus a nasal cavity). The palatine processes then come together from either side of the maxillary (the tongue, which had previously been lying between them, being directed downwards) and fuse with the front of the maxilla to form the hard palate. The fusion begins at the front (at the premaxilla) and gradually extends backwards, forming the roof of the mouth and finally the soft palate. The whole area is formed by the end of the third month.

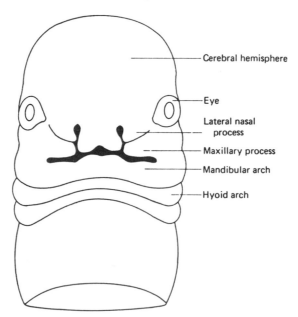

Figure 5.1 Head of human embryo (about 7 weeks) showing the developing nasal and maxillary processes

---

[39]The widespread term 'hare lip' is not usually used in the scientific study of the phenomenon.

While there is plainly a single extensive process of oral formation taking place here, it is also possible to group the developments into two main stages: the first stage deals with the completion of upper lip, floor of the nose and premaxillary process; the second deals with the palatal fusions that take place subsequently. It is this distinction which forms the basis of the most widely used systems of cleft palate classification (for example, by the American Cleft Palate Association (ACPA)). Whatever it is that causes the fusion processes to be incomplete,[40] the results can be clearly distinguished in terms of whether the first set of developments have been affected, or the second, or both. Terminology varies a great deal, but one widely used system has the following labels (see also Figure 4.11).[41]

The first category, involving clefts in the area in front of the *incisive foramen*,[42] is described as constituting clefts of the *primary palate* (or *prepalate*, in the ACPA terminology). (The incisive foramen is chosen, as this is the point of anatomical junction between the two stages of development, when they finally fuse in normal embryonic development.) The second category, involving clefts behind the incisive foramen, is described in terms of clefts of the *secondary palate* (or simply *palate*, in ACPA terms). The following subdivisions are then made. Clefts of the primary palate may be *unilateral* (left or right), *bilateral* or *median* (see Figure 5.2 a–f, which includes frontal views of the lips). The clefts may be *complete, incomplete* or *submucous* (in which the surface tissues of the palate have united, but the underlying bone and muscle structures have not) (see Figure 5.2 g)). In the ACPA classification, the varying degrees of incompleteness, in both lip and palate, are given a more detailed subclassification. When clefts of both primary and secondary palates occur together (Figure 5.2 h), the resulting classification is based on an application of the categories so far recognized.[43]

The therapeutics and management of cleft palate patients form a highly complex area, which it is not possible to go into in this book. But what we do need to remember is the constellation of factors that have to be borne in mind when intervening surgically to correct the damage: a

---

[40]The causes of this condition are unclear: genetic factors have been proposed (and moreover different genetic factors for the different categories of cleft), as have environmental factors (such as viruses or deficient oxygen supply to the womb at the crucial points in development). For information about incidence, see p. 223.

[41]See D. A. Kernahan and R. B. Stark (1958), 'A new classification for cleft lip and cleft palate,' *Plastic and Reconstructive Surgery* 22, 435ff.

[42]A *foramen* is an opening in a structure through which nerves or blood vessels may pass; *incisive* refers to the aperture behind the central incisors through which pass a main nerve and artery supplying the palate: see Figure 5.2 d.

[43]Some clinicians relate cleft palate conditions to the underdevelopment of the lower jaw, or mandible, which is characteristic of certain syndromes (such as Treacher Collins or Pierre Robin syndromes): the phenomenon is known as *hypomandibulosis*.

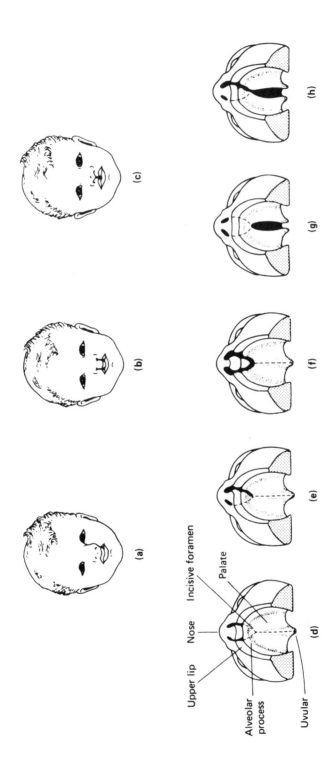

Figure 5.2 (a) Unilateral cleft lip; (b) bilateral cleft lip; (c) median cleft lip; (d) bilateral cleft lip, basal view; (e) unilateral cleft involving lip and alveolar process; (f) bilateral cleft involving lip and alveolar process; (g) complete cleft of secondary palate; (h) complete (unilateral) cleft of primary and secondary palates

person needs a whole palate in order to eat satisfactorily, speak satisfactorily and appear satisfactorily to others. Surgeons thus have to decide when to intervene, taking the interrelationship of these variables into account: if they leave the operation until after the first year or so, it will become increasingly difficult to correct the faulty patterns of articulation which by then will have become well established; on the other hand, if they intervene in the earliest months, they must be sure to allow for the natural growth in facial processes yet to take place, so that their surgical correction does not interfere with this. Most cleft palate operations in the UK are in fact performed within the first year of life; the prognosis for speech is therefore very promising.

What is the nature of the speech problems which result from the cleft palate syndrome? Obviously, articulation will be affected – and in particular those articulations which are made involving the lips and palate. Resonance – hypernasality or excessive nasal airflow – can be a problem even after surgery to repair the cleft has taken place. There may be insufficient tissue in the region of the palate to allow the soft palate to close against the wall of the pharynx, or scar tissue in the region of the palate may limit and slow movements of the palate. In such cases, further surgical intervention is often required. But even if surgery to repair the cleft has been successful, various aspects of articulation may be impaired. If you have been breathing through your nose and mouth simultaneously for several months, and then find yourself having to operate with separable oral and nasal cavities, it may take some time to learn to control the valving of nasal versus oral air-flow. There will be erratic control of the soft palate, and nasalization will affect many consonants and vowels. It will be particularly difficult to keep up sustained pressure in the mouth, such as is needed for fricative and stop production. Tactile feedback from the mouth may take time to be established, or may be permanently impaired.

If surgery has been left or has been unable to establish adequate oral–nasal valving until after the beginning of the period of phonological development (not within the first two years), idiosyncratic realizations of phonological contrasts may have become established. Instead of saying *pin* and *bin*, an individual might have learned to say [ɪn] and [ʔɪn] (i.e. to use a glottal stop to signal a voiced plosive). 'Unlearning' such realizations may be quite complicated, even after the time when the real plosive contrasts are quite within the individual's articulatory capabilities.

In addition to articulation and resonance abnormalities, there may be associated phonation disturbances – a husky voice, or a weakly intoned voice, due to the increased incidence of upper respiratory tract infections in these individuals. This raises an additional complication: the infection moves via the Eustachian tube into the middle ear, resulting in otitis media (compare p. 142). The middle ear may also be poorly aerated, because of poor muscular control of the tube's opening by the tensor palatini muscle (compare p. 123). As a result, hearing problems are common in this group of patients: about half the population of cleft palate patients have a bilateral loss of between 30 and 70 dB (depending on the extent of the cleft). It should also not be forgotten how much at risk these children are, especially when they are infants. There is a persistent risk of suffocation or pneumonia (due to inhalation of fluids). They are also a poor anaesthetic risk – and we must remember in this connection that some 40% of cleft palates occur in conditions of multiple handicap (associated heart disorders, for example). Last, there is a real but unexplainable language delay with many of these children – presumably because of the interference from some of the factors already described, and the repeated hospitalization and emotional trauma to both parents and child which accompanies the condition. The amount of speech heard by the cleft palate infant may also be down on normal: if one is being fed for six to eight hours a day, in the first months of life (feeding problems are inevitably very great), there is relatively little chance to play, to listen or to practise one's babbling.

Cleft palate is a condition in which there are potentially multiple disruptions of components of the communication chain, and the condition cannot be viewed solely as one of motor execution. The condition needs careful assessment and management of the needs of the child and the family. Instrumental techniques are likely to have an increasingly important role in the treatment of the phonetic-articulatory disorder. Precise measurement of the degree of nasal airflow during speech is important in charting progress in achieving control of velopharyngeal closure. Similarly, techniques such as electropalatography (p. 36) can be useful in establishing awareness of intra-oral movement in the patient with impaired oral sensation.[44]

Pathologies of Reception

In the remaining sections of this chapter we will consider disruptions in the process of receiving messages. The process of reception may be impaired at a variety of levels. At the beginning of the communication chain, a hearing impairment will disrupt the ability to receive acoustic stimuli, whereas at the end point of the chain there may be failures in the decoding of linguistic and other communicative information within the message. Patients with pathologies of reception will all have some degree of difficulty in receiving and/or understanding messages, but beyond this obvious similarity there will be many qualitative differences between them. Again we can see the need for detailed psycholinguistic investigation of the behavioural deficits experienced by patients, but we

---

[44]Further reading, see M. Edwards and A. C. H. Watson (eds), *Advances in the Management of Cleft Palate* (London, Whurr, 1993); P. Grunwell (ed), *Analysing Cleft Palate Speech* (London, Whurr, 1993).

find that there is less study of receptive deficits than of pathologies of production. The source of this disparity is not difficult to locate. A pathology of production results in 'hard' data for the investigator to study – that is, the patients' observable linguistic behaviour, including any errors they make. By contrast, comprehension failures do not produce such definite evidence.

We may administer a language-comprehension test to patients and glean some evidence of their ability to decode linguistic information, but the interpretation of the test performance is by no means simple or unambiguous (p. 81). Do all failures indicate a failure of language comprehension? Clearly some may do so, but patients may also fail for non-linguistic reasons – perhaps they are bored and inattentive, or maybe confused by the test situation, or anxious to do well, with anxiety disrupting their performance (see further Chapter 6). Similarly, successes on the test may not provide evidence of adequate linguistic processing. Patients may be using other sources of information to interpret the clinician's language. On a test which requires a patient to listen to words and then point to a matching picture to show that they have understood each word, successful performance may simply be through chance. If the patient has to select the target picture from a choice of four, then we would expect a 25% correct score just through chance. Non-verbal information may also allow patients to perform successfully. It is very difficult when administering such tests for the clinician not to look at the target picture (a behaviour called 'eye-pointing'). The patient may follow the direction of the clinician's gaze and guess that this is the target picture. It takes considerable practice on the part of the student clinician to avoid giving non-verbal clues of this type. Investigation of receptive behaviour is therefore difficult and, to some extent, indirect – with behavioural successes and failures needing careful interpretation. These difficulties lead, inevitably, to comparatively few detailed studies of language comprehension deficits.[45]

Hearing impairment

Humans can hear sounds in the range from 20 to 20 000 Hertz (Hz), although speech frequencies are drawn from the narrower range of 250 to 8000 Hz. In terms of intensity, normal conversational speech at about one metre distance is at a level of 60 decibels (dB: p. 135). Inability to detect sounds at these frequencies or intensity will lead to a hearing impairment which may have consequences for communicative ability. This will include difficulties in speech reception and, if the hearing loss is experienced early in life, problems in the acquisition of normal speech.

---

[45]See D. Howard and S. Franklin, *Missing the Meaning* (Cambridge, MA, MIT Press, 1988).

Given the nature of the auditory apparatus (see Chapter 4), it will be plain that loss of hearing is not a single homogenous category. Rather there is a potentially infinite range of degrees of hearing impairment, ranging from a very slight inability to respond to a few low-intensity frequencies (which will hardly interfere with normal communication) to a loss where there is no detectable response to any frequency no matter how intense the sound. This latter condition we might want to call 'deafness', but it is in fact fairly uncommon: the vast majority of people diagnosed as deaf do have some degree of response to sound (they have some 'residual hearing'). Most people, in other words, are spread over the scale of hearing impairment, in a way which makes it impossible to draw anything other than the grossest of distinctions. But distinctions have to be drawn.[46] For young children suffering from hearing loss, decisions must be made as to how they are to be educated. In Britain, various types of institution are available: there are special *schools for the deaf*, which cater for the more severely impaired child; there are a few *schools for the partially hearing*; and there are *partially hearing units*, usually attached to normal schools, which cater for the less impaired. Partially hearing children are also often placed in normal classes, receiving special assistance from a peripatetic teacher of the deaf. Unfortunately, it is not always obvious which type of institution will best meet the needs of children with a considerable, but not particularly severe, degree of hearing loss; a lot depends on the use these children are making of whatever hearing is available to them, and it is in such circumstances that the theoretical problems of defining deafness become practical and social ones.

Investigating hearing loss involves three interrelated decisions: where is the cause of the deafness located? how great is the degree of hearing loss? and what type of hearing loss is it? The otologist is responsible for the first of these questions (compare above, p. 142); the person responsible for the other two is the *audiologist*. *Audiology* is the study of hearing and its disorders. It is specifically concerned with assessing the nature and degree of hearing loss and conservation, and with the rehabilitation of people with hearing impairment. When the focus is on children, the specialized techniques involved are known as *paediatric audiology*. *Audiometry* is the scientific measurement of hearing, using, in particular, the audiometer (compare p. 136). A wide range of *audiometric tests* is available, to determine the nature and degree of hearing sensitivity. One of the most widely used techniques is *pure-tone audiometry*, which uses a specially calibrated machine to generate pure tones at different frequencies and

---

[46]For example, one system of classification distinguishes degrees of hearing impairment as follows: mild – loss of 27–40 dB; moderate – loss of 41–55 dB; moderately severe – loss of 56–70 dB; severe – loss of 71–90 dB; profound – loss of 91+ dB.

intensities; these are presented to the patient one ear at a time through headphones (in an *air-conduction test*), or through the bone behind each ear (in a *bone-conduction test*). Patients indicate when they sense a sound, and the results are plotted as an audiogram (Figure 5.3, compare Figure 4.18). *Speech audiometry* aims to obtain a measure of the patient's response to speech, as opposed to pure-tone stimuli. It may be carried out impressionistically, with the audiologist speaking at different levels and distances from the patient; but a more precise estimate can be achieved by recording a series of words or sentences representing the various kinds of speech sound and playing these back to the patient at known intensities under various conditions. Other important audiological assessments include *tympanometry*, which evaluates the efficiency of the middle ear vibratory system, and *auditory evoked potentials*, which measure the electrical activity in the brain following the presentation of sound. The latter technique is important in testing the hearing of very young children and other individuals who are unable to comply with the demands of test techniques such as pure-tone and speech audiometry.

Using these techniques, one can make a major differential diagnosis of hearing loss into two broad categories, based primarily on where the lesions occur in the auditory pathway: *conductive* deafness and *sensorineural* (or *neural*, or *nerve*) deafness. Conductive deafness refers to any interference with the transmission of sound to the inner ear; sensorineural deafness refers to interference arising from the inner ear itself, or in that part of the auditory nerve as far back as its first synapse in the brain stem. Sensorineural deafness is further divided into the common *sensory* (or *cochlear*) deafness, due to inner ear damage, and the rarer *neural* deafness, due to nerve VIII disease, typically a tumour (*acoustic neuroma*). Figure 5.3a illustrates a case of moderate conductive deafness; there is a fairly uniform reduction in intensity throughout the frequency range. This might have been caused by any of the outer/middle ear problems outlined in Chapter 4. A case of sensorineural deafness is illustrated in Figure 5.3b: here, the patient has had particular difficulty responding to the high frequencies ('high-tone deafness'), indicating that there has been some specific damage to the receptor cells in the organ of Corti which handle these frequencies, or to those nerve fibres which transmit these frequencies to the brain. An important factor in the diagnosis will be the ability of patients to respond differentially to air-conduction and bone-conduction tests (the audiograms in Figure 5.3 were air conduction only). If they cannot hear sounds through the air, but can hear them through the skull, it suggests that a conductive deafness is present; conversely, if there is no difference in hearing between these two modes, the damage must be neural. More complex, 'mixed' cases of deafness also occur.

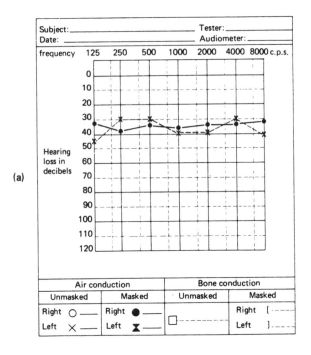

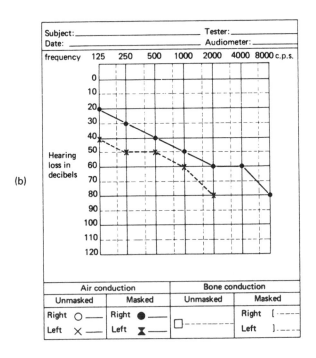

Figure 5.3 Audiograms of two types of hearing loss: (a) conductive deafness; (b) sensorineural deafness

A specific example of (fluctuating) neural deafness occurs in *Ménière's disease* (described by the French physician, Prosper Ménière, in 1861), along with tinnitus, giddiness (*vertigo*) and vomiting. *Tinnitus* itself is little understood: it refers to noises in the ear, which may take on several different qualities – ringing, buzzing, hissing, pulsating . . . Most of us have experienced a mild tinnitus (e.g. 'ringing in the ears'), and any slightly abnormal condition, such as excessive wax, might produce it. But it often occurs in acute form (as in Ménière's disease), in which the noise levels can be desperately irritating and painful – a condition that the sufferer can only learn to live with, by attempting to ignore it or mask it in some way. It is generally felt that the cause lies deep within the cochlea, but the reason for the specific qualities of sound (e.g. whether the cochlea is in some way picking up sounds from the circulation of the blood) is unknown.

Conductive and sensorineural deafness are sometimes grouped together under the more general heading of *peripheral deafness*, and opposed to the little-understood phenomenon of *central* (or *cortical*) *deafness*. Central deafness refers to the loss of hearing sensitivity due to damage of the auditory nerve in the brain stem or in the hearing centres of the cortex (compare p. 107). It is sometimes referred to as 'auditory imperception', and this term illustrates the issue that is involved: the ear seems normal, as can be shown by a pure-tone audiogram, which will produce normal results; but the patient will respond poorly to speech audiometry, being unable to integrate and interpret the sounds of speech. The problem of diagnosis here, of course, is in deciding whether this is purely an auditory problem, or whether a more fundamental linguistic pathology is involved (as in Wernicke's aphasia, see p. 107), or something even more deep-rooted (as in the failure to respond of severely autistic children, see p. 161).

Other variables may enter into the classification of hearing impairment. Apart from the above distinctions, we must obviously allow for 'mixed' types of deafness, in which both conductive and neural elements are involved. This is particularly noticeable as part of the neural process of hearing loss associated with age (*presbycusis*): sounds become fainter, generally, but with certain sounds (usually the consonants involving the higher frequencies) causing particular problems. Speech will get through, but it will be full of 'gaps'; it will thus take much longer to interpret, and it is this which accounts for the slow response of many old people to speech, even when it is shouted (shouting will usually not help: what they need is *time* to decode the partially received signal). Unfortunately, such slow responses are often interpreted as a diminution in the person's mental faculties – which is by no means necessarily the case.

An important further distinction is whether one or both ears is involved. If the problem affects only one ear, it is referred to as *monaural* or *unilateral*; if two ears, it is *binaural* or *bilateral*. It is usual to refer to patients' hearing abilities with reference to their 'better ear', if they have one.

Yet another distinction to note is that between *congenital* and *acquired* deafness. The former means 'present at birth', insofar as this can be established, and usually subsumes cases of genetic origin as well as those where the deafness was caused by disease or trauma in the womb or during birth itself. Acquired, or *adventitious* deafness, refers to the later onset of this disorder, as a result of disease or trauma, throughout the whole period of child and adult life. In relation to this distinction, three points should be stressed:

1. The need for routine auditory screening at or shortly after birth is paramount, but is infrequently carried out. Over 95% of the babies born deaf have some degree of residual hearing, and the earlier that auditory training can be established with such children, the better the prognosis for the later development of speech.
2. An important issue, in relation to acquired deafness, is whether the change took place before or after the onset of the learning of language. If some language input has taken place before the advent of the deafness, the teacher of the deaf is much helped in the attempt to facilitate the language learning process.
3. If deafness is congenital, or acquired in the first months of life, when will it be first noticed? One factor to remember here is that deaf infants do cry, coo, and babble in the early months of life; they do not remain silent. Studies are few, but those that have been made suggest that there is considerable variation in the early babble of deaf infants, though it tends to be less in quantity and (as time passes) less purposeful than with hearing infants.

By the end of the first year of life, some indication of the presence of deafness is normally present in the 'flattened' tones of the child's babble, compared with the developing intonation of hearing children, which will become more and more language specific as time goes by. It is possible to begin telling apart the language backgrounds of infants, on the basis of their early babbling and attempts at speech, from as early as 9 months; and it is from this time, accordingly, that a phonetic analysis (of non-segmental vocal effect, compare p. 42) might be able to contribute to diagnosis.

Later work with the deaf is a complex and time-consuming business. There are of course a variety of aids available, but it should be noted that as a rule hearing aids only amplify sound presented to the ear – they cannot help in the interpretation of that sound. Moreover, *all* sound in the environment of the person may be amplified – including the background noises to speech. Lip-reading skills also constitute an important additional aid to comprehension. But what about speech production? The difficulty which deaf children have in learning to speak is well illustrated by the traditional (and misleading) term 'deaf and dumb'. The term is misleading because it does not at all follow that if you are deaf you will be unable to speak. Everything depends on the kind of deafness involved, the amount and quality of your exposure to speech, the kind of teaching you receive, and so on. But it is a fact that, for whatever reason, most congenitally deaf people grow up with a functionally inadequate speech level, i.e. they cannot produce intelligible speech for the whole range of occasions when they want to communicate. Partly as a result of the apparent failure of this mode of language learning, many teachers of the deaf in recent years have focused their attention on the possibility of teaching the deaf to communicate by means of developing their natural *signing* capacities. All of us have an ability to gesture our meaning, on occasion, but the range of meanings which we can signal in this way is very limited. In so-called *sign languages*, however, a range of several thousand meanings can be communicated, and whole communities of the deaf have learned to use these systems. Some of these systems have developed naturally, from within the deaf communities (such as American Sign Language (ASL), or British Sign Language (BSL)). Others have been artificially constructed to meet a particular purpose (such as the Paget-Gorman Sign System, which attempts to reflect in its sign sequences the grammatical rules of English sentences).[47]

Other forms of signing behaviour have been devised to help the deaf. *Finger-spelling* (or *dactyology*) provides a manual alphabet (there are both one-handed and two-handed versions) which enables anyone to spell out words on their fingers. The alphabet used by the British Deaf Association is illustrated in Figure 5.4. Then there is *cued speech*, a system devised by Orin Cornett, an American researcher in deaf education at Gallaudet University, Washington; this supplements the movements of the lips by a series of signals representing some of the main sound contrasts involved in speech, thereby aiding the deaf person's comprehension. And there are many other schemes. Reaction to all forms of *manual* communication has been mixed, over the years. Indeed, in the world of the deaf, it is commonplace to find educators who are fiercely in favour of signing (so-called 'manualists') and those who are fiercely against it (so-called 'oralists'). There are also others who try to make use of both systems of communication in their work. The arguments on both sides are important and far-reaching, but are often

[47]The sytem was invented by Sir Richard Paget, and developed by his wife after his death, in collaboration with the librarian of the RNID in London, Pierre Gorman. It was published in 1976 as *The Paget-Gorman Sign System Manual* (London, Association for Experiment in Deaf Education Ltd.).

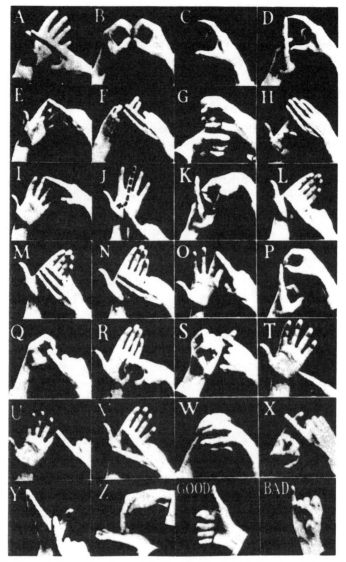

Figure 5.4 British finger-spelling alphabet (© The British Deaf Association)

obscured because of the emotion which is engendered when the issue is discussed. The main argument against signing is that it is setting deaf people apart from all but their own small community, labelling them as deaf and different, and not helping them in their desire to communicate with the outside world. To which argument the manualist might well respond that this is no worse than the situation which exists for deaf people who have been trained in an oralist tradition: they cannot communicate with the outside world either, and are readily labelled as deaf, on account of their absent or unintelligible speech. A manual system of communication is a positive gain, the manualist might argue, for people who have nothing else, and it is moreover capable of providing a very wide range of communicative experience in social and artistic life. To which the oralist might respond that the weaknesses in oral methods can be circumvented by the development of new techniques of language teaching, such as the devices now available for displaying features of the voice visually (e.g. the *laryngograph*, which makes the larynx frequency visible, and thus motivates deaf people to improve their voice pitch). And so the argument continues. When such matters as a person's identity and the fullness of life enter into an argument, it is evident why emotions are easily roused. But one fact cannot be obscured by the arguments of both sides – the pressing need for research into all aspects of deaf communicative behaviour. What stages of language do deaf children pass through as they begin their acquisition process? To what extent do deaf children develop a system of their own, when learning language – a kind of 'deafish', as it has sometimes been called? Which structures of the adult language cause particular problems of comprehension for the deaf, whether child or adult? Are there limits to the amount of visual discrimination, which might affect the learning of a sign system? These and many other questions remain to be investigated systematically.[48]

To illustrate the kind of linguistic problems encountered in analysing the language of deaf children, four samples of their free writing (the first two in response to a picture stimulus) are given below. The first is from a $12^1/_2$-year-old girl (A), whose audiogram is given in Figure 5.5a.

The guinea pig

There is a guinea pig. The guinea pig name is Funny. The guinea pig got black and white. The guinea pig got pink nose. The guinea pig is standing. The guinea pig is waiting the food. The guinea pig got pink ears. The guinea pig got four leg. The guinea pig is standing on the table. The guinea pig look at the boy.

The second is from a $14^1/_2$-year-old boy (B), whose audiogram is given in Figure 5.5b.

White horse

There is a white horse in a forest he has large ears and big brown eyes. He have got lots of hair all over his eye on one side. His nostrils are about 2 cm wide. He is very wild horse. The forest are black the grass are nice and green. He has got a brown harness. Sometime he ran away and eat people apple in the garden. His eyes looks as they are coming out.

Several of the deaf child's linguistic difficulties are illustrated by these extracts. There is an extremely restricted range of sentence structure, most

---

[48]For further discussion of deafness, see J. Ballantyne, M. Martin and A. Martin, *Deafness* (London, Whurr, 5th edn, 1992).

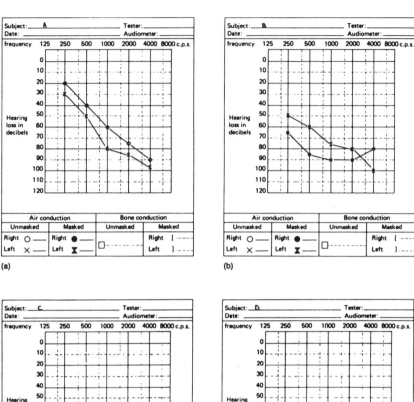

Figure 5.5 Audiograms of the four children whose writing is analysed in the text (pp. 217–19)

noticeable in the stereotyped sentence openings in the guinea-pig story. There are problems with articles (*He is very wild horse*), tenses (*Sometime he ran . . . and eat*), prepositions (*is waiting the food*), agreement between subject and verb (*he have . . ., the forest are . . .*), omission of auxiliary verbs (*the guinea pig look at*), and omission of certain word-endings (*the guinea pig name*). It is sometimes difficult to be sure what sentence is intended: how, for example, would you correct A's third sentence – *The guinea pig is black and white?* or *. . . has a black and* *white coat?* The third extract illustrates this problem in extreme form. It was written by a $16\frac{1}{2}$-year-old boy (C), whose audiogram is given in Figure 5.5c. The analysis of this kind of language presents major problems to the language pathologist, whose aim is to establish how many of these data have an underlying pattern. It also illustrates the need for as early intervention as possible with such children, with the aim of teaching a stable basis of linguistic structure, and thus preventing the development of such ungrammatical sequences.

Star Wars

The Star Wars was the two spaceship a fighting opened door was coming the Men and Storm trooper guns carry on to Artoo Detoo and threepio at go the space. The Earth was not grass and tree but to the sand, R2D2 and C3PO at going look for R2D2 walk the sand people carry away Artoo Detoo sleep. The Luke Skywalker Came was van Horrible and the his was Came C3PO to walked the to R2D2 the Man said No and to other one Small Came was bomb as no good. The C3PO ask to man was oh! yes with came to R2D2 yes very good. The R2D2 going long away the his said C3PO as the Nobody was long away as the his bring Binoculars For Look round not they was the car float as but the very fast and you are found R2D2. The spaceship to away the Earth space-metal the long away very big Earth.

A much more satisfactory outcome is illustrated by the fourth extract, from a $16\frac{1}{4}$-year-old girl (D), whose audiogram is given in Figure 5.5d.

Snow

It was Saturday morning, I woke up and I got dress. Then I drew the curtain.

I looked through the window and found that everything was white and the water had changed into ice. I sat down on a chair by the window.

I was looking everywhere. On the long lake beside my house was a small white bridge and under the bridge were a long icicle drop. The drop had made a small hole in the frozen lake. In the small hole, I could see two little fishes swimming about. The lake looked like glass with a small hole in it.

The grass was cover in snow and it looked like a very big white carpet with some footmark. I didn't know who made the footmark. I was thinking who come to my door and goes back again. I follow the footmark to see if I get any clue. Then I found there were three bottles of milk so I thought it must be the milkman.

Agnosia

An intact hearing mechanism is necessary to relay an acoustic input, converted first into mechanical vibration and then into an electrochemical impulse, to the auditory processing areas of the brain. We have already seen how reception of sound by the ear and the auditory centres of the brain can be interfered with at various points, and the clinical distinctions involved are classified as the main categories of deafness. But the fact that the brain receives sound does not mean that it has the ability to *recognize* the sounds it perceives. The term *agnosia* is a general one, which is used whenever the brain apparently lacks the ability to recognize familiar percepts, despite adequate sensory input. We have already mentioned the difficulties in differentiating central (or cortical) deafness from disorders of linguistic decoding (see p. 213), and indeed when discussing disruptions in the perception, recognition and decoding of sensory inputs, distinctions are often easier to make in theory than in practice. Thus the differentiation of central deafness (a disruption in the cortical reception of auditory information) from auditory agnosia (a disorder in the recognition and classification of the input) is not easy, and similarly both of these disabilities can be confused with failures in linguistic processing that occur in developmental language disorders and aphasia.

An agnosia may affect any of the senses. There is the phenomenon of *visual agnosia* – inability to identify visual stimuli. Patients are not blind – they do not bump into objects as they move about the environment – but they fail to recognize what they are seeing. Every object is seen as if for the first time. The faces of family members may not be recognized, although if they speak, they could be identified by their voice.[49] *Tactile agnosia* (or *astereognosis*) is an inability to identify objects by touch. And in *auditory agnosia* the patient may have problems in identifying two instances of the same word, or sound, as being the same. Sounds that distinguish word meanings would be regularly confused, with profound consequences for the ability to understand speech. 'I can hear you talking, but I can't translate it', said one such patient. Patients may, like the hearing-impaired, use visual information from lip-reading to assist their understanding, and in milder forms of the disorder, where they may have difficulties only in discriminating sounds which are acoustically very similar, they may be unable to recognize all of the input, and have to 'fill in the gaps' from knowledge of the context of the utterance.

Auditory agnosia is difficult to differentiate from difficulties in the subsequent decoding of the meaning of an auditory input – for example, difficulties of the type found in aphasia of the Wernicke's type, i.e. with severe speech comprehension difficulties (p. 170). A differential diagnosis can be made only by careful psycholinguistic assessment and detailed analysis of the patient's behaviour. Take, for example, the following two situations.

1:

T   'show me the tàble/
P   oh yés/ tàble/ [*but not pointing at it*]
T   yès/ the tàble/ where ìs it/
P   'one of those tàbles/ [*still not pointing*]
    well I sup'pose it 'might be [*looking around*] in a róom/
T   yés [*encouragingly*]
P   thère/ [*pointing to a chair*]

---

[49]The title of Oliver Sacks' book *The Man Who Mistook His Wife for a Hat* (London, Pan, 1986) is based upon a case-study of a patient suffering from visual agnosia.

2:
T 'show me the tàble/
P [*points, correctly*]
T now tèll me/ 'where's the tàble/
P [*looks uncertainly at her*]
T lísten/– 'where's the tàble/
P ta – ta –
T [*carefully*] tàble/ – tàble/
P 'ta-'ble/ òh/ tàble/ [*points, correctly*]

In the first extract, the evidence seems to support, fairly certainly, a diagnosis of aphasia. The patient seems to be having difficulties in decoding the meaning of the word *table* and ultimately makes a semantic error, interpreting *table* as 'chair'. In the second case, the patient seems to be having a more fundamental difficulty in processing the phonological information in the input. There is variability in the performance – one moment the patient recognizes the word correctly, and the next, recognition appears to fail. Situations such as these are typical in clinical contexts. Of course, there are several strategies and tests available which can help to make a decision in such cases, but it would be wrong to leave the impression that it is always possible to sort them out. Indeed, diagnosis is often an uncertain and controversial matter.

Linguistic and message-decoding disorders

We include this section for the sake of completeness, but our discussion of language disorders and cognitive disorders (p. 155) has already shown that both of these categories of disorder may be characterized by difficulties in encoding as well as in decoding messages. In developmental language disorders, patients may have difficulties in understanding language as well as in formulating it. The aphasic patient is also likely to have deficits in language comprehension, in addition to more obvious difficulties in encoding linguistic messages. As with the linguistic encoding difficulties of patients, there is a very broad range of comprehension deficits that may occur – both in severity and in the levels of language organization which are impaired – with the consequence that each patient requires detailed and meticulous assessment in order to identify and treat difficulties. Patients with disabilities which have been grouped together under the heading of 'cognitive disorders' may also have problems in understanding the messages of others, in addition to their difficulties in formulating appropriate and coherent messages of their own. Schizophrenic patients, in addition to sending chaotic and incoherent messages, may misinterpret the messages sent to them by others. Thus, for example, misunderstanding of the linguistic or voice quality information, or misinterpretation of the speaker's intent, may result in the schizophrenic patient being placed in a state of terror at what may have been intended as a perfectly innocent or neutral utterance.

Comprehension disorders are usually more difficult to detect than language production difficulties. The reasons for this were discussed in Chapter 3 – in particular, the possibility of using information sources other than language in an attempt to understand a message. Non-verbal information, voice quality, and contextual knowledge can all be used in an attempt to reconstruct the meaning of a linguistic message, when that message itself has not been understood. Patients who can use such information may be described as having good 'functional' comprehension, often despite serious language comprehension deficits. Undoubtedly many basic communicative acts can be understood on the basis of such information – for example, greetings and other social pleasantries, and communication within contexts where there is a high degree of routine. But there are many situations in which, without an ability to understand language, the patient will not cope: understanding what is happening in a classroom, or courtroom, or during a medical consultation are representative examples.

Epidemiological Issues

We have referred frequently throughout this chapter to the need for precise descriptions of the behaviour involved in linguistic disabilities, and for careful analysis of these behaviours in relation to the medical conditions underlying them. Without such information, it is difficult to arrive at any conclusions about the extent to which a disorder occurs within a population, and thus the extent to which there is a clinical need that has to be met – for instance, by the provision of special facilities within the health service. The science which deals with the prevalence, distribution and control of disease in a population is known as *epidemiology*, and in recent years, considerable progress has been made in our understanding of linguistic disorders from the epidemiologist's point of view; but there are several basic problems.

The question, 'How many cases are there of such-and-such a disease in a country?' is deceptively difficult to answer. Everything depends on how you identify the disease in the first place. How many speech impairments are there? If by 'speech impairments' you mean everything from the slightest detectable error in articulation to the most obvious forms of disturbance, then your figure will be relatively high; on the other hand, if you mean only disorders of articulation, the figure will be much lower; and if you mean only those disorders of articulation that are sufficiently severe to need therapy, the figure will be lower still. Reviewing the literature on the prevalence of speech disorders, a 1972 British government report concluded that about 3% of children in ordinary schools suffered from some kind of speech disorder, but only about 2% were in need of speech therapy. Age is another variable: in the pre-school child, that report concluded that nearer 3% of the children might need the services of a speech therapist (about 60 000 altogether, in 1972).[50]

A similar percentage has been suggested for the USA. An identical problem would face anyone interested in studying the prevalence of hearing loss in the community: how much hearing loss is included under this heading? Under what kinds of circumstances? One estimate that has been given is $2^{1}/_{2}$% of the population.

Such gross figures can be accumulated for any disease, if the information is available. There are many ways of obtaining the data – using interviews, analysis of case records, direct examination of samples, study of death registration records, and so on. In linguistic disorders, a factor which is of considerable importance is the adequacy of the medical history and the accuracy of the behavioural description. In so many cases, accurate accounts of medical and behavioural factors are lacking. This is one reason, it is said, why estimates of so many syndromes vary so much. Because birth records are often not clear, estimates of the cleft palate condition, for example, have ranged from 0.80 per 1000 to 1.70 per 1000 births. We can average this out and say that cleft palates are a little over one in 1000, and this is the figure usually quoted; but there is plainly a need for caution in interpreting this.

Such gross figures, also, are not necessarily the most interesting. Many people are more concerned, not with the overall statistics, but with a more detailed breakdown in terms of age, sex, and social background, on the one hand, and type and degree of severity of the condition, on the other. For example, it is important to know that in most spoken language disorders, boys are twice as likely to be affected as girls. In cleft palate, for instance, one study showed that for clefts of primary and secondary palate together, boys were more frequent than girls in a ratio of 2:1, whereas for clefts of the secondary palate only, the ratio was reversed.

Another important factor, in discussing these issues, is to ensure that a careful distinction is drawn between the notions of *prevalence* (which we have been discussing above) and *incidence*. Prevalence refers to the number of cases of a disease in a population at any given time. Incidence refers to the number of *new* cases of disease within a specific period (the 'attack rate'). This distinction is not just a terminological one: quite different pictures of a disease are obtained. For example, the incidence of acute otitis media (compare p. 142) is 100 per 1000 of population per annum. However, the average duration of a case is only about a week, so that at any given time only 2 people in 1000 will be suffering from the disease.

The Quirk Report's (1972) estimates of the numbers needing speech therapy provides an interesting perspective for this chapter. It

---

[50]*Speech Therapy Services* (London, HMSO, 1972). The committee of enquiry was under the chairmanship of Professor Randolph Quirk, and is generally known as the 'Quirk Report'.

concluded, as an 'informed guess', that well over 300 000 children and adults were in need of speech therapy services in the UK – a figure which, it says, 'can err only in being too low' (p. 78).

Revision Questions

1. Write the stages in the model of the communication chain. Alongside each stage, write the name of a communication disorder which represents an impairment of that stage and list its core characteristics.
2. Why do disabilities such as cleft palate and hearing impairment present a challenge to the structure of the communication chain model?
3. What is the difference between a pre-linguistic and a linguistic disorder? Illustrate your answer with reference to a disorder in each category.
4. What is the difference traditionally claimed between a speech disorder and a language disorder? Illustrate your answer with reference to a disorder in each category.

Tutorial Activities

1. The issue of 'politically correct' language to refer to elements of disability was raised at the beginning of the chapter. Consider the following pairs of terms. What are the connotations attached to each term and which do you feel might be considered 'politically incorrect', and by what kind of person? Compare your intuitions with those of fellow students.

    patient – client
    speechless – dumb
    disabled – handicapped
    visually impaired – blind

    Are you able to identify any other terms used to refer to the disabled, or categories of disability, to which the political correctness arguments might apply?

2. The notion of normality and abnormality in language and communication appears, at first glance, a very obvious one. But defining normality is not as simple as it first might appear. We might start off defining normality as 'the way I speak'. Reflect on this statement. Can you identify ways in which your language is different from others, and then can you link these differences to other variables such as age, gender, regional background etc.?

    Once you have done this, find an anthology of poetry. Select a range of poets' work. Would you describe their use of language as normal or abnormal?

Consider the following case descriptions and decide on the type of communication disorder(s) involved:

(a) Sarah is 3 years old. Her birth history was normal and her subsequent medical history suggests nothing to indicate any interference with normal growth and development. Her early developmental milestones show a slight delay (for example, walking at 15 months, first words at 16 months). Both of her parents work, and Sarah is looked after by an elderly grandmother. The grandmother is rather deaf and not very active. Sarah has been referred to a language pathologist because she does not talk very much. Her hearing has been tested, and the test indicated a mild hearing loss, but the audiological assessment is due to be repeated because she had a cold on the day of the test.

(b) Simon is 30 years old. He was knocked down by a car as he crossed a road. This accident resulted in multiple injuries, including a fractured skull, and damage to both cerebral hemispheres and the brain stem. He was in a coma for 23 days and then slowly recovered consciousness. Four months after the accident, Simon has difficulty moving all four limbs, with particular weakness on the right side of his body. He is fed by tube because of a swallowing difficulty. He is not very communicative, and when he does speak his speech is not clear. He answers questions by nodding or shaking his head. He usually, although not always, answers such questions appropriately (e.g. 'Is your name Simon?'). His attention span is very short and he is easily distracted.

(c) Annie is a 45-year-old market trader. She is a heavy smoker. She has been referred to a speech pathologist by the ENT department of a local hospital. Her voice is very hoarse, and Annie reports particular difficulties in using her voice towards the end of the day. She reports that she has a sore throat, but an ENT examination revealed no abnormality in the structure of her vocal folds. She uses her voice a lot in her work and is very anxious about the voice problems she is experiencing.

(d) Richard's parents are very concerned about his speech development. He is 3 years old and does not produce the following sounds: /s, z, ʃ, ʒ, ʧ, ʤ/. His birth and medical history are normal and his development in all other areas is giving no cause for concern. Richard is using sentences, sometimes containing three or four elements (e.g. *We go home now*). His vocabulary is extensive. His understanding of language is normal for his age.

Chapter 6
Assessment and Treatment of Communication Disorders

In earlier chapters we have reviewed the range of pathologies of spoken language that may occur, and the different approaches that the language pathologist might use in the investigation and remediation of these disorders. The task faced by clinicians is not an easy one. They may, in the course of any working day, be faced with very different challenges. One patient may come to the clinic with an organic disorder – for example, cleft palate – in which the language pathologist would need in-depth knowledge of the anatomy of the speech organs, and understanding of the effects of the condition on speech production. Detailed information on the syndrome of cleft palate is also necessary so that the clinician is aware of other potential complicating factors such as hearing loss and its consequent effects on understanding speech and, in turn, language development. Other patients may appear at the clinic suffering from problems with no obvious physical cause, but displaying profound linguistic and cognitive impairments. In such instances, clinicians would be required to call upon their knowledge of the behavioural sciences, especially linguistics and psychology, in order to tackle the problems displayed by patients. Clinicians often choose to specialize in particular areas of linguistic disability, but, ironically, it is often the relatively inexperienced clinician who has to deal with a very broad spectrum of disorders. What, then, is the education and training this individual must complete in order to be able to perform this task?

Throughout this book, we have concentrated on presenting language pathology as an intellectual field of inquiry, which takes the data of clinical and other communicative situations and attempts to provide a coherent frame of reference which will account for those data. Only on the basis of this, we have argued, is it possible to devise adequate procedures for management and rehabilitation of the patient. A strong theoretical foundation is at all times essential, to guarantee consistency in the tasks facing clinicians (such as the description and analysis of patient behaviour) and to enable them to make headway in explaining awkward cases. It is not only the successful cases which a theory is called upon to explain, but also the failures: why has a remedial procedure *not* worked, in a specific instance? Chapter 5 has indicated the need to be critical of terminology, the search for analytic criteria, the concern for adequate data bases – these are issues which turn up repeatedly. Probably the biggest problem facing the language pathologist, though, is the need to integrate and interpret the findings from a multiplicity of different disciplines and academic traditions, each of which has an important contribution to make concerning linguistic disability. We have encountered several of these disciplines in the course of this book, as we reviewed the implications of working in medical and behavioural terms. It remains now to bring these disciplines together, in order to see clearly the academic breadth of the subject and to anticipate what is involved in the assessment and treatment of communicative disability.

For those readers who are anticipating linguistic pathology as part of a career (in speech and language therapy, in particular), this perspective is very necessary. A common enquiry relates to the best kind of preliminary training needed in order to become an efficient clinician. It should be plain from the range of topics reviewed in this book that there can be no single simple answer. Apart from the personal qualities necessary for successful clinical practice (a discussion of which falls outside the purview of this book), there are several academic and academically inspired skills involved, which cut across the traditional division between arts and sciences. The two main foundation areas were reviewed in Chapter 2: medicine and the behavioural sciences. The former subject can be broken down into its main subdisciplines, of which the following would form the core of medical training in the various degree courses in the subject:

anatomy   orthodontics
physiology   psychiatry
neurology and neuropathology   audiology
otorhinolaryngology   paediatrics

with some reference to embryology, genetics, general pathology and geriatrics. The behavioural sciences relevant to training are primarily linguistics and psychology. Under the heading of linguistics, we would expect to encounter courses in the following subjects:

phonetics and phonology
grammar
semantics
pragmatics and discourse

psycholinguistics (including language acquisition)
clinical linguistics[1]

Under the heading of psychology, the following range of subjects would
be relevant:

developmental psychology
social psychology
cognitive psychology
abnormal psychology
neuropsychology and neuroscience

Several other fields of study would make their appearance, including:

acoustics
education
contemporary institutions (such as the health service, social and
welfare services, relevant aspects of the law)
research methods and statistics

In addition to these contributory subjects, there are the core topics of
communicative pathology, providing coverage of the full range of
disability. The difficult task for the trainee clinician is to apply to language
pathology the theory, methodology and empirical findings of the various
contributory disciplines. Thus, alongside linguistics, in its various
branches, there is the clinical application of these ideas to the various
pathological areas – such as the use of grammatical and phonological
models in carrying out assessments, or motivating remedial programmes.
Alongside psychology, there are the various applications of that subject –
for example, taking theories from developmental psychology of how and
why children learn, and using them in clinical teaching situations.

The multidisciplinary nature of the education of language clinicians
reflects the multifaceted nature of communicative disability. Patients
may have complex conditions which require an understanding and
description of their communicative basis, of the physical limitations of
the patient's anatomy and physiology, and of the possible cognitive,
social-emotional, educational or occupational consequences of the
disability. It is often the case, therefore, that the language pathologist is
working as part of a multidisciplinary team. The size of the team is
variable, but the range of other professionals who might be involved
from time to time would include:

---

[1]Clinical linguistics is one of the newest branches of applied linguistics, which takes
the methods and theories of linguistic science and applies them to language
pathology. Work in this field has mushroomed in the past two decades with the
appearance of new journals such as *Clinical Linguistics and Phonetics* and books
such as D. Crystal, *Linguistic Encounters with Language Handicap* (Oxford,
Blackwell, 1984); D. Crystal, *Clinical Linguistics* (London, Whurr, 1981); and
K. Grundy, *Linguistics in Clinical Practice* (London, Whurr, 2nd edn, 1995).

educational psychologists
clinical psychologists
social workers
hospital medical teams
general practitioners
health visitors
school medical officers
teachers
physiotherapists
occupational therapists
audiologists
hearing therapists

All of these professionals have an area of expertise which, although overlapping with that of the language pathologist, is distinct. If the members of the multidisciplinary team work effectively – recognizing the limits of their own expertise, knowing when to refer to the relevant profession difficulties which are beyond their area of knowledge, and communicating their findings to others in the team, a complete picture of a patient's difficulties can be built up, which in turn allows for effective management.

The language pathologist, then, may work as part of a multidisciplinary team and, like all other members, has a distinct area of expertise within that team. What are the roles that language clinicians should fulfil as part of their professional responsibilities? The most obvious roles are the assessment and treatment of communication disorders, and as these are central we shall consider them in some detail below. But other areas of responsibility can also be identified. First, the language pathologist has a role in preventing communication disorders. This is perhaps a surprising claim, because many of the disorders we have reviewed in Chapter 5 have causes which are beyond the language pathologist's area of control. Hence programmes to improve maternal health in pregnancy (e.g. through reducing smoking and improving diet) might have an influence on the incidence of damage to the foetus, and health programmes to control hypertension in the adult population (through control of diet, stress and smoking, and the regular monitoring of blood pressure) might reduce the incidence of stroke, but it is difficult to see a specific role for the language clinician in these activities. They are clearly the remit of those involved in health education – medical and nursing staff in particular.

However, there are areas of preventive intervention which are clearly within the remit of the language clinician. One such example might be with infants who are identified as being 'at risk' of a subsequent developmental handicap.[2] If a child is born with a severe physical or intellectual disability, it is essential that the child is placed in an environment which

[2]The 'at risk' concept derives from the observation that certain factors (e.g. low birthweight) correlate with subsequent developmental problems. Children who are identified as being at risk of future developmental or health problems can be closely monitored, and intervention may begin as soon as any difficulties emerge.

provides maximal opportunities for subsequent language learning. The environment should be carefully structured so that the input is in tune with the child's current level of function. Opportunities can be provided for the child to practise and develop new skills, and attempts at new learning should be reinforced and encouraged. This might appear to be stating what is obvious, but the disabled child may not be in an environment which will maximize opportunities to learn. It is not difficult to imagine the effect that the birth of a child with a disability has on both parents and other members of the family. Parents who are shocked and distressed may not interact with the disabled child in an entirely normal way. An understandable response to the knowledge that a child has a profound hearing impairment is to assume that talking to this child is a futile exercise. Few individuals with hearing impairments are, however, completely deaf – there may be some degree of residual hearing (p. 210). The task for the carers of hearing-impaired children is to try to ensure that they receive maximal auditory input, that the amount of distracting ambient noise in the environment is controlled, and that they are able to see the speaker, in order that incomplete auditory information is supplemented by visual information from lip-reading. Similarly, children with a profound intellectual handicap require that the task of language learning is simplified for them. A situation where different adults refer to a single object by different names (e.g. a teddy bear as 'teddy', 'cuddly' or 'Fred' (p. 161)), will not simplify the task of the disabled child in learning language. In both these examples it is the behaviour of carers, as opposed to that of patients, which is modified. This is an important model of intervention in language pathology, and very different from therapeutic approaches adopted in medical science, where treatment is solely directed at the patient.

A preventive approach is not just restricted to early intervention with developmental disorders; it also has applications for some acquired disorders of communication. An important adult population to target for preventive intervention is the so-called 'voice professionals' – individuals who use their voices extensively as part of their occupation. Teachers, actors and singers are in a high-risk group for voice disorders, partly because of their heavy use of voice, but also because they use their voices in far from ideal conditions. A teacher, for example, may have to be heard over a large space and in competition with high ambient noise. Preventive work with trainee voice professionals can suggest ways in which problems can be avoided, and if voice difficulties do begin to develop, action can be taken at an early stage to prevent a voice disorder becoming established.

A second general role for the language pathologist is to act as an information provider on the subject of communicative pathology. We have already emphasized that language pathology is a coherent field of intellectual enquiry which requires that its practitioners draw upon a body of knowledge from both behavioural and medical sciences. The language pathologist needs to integrate these approaches and then to put them into practice. This means that the language pathologist has a unique set of knowledge and skills and is equipped to act as a source of information on communicative disability to society generally, to other professionals (e.g. medical practitioners and teachers), and most importantly, to patients and their families. Society, represented by its various institutions, needs information on the nature, incidence and needs of those with communicative disability in order to plan and cater for these needs. Other professionals require the language pathologist to provide accurate information on an individual's communicative difficulties in order to inform their own assessment and treatment decisions, and also to contribute to their professional development by expanding their knowledge of communicative disability. The importance of patients and their families understanding the nature of a communicative difficulty cannot be over-emphasized. Knowledge and insight into a disorder reduces fear and anxiety of the unknown. Patients and their carers can make predictions as to which situations are likely to cause particular communicative difficulties, and so make plans to control and ameliorate the effects of these situations.

The third general role of language pathologists is in research and development. Because clinicians have a unique blend of theoretical knowledge and the ability to put this knowledge into practice, it is important that they take responsibility for identifying areas where knowledge is short, or where techniques of assessment or intervention are in need of development. It is essential for the development of language pathology as a coherent academic field that it develops a flourishing research base. It would be quite possible for language pathologists to surrender the research role to psychologists, linguists and neurologists, and to become consumers, as opposed to generators, of research. But the consequences of this would be profound in terms of the health of the profession. In failing to ask questions, and to seek to supply answers to questions, a profession can lose its intellectual integrity. Language pathologists are often busy practitioners, but working in collaboration with colleagues and other behavioural and medical scientists time can be created for research. This is particularly true now that single-case study research is widely reported in academic journals. The single-case study is a detailed report of an individual patient – often relating the findings from the study of the patient to theories of language processing. It represents an alternative to the research methodology which has been pre-eminent in both medical and behavioural science – the large-scale group study. The latter research design, which involves large numbers of research subjects, and often relatively superficial assessments and measures of behaviour, is difficult for the practitioner to effect. One could argue, as we have done throughout much of this book, that in order to expand our knowledge of language pathology, only detailed descriptions of disordered communicative behaviour will suffice.[3]

These are some of the less obvious roles of the language pathologist. The central roles are those of the assessment and treatment of communication disorders, and it is to the more detailed consideration of these responsibilities that we now turn. When patients (and, to a degree, their carers and usual interlocutors) are referred to a language pathologist, they enter a process which has the following steps: initial or screening assessment, full assessment, treatment, reassessment and re-evaluation of treatment. The initial assessment is a quick and relatively superficial evaluation, the purpose of which is to decide whether or not a person does indeed show any evidence of linguistic disability. If the initial assessment indicates no obvious disability, or perhaps a very minor difficulty, the language pathologist will inform the patient and the referring agent of this finding. If the difficulty is minor, and the clinician predicts that it will resolve without professional intervention, the patient may be asked to return to the clinic after an interval, at which point progress will be reassessed. If, however, the screening assessment detects the presence of disability, the patient's communicative skills will undergo detailed assessment, which incorporates methods from both the medical and behavioural sciences. Thus the child with unintelligible speech will receive an evaluation of the speech organs, and potentially also be referred to an audiologist for a hearing assessment, and at the same time the child's speech will be recorded and a detailed phonetic-phonological analysis undertaken. The in-depth assessment should reveal behavioural and medical parameters of the disorder. This information, together with a detailed case history (taken from the child's parents) should suggest possible causes of the deficit and possible behavioural interventions to improve the situation. Any causative factors can be eliminated, or at least diminished; for example, any hearing loss would be treated by appropriate audiological intervention. At the same time, the language pathologist can identify the behavioural parameters of the disability; for example, determining whether the child is using a large number of substitutions, or whether certain sounds are being used with little consistency (p. 202). Once the behavioural deficits are identified, the clinician is then in a position to initiate treatment.

Treatment can be viewed as a process of hypothesis testing. From the assessment, the language pathologist develops one (or more) hypotheses which might account for the patient's problems. Treatment then tests out these hypotheses. If the working hypothesis is that the child's unintelligible speech is due to a deficit in tactile feedback from

---

[3]The issues in single-case study research are discussed in D. H. Barlow and M. Herson, *Single Case Experimental Designs: Strategies for Studying Behavior Change* (New York, Pergamon, 2nd edn, 1984).

the oral cavity, and a therapy programme has been targeted at this deficit, then if the hypothesis is correct the child's speech should improve. If it does not, the hypothesis may be wrong or the intervention poorly planned or implemented. Alternatively, the reason for the absence of behavioural change may be because of a factor which is not so easily within the clinician's control, such as a lack of motivation in the patient or the carers. Whatever the cause of the failure, it is clear that the clinician must re-evaluate the treatment plan and the hypotheses which underlie it. The reasons for failure must be identified and appropriate alterations made: the initial hypothesis might be rejected or modified, the intervention procedures changed, or the limited motivation of the patient and carers addressed. The process of continual re-evaluation of the working hypothesis and the intervention means that assessment and treatment are closely linked. The patient's behaviour is regularly re-assessed, and performance after treatment is compared to behaviour prior to treatment. Pre-treatment performance is usually described as 'baseline' behaviour, and the evaluation of the effectiveness of intervention involves a series of baseline to post-treatment comparisons.[4] This process is not simply one of trial-and-error; the patient and the clinician's employers do not have an endless supply of time and patience until the clinician happens upon the correct hypothesis and the appropriate intervention! But as more is known about the characteristics of language disorders, their causes, and the types of intervention that prove effective, clinicians will be able to act quickly and efficiently to tackle disabilities.

Management of Communicative Pathology

The assessment and treatment of disorders of communication are the core responsibilities of the language clinician and in the following sections we will consider some of the issues involved in these activities. Before we do this, we will address some general factors which are fundamental to the holistic management of communicative problems and which are relevant to both assessment and intervention. The first of these is that language involves interaction, and there is a minimum of two participants in a communicative exchange. Linguistic procedures such as conversational analysis (p. 49) have illustrated that the

---

[4]The situation is complicated by the possibility of *placebo* effects in treatment. These are positive effects of treatment which do not stem directly from the intervention procedures themselves – for example, the psychological benefits of coming to a clinic for treatment and having a sympathetic clinician taking time and effort to tackle problems. In order to make a valid claim that behaviour has changed as a result of treatment, other behaviours which are not treated are measured. A claim that an intervention programme has proved effective would be valid only when non-targeted behaviours are not significantly changed, whereas targeted behaviours show significant gains.

interaction of participants is patterned and that linguistic behaviour of one participant determines what is likely to occur in the turns of another participant. If one participant asks a question, it is likely that a second participant will provide an answer or some other linked response to the question. Language pathology traditionally has focused both in assessment and treatment on the patient, which is part of the inheritance from a medical approach to disease. But given that the communicative behaviours of other participants have a significant effect on the patient's behaviour, more contemporary behaviourally motivated approaches to management advocate assessment of the behaviours of both patients and their usual interlocutors.

The type of questions that an assessment of interlocutor behaviour might address would be: does the communicative partner produce utterances which the linguistically-impaired listener will be able to process and understand? Do non-impaired participants give the patient sufficient time to formulate and produce a response? If the patient gets into difficulties, does the non-impaired participant produce helpful behaviours which allow the interaction to be continued or does the conversation break down irretrievably? The issue here is not only of assessment and description of the communicative environment of the patient, but also potentially one of treatment. The language clinician might choose to intervene to modify the behaviour of carers: for example, if carers are quite unconsciously using interactional behaviours which are facilitatory to the communication of the patient, these behaviours might be highlighted by the therapist, and their use encouraged yet further. Alternatively, if an analysis of the interaction between the patient and the usual interlocutors reveals the presence of behaviours which are not assisting communicative exchange – for example, the use of irony and complex metaphors is unlikely to assist the comprehension of a patient with Alzheimer's disease – such behaviours can be identified and reduced. This type of intervention is particularly important in disorders which are chronic (or long-lasting) and which represent serious disruptions of cognition or language; the ability to learn new information or new ways of behaving is likely to be slow for an individual with serious brain damage or an intellectual impairment. In this situation, intervention which is directed at carers who suffer from no such limitations in their ability to modify and change their behaviour may be a more viable management strategy than treatment directed solely at the communicatively-impaired individual.

The issue of management of chronic disorders of communication leads to the second general issue which spans concerns in both assessment and treatment. In this book we have been using the terms *impairment*, *disability* and *handicap* interchangeably, but they have come to have specific and different meanings in discussion of the management of chronic conditions. The distinctions between the three terms were originally made by the World Health Organisation (WHO) in 1980, but they took a considerable time to permeate the vocabulary of language pathology.[5] These terms attempt to isolate different components of a disorder and suggest that the total or holistic management of a condition should address all three issues. An *impairment* is the underlying anatomical, physiological or neurological deficit. This can be defined in medical terms, such as a lesion to the temporal regions of the left hemisphere, or in behavioural terms, as in a psycholinguistic deficit such as a failure of the lexical retrieval system. The *disability* is the consequence of the underlying impairment for surface behaviours and, continuing with the example of lexical retrieval failure, this might result in conversational breakdown as the speaker is unable to convey his or her intended meaning. *Handicap* addresses the consequences of the impairment and disability for the activities and roles an individual can undertake in society. For example, a communication disorder might limit an individual's ability to form social relationships and to take up certain forms of employment, such as teaching, or a job involving extensive use of the telephone. The restriction in activities might be due to the intrinsic limitations of an individual's abilities caused by the impairment, but it might be caused by the attitudes that societies have towards individuals who have disabilities.

The content of this book has been directed largely at the impairment and disability components of communicative problems. First let us show that the distinction between the two terms is a clinically useful one, in that we can identify situations where level of disability is not entirely predictable from the impairment. An example of this nature can be seen in the transcript of the fluent aphasic given in Chapter 5 (p. 169). This individual has very marked lexical retrieval difficulties, and we might hypothesize that his underlying impairment represents a failure of the mental mechanisms involved in accessing and retrieving items of vocabulary. A word-finding test might reveal a fairly pronounced degree of impairment, but when we examine this albeit short transcript, we perhaps form the impression that the patient, with the assistance of a helpful interlocutor, is really rather successful in communicating his intended meaning. In this example, the level of linguistic impairment does not translate in a direct way to the degree of communicative disability. The interlocutor's willingness to collaborate in locating the intended meaning is one reason for this, but there are also the behaviours that the patient has developed, such as circumlocutions, gestures and the cueing of the listener, which contribute to the success of the interaction. Given that the aim of clinicians is to improve their patients'

---

[5]*International Classification of Impairments, Disabilities, and Handicaps* (World Health Organisation, Geneva, 1980). Changes to the terms are currently being considered, as they are now regarded as stigmatizing by many in the disability lobby.

competence in everyday communicative situations – the playground, the classroom, work, conversation with family and friends, and so on – it is clearly important to extend the scope of assessment and treatment to address issues both of disability and impairment.

Assessment

Assessment is of central importance in any endeavour in language pathology. In research, it is the key to identifying the behavioural characteristics of disorders, whereas in clinical intervention treatment can begin only after assessment has revealed the behavioural strengths and weaknesses of the patient (and interlocutors). The purpose of assessment is, first, to allow the language pathologist to answer a series of questions which are posed by the referral of a patient. These questions are: does the patient have a communication problem? What is the exact nature of the problem (the *diagnosis*)? and how should the difficulties be managed? A second, related, purpose is to quantify behaviour. This permits comparisons of behaviour to be made: the patient's behaviour can be compared to establish normative behaviour (see p. 153), or, alternatively, across two points in time (e.g. prior to treatment and post-treatment), or across two communicative contexts (e.g. degree of non-fluency when talking in a high-stress versus a low-stress situation).

In answering the first of the questions posed by the referral of a patient (does he or she have a communication disorder?), the clinician will first collect preliminary case-history information. The content of the case-history will vary depending upon the type of condition which is being considered. In a developmental disorder, the clinician will focus on aspects such as early medical history and progress towards a range of developmental milestones – for example, the age at which a child took his or her first steps. The aim here is to establish whether there might be any pre-natal or post-natal factors which might affect development (e.g. evidence of birth trauma) and to establish an overall perspective on the child's development (e.g. is the case displaying a delay in development affecting language alone, or a broad pattern of delay of which a language deficit is just one component?). If the disorder under consideration is one of voice, the content of the case-history will obviously be different. The clinician will again be interested in any medical factors that might affect the functioning of the speech organs (e.g. information from the laryngologist regarding laryngeal structure and function), but will also seek information on the patient's patterns of voice use. The clinician here will be looking for any evidence of misuse of the voice, such as excessive shouting, or evidence of abnormal tension in laryngeal muscles. In addition to collecting broad background information from the patient and perhaps from other professionals involved (such as doctors and teachers), it is important to establish the patient's perspective on the disorder. Clearly, if the patient and the family feel that they have little or no handicap, their willingness to attend the speech and language clinic, and to comply with any treatment, will be limited.

Once preliminary case-history information has been collected, the language pathologist will then move to an initial or screening assessment of the patient's behaviour. This should provide an answer to the question 'is there a disability here and is it deserving of further assessment?' If this question is answered in the affirmative, the clinician will move on to a detailed assessment of the patient's behaviour. The initial assessments are usually informal and unpublished procedures often devised by clinicians themselves. These have the advantage of being quick, but the disadvantage of not being familiar to other clinicians, so that the findings of an informal assessment procedure cannot be easily communicated to others. This is one of the major reasons for switching to published assessment procedures in the next stage of the analysis of the disorder.

The use of *screening* in this context deserves some discussion. When we hear of 'screening' programmes, we generally think of assessments which are applied to a very wide population in order to identify medical or behavioural abnormalities. Most developed countries run infant-screening programmes – blood samples are taken from neonates to check for diseases such as phenylketonuria (see p. 160). As part of child-health programmes, professionals keep a check on the general development of the child so that any difficulties can be identified early and intervention can begin before difficulties become compounded. Similarly, groups within the adult population who are identified as being 'at risk' of certain disorders – for example, middle-aged woman identified as being at risk of breast cancer – can receive regular screening checks. When we talk of screening assessments in language pathology we are discussing screening on a more modest scale. Rather than scrutinizing a total population for possible communication disorders, a very small sample – often preselected by other professionals (such as doctors or teachers) – is subjected to the screening process.

Once a screening assessment has indicated that the patient is displaying some degree of communicative disorder, the process of full assessment begins. The first step in this is informal observation of the patient in a relatively natural communicative context – for the child this might be play, and for the adult it is usually conversation. In this context the clinician can form a rapid impression of the extent of the patient's disability, which is an important perspective to establish before various psycholinguistic impairments are examined. In selecting subsequent tools for use in assessment, language clinicians have a number of options open to them. One option is a *checklist*. This type of assessment lists a series of behaviours, and the clinician records the presence or absence of any of the pr-selected behaviours. A checklist of grammatical development might list behaviours such as the presence of

Subject–Verb–Object or Subject–Verb–Object–Adverbial structures in the patient's speech. Clinicians base their judgements of whether certain structures are present either by directly observing the child's speech or by asking parents to report on the type of structures their child uses. The former approach is more likely to be an accurate record of the child's speech in one particular sampling situation – for example, playing with toys in the language clinic. The use of parent-reports is likely to result in less accurate data; parents may not be so clear as to what the behaviours are, and their recall of the child's competencies may not always be correct, particularly if there are a number of young children present in the home. However, although parent-report data may be less accurate, they do have the advantage of being more comprehensive. Parents have the opportunity to record their child's behaviour across a variety of communicative contexts and thus have access to a much broader database than does the clinician. This factor is of importance when assessing skills for which performance across a variety of contexts is essential. Hence checklists are particularly suited for the assessment of vocabulary production or of pragmatic ability. Checklist assessments are quick measures, and also have the advantage that, if carer-reports are used, the clinician can gain insights into the patient's behaviour in contexts outside that of the clinic. The speed at which an assessment can be completed, however, often has costs. The quicker a procedure is, the more likely it is to prove a rather superficial analysis of complex communicative behaviours. The major difficulty with checklist assessments is that they preselect behaviours for analysis. Although they may prove efficient in identifying the presence or absence of those behaviours, what happens if the patient is demonstrating other behaviours which are also potentially significant in understanding the nature of a disorder and planning its remediation? Speed of assessment is therefore bought at the expense of comprehensiveness.

A second option in assessment is the use of a speech or language *test*. This is a popular and widely used technique of assessment. Tests can be directed at various components of linguistic performance – some at very broad aspects of behaviour (e.g. 'receptive language' or 'expressive language'); others at more specific components of language competence (e.g. the understanding of grammatical structures). In addition to tests directed at language, clinicians are also likely to use tests of other cognitive skills linked to language, such as symbolic ability, attention or memory skills. Tests are particularly useful when a therapist wishes to evaluate a specific hypothesis such as 'the patient has difficulty in finding words which occur infrequently in a language versus those which are frequent'; or 'the child has difficulty producing a particular sound when it occurs at the end of a word, but not in a word-initial position'. Often tests are described as 'standardized' assessment procedures. These are tests in which there is strict control of the materials and the administrative procedure. Because these tests often include normative data (i.e. information on the scores that non-disordered subjects achieve on the test) and also the typical pattern of scores obtained by groups of disordered subjects, it is essential that the patient who is being compared to the norms is administered the test in an identical manner to the subjects from whom the normative data are drawn.

Standardized tests are a widely used method of assessing language behaviour. Their popularity is due to the fact that they are relatively quick procedures – particularly when compared to an alternative such as producing a detailed linguistic profile of behaviour (see p. 240). The administration and scoring of tests is also relatively straightforward, and this simplicity is also an advantage to the busy clinician. Often the scorer has to decide only whether the patient selected the correct picture, or manipulated objects in a way consistent with a command. Alternatively, in language production tests, the decision may be based simply on whether the description of an object or picture is acceptable, and often the test provides a criterion by which correct responses can be identified. A further reason for the popularity of tests is that, very often, they provide normative data. The patient's test performance can be compared against that expected of a normal 4-year-old, or a normal adult, and where there are significant discrepancies between the patient's behaviour and normative patterns there is strong evidence for some form of unusual language behaviour. Such data help the clinician to answer the question 'does the patient have a communication problem?' The standardized test may also assist the process of exact diagnosis of particular linguistic pathologies if it gives details of the typical profiles of different groups of language-disordered patients. Thus, if a profile of a typical agrammatic aphasic patient is given, or a child with a typical semantic-pragmatic language difficulty, the test performance of a particular patient can be compared to these typical patterns, and areas of similarity or difference can be highlighted. A further advantage of the language test is a consequence of its popularity among clinicians. Procedures which are popular are also likely to be familiar to a large number of professionals. Additionally, the standardized test, with its carefully controlled materials and procedures, should produce the same score whether the test is administered by clinician A or by clinician B. As a consequence, standardized tests are valuable in assisting communication between different professionals. If a patient moves from one clinic to another – perhaps from a general clinic to a specialist one, or from one part of the country to another – a second clinician can review the patient's test results, derive an impression of areas of strength and deficit, and so will not need to begin the assessment process from the very beginning.[6]

---

[6]See J. R. Beech, L. Harding and D. Hilton-Jones (eds), *Assessment in Speech and Language Therapy* (London, Routledge, 1993) for an overview of issues in assessment, and reviews of many standardized tests of speech and language.

Language tests have very clear advantages, but there are also significant problems which need consideration so that a balanced evaluation of their role can be obtained. Tests suffer from the same disadvantage as checklist assessments in that they are selective in what they measure. Only a small set of predetermined linguistic structures is probed, and these may not address the significant components of a patient's difficulty. Major difficulties also concern the question of the *ecological* validity of the test performance (p. 33), or whether the results of a test can be used to predict communicative performance in less artificial situations. Tests do not always yield valid measures of behaviour, perhaps because the person being tested is bored, or made anxious, or is simply confused by the artificiality of the situation. (One test of aphasia includes comprehension questions such as 'Are you a man?' (to women) and 'Are you a woman?' (to men).) Most tests are designed to examine isolated components of language (e.g. comprehension of different grammatical structures, retrieval of vocabulary), and to give detailed accounts of impairments within component systems. It is left to the clinician to put the component systems together and to combine descriptions of various impairments with an acknowledgement of the various compensatory mechanisms that the patient may be using to great effect. A word retrieval test may suggest that a patient has very great difficulty in locating and producing the target words, but requires the clinician to note that all non-retrieved target items were successfully communicated via gesture, circumlocutions or drawings.

In the face of these difficulties with tests, a further option in assessment is to base an analysis on a sample of behaviour obtained in a naturalistic context – for the child, this would be play, and for the adult, conversation. The patient's communicative behaviours are then analysed, with the clinician usually targeting particular aspects of behaviour for detailed analysis – for example, grammatical ability. The results of these analyses are often displayed on a profile chart, so this method of assessment has come to be known as *profiling*.[7] Profiles are often based around levels of linguistic organization – grammar, semantics and phonology – but can also be targeted at other facets of communication, such as patterns of eye contact. As the sample upon which the profile is based is usually collected in a natural communicative context, it is more likely to be typical of the patient's performance outside the clinical context. As such it is more likely to give the clinician a clearer sense of the communication difficulties experienced by the patients and their families. Because tests generally use controlled materials (such as a set

---

[7]See D. Crystal, *Profiling Linguistic Disability* (London, Whurr, 2nd edn, 1992) for further discussion and D. Crystal, P. Fletcher and M. Garman, *The Grammatical Analysis of Language Disability* (London, Whurr, 2nd edn, 1990) for an example of a grammatical profile.

of pictures or objects), the patient is communicating already known information to the clinician. In deciding on a patient's intelligibility, if the clinician or any other listener knows what the intended target of an utterance is, it is possible to over-estimate the ability to produce it accurately. Using natural conversation as the basis for a communicative assessment places the clinician in the same – often frustrating – position as the carers of the communicatively disordered individual, and allows a real estimation of the patient's communicative difficulties.

The behavioural profile therefore has advantages over speech and language tests in that it avoids the sometimes bizarre and unnatural interactions of the test context. It has other advantages too. Whereas both tests and behavioural checklists measure only a predetermined set of behaviours – for example, a particular set of grammatical structures or vocabulary – the data yielded by a profile are more comprehensive. Because the situation is not constrained by the test materials, or by the checklist items, patients may display a much wider range of their behavioural repertoire. The difficulties of patients who show interactions between various components of their linguistic performance are also more likely to be revealed by analysing a full behavioural sample. One school-aged child was referred to the speech clinic because his teachers reported that his speech was unintelligible. The speech pathologist administered a test of phonetic and phonological abilities, which consisted of asking the child to label pictures (the targets being known to the clinician and requiring single-word responses from the child). The analysis of the results revealed few difficulties, and this information was relayed back to the class teacher. The teacher was perplexed by this result, and asked for a reassessment. The equally perplexed therapist complied with the request, but this time recorded a sample of the child's speech while he played with toys in the clinic. The interaction and the subsequent analysis revealed that the child was indeed very difficult to understand – but only in connected or conversational speech. His difficulties were described as those of cluttering (see p. 194), where the rhythmic structure of speech was disturbed. In the course of an utterance, his rate of speech gradually speeded up, to the point where the time-frame for each articulatory movement was so short that movements were not fully executed. As a consequence, each articulatory movement influenced its neighbours in abnormal ways, resulting in a large number of assimilations between sounds. Only by basing the assessment on a full behavioural sample was this deficit revealed, and, in particular, the problematic interaction between articulatory accuracy and the utterance length. The example also illustrates the need for clinicians to place themselves in the same situation as the patient's usual interlocutors (i.e. communicating unknown information), because only then are they really able to appreciate the difficulties likely to be experienced in communication.

The profile based on natural conversation therefore has significant advantages over testing as a method of assessment. But, as always, in addition to benefits, there are costs associated with profiling. The two most significant costs are time and clinical skill. At a number of points already in this book we have indicated the need for detailed assessment procedures in order to extend the theoretical basis of language pathology. The reason such analyses are not performed routinely in speech and language clinics is that they are extremely time-consuming. Basing an assessment on a sample of natural communication requires that the patient – clinician interaction is recorded. In terms of time this is a relatively insignificant procedure; the time expenditure comes when the audio- or video-recording of the interaction is transcribed (p. 35). A 30-minute interaction might take several hours to transcribe in any detail. Then the transcription must be further analysed, for example a grammatical analysis completed, and the results of this analysis evaluated for significant features. Clearly, the behavioural profile can be a time-consuming procedure, which perhaps only automatic (computational) procedures can significantly alleviate.

The second cost is the degree of clinical skills required to elicit and analyse data. The collection of samples of interactions from patients with communication disorders is not a simple or obvious procedure. Many young children are reluctant to talk to strangers. Adults with communication difficulties may be unwilling to talk and reveal those difficulties. Interactions can consist of clinicians asking lengthy questions and patients responding with monosyllabic *yes* or *no* answers. An analysis of a data sample consisting of 300 instances of *yes* or *no* is clearly going to reveal little of the patient's expressive linguistic difficulties! The clinician needs considerable skill in eliciting communicative behaviours from individuals who, for one reason or another, are unwilling to talk.

We have reviewed a number of alternative assessment procedures. All of them have a place in the language pathology clinic as, to a great extent, the advantages of one method offset the disadvantages of others. Thus checklists allow access to behaviours which occur outside the clinic, whereas tests do not. Tests are completed by the clinician, and avoid inaccuracies that may stem from reliance on a carer-report of behaviours. Tests are quick, but at times fail to produce results which generalize to natural communicative situations; profiles are time-consuming, but yield detailed and comprehensive behavioural data. It is important for the clinician to perform a cost-benefits analysis on each type of assessment procedure, and then to decide what is most appropriate for each client. At the end of the process of detailed assessment, the clinician should have answered the questions 'What is the nature of the disorder?' and 'How can the disorder be treated?' A good assessment procedure should, at its conclusion, give the clinician strong indications of which routes might be productive to follow in treatment.

Treatment

In the treatment of language pathology, the clinician works with the patients and their carers to maximize the effectiveness of communication. The techniques used in treatment are immensely varied as clinicians may focus on different components of a condition: addressing issues linked to social handicap may result in the use of counselling and psychotherapeutic techniques, which aim to help patients to understand the nature of their disorder, and to deal with the anxiety, frustration and depression that communication difficulties might engender; at the other extreme, the use of computers can help to remediate impairments in speech production. As a consequence of this breadth we can do no more than give an overview of broad approaches which can be used in intervention, and focus only on treatment approaches targeted at speech, language and communicative functioning rather than those dealing with the psychological and social elements of a handicap.[8] But even within this narrowed area, there is a huge diversity of approach. There are very few formalized treatment programmes for linguistic disorders. Treatment programmes are tailored to fit the individual client, and are created from the careful evaluation of assessment results. Moreover, the treatment process is informed by both medical and behavioural approaches, and both need to be taken carefully into account.

A scientific approach, whether motivated by medical or behavioural sciences, suggests that a key component in intervention is to remove the causes of a pathology (p. 24). Thus, if a child's slow acquisition of language is viewed as a consequence of living in an environment where there is little or inappropriate stimulation, the language pathologist will act to modify this environment. If a patient's voice difficulties are thought to be a consequence of vocal misuse, intervention will attempt to reduce or eliminate harmful behaviour. Elimination of the causes responsible for the genesis of a disorder is likely to have a profound effect on certain disorders – potentially eliminating the pathology without any further therapeutic intervention. An additional example is the reduction of parental anxiety when a child is normally non-fluent during the course of language acquisition; this would prevent the behaviour being perceived as 'stuttering' and the child developing anxieties about speech (see the 'diagnosogenic' theory of stuttering, p. 193).

Other disorders, however, have no clear causes. A child may fail to learn language at a normal rate despite being raised in a perfectly adequate environment, and in the absence of physical or intellectual deficits. Other disorders – for example, aphasia as a result of a stroke, or the intellectual and communicative deficits of Down's syndrome – may

---

[8]See W. Rollin, *The Psychology of Communication Disorders in Individuals and Their Families* (Englewood Cliffs, Prentice-Hall, 1987); and P. Dalton, *Counselling People with Communication Problems* (London, Sage, 1994).

have a clear cause, but this cause cannot be directly remedied. In these instances, behavioural approaches come into prominence, suggesting that the clinician should identify the patient's current stage of communicative ability, define where there are significant discrepancies between this and normal performance, and then seek to move the patient's behaviour as near to the norm as possible in a series of steps. As well as providing the motivating principle behind treatment, branches of the behavioural sciences provide valuable components of the treatment process. The methods of linguistic science enable the clinician to produce a detailed evaluation of language behaviour at the various levels of language structure.

Linguistics and developmental psychology together suggest the first structures that should be introduced to the patient as part of a treatment programme. Clinicians will usually follow the sequence in which behaviours normally develop. In the area of phonological intervention, for example, early acquired sound contrasts, such as contrasts between oral and nasal sounds, will be introduced before those later acquired, such as contrasts between stop and fricative sounds. Procedures of this kind are standard practice when working with children; interestingly, they are also often employed when working with adults. But can the use of developmental hierarchies be justified with acquired disorders such as aphasia and apraxia, or are there other ways in which linguistic structures can be graded for complexity which might prove more appropriate to adult language? Both the method of recognizing the relative difficulty of structures and the actual content of any hierarchy are subject to much debate – and very little consensus – within psycholinguistics. In the absence of other agreed ways of defining linguistic difficulty, accordingly, the use of developmental hierarchies in planning a sequence of stages in treatment is widely practised. Linguistically, aphasics have to stand before they can walk, and walk before they can run, and a developmental model suggests one practicable direction in which they can move.

Intervention in language pathology may target any of three components of a communicative interaction. Communication involves a minimum of two participants and the exchange of messages in a context in which the interaction takes place. In a situation where communication has failed, it may be possible to facilitate a more successful interaction through intervention directed at any one of these variables. Treatment may be focused at the patient's ability to send and/or receive messages efficiently – a *patient-centred* model of intervention. Here, intervention may endeavour to increase the patient's linguistic knowledge, or to use this knowledge effectively. A second option is to direct therapy at the patient's usual interlocutors – a *carer-centred* model – encouraging them to behave in ways which facilitate the patient's understanding, or their understanding of the patient. Third, the environment in which communication takes place can be modified in ways which enhance communication – a *context-centred* model of intervention.

The first of these models is the most familiar; it is, after all, the system of treatment that we receive when we go for a medical consultation. Patients report the symptoms they are experiencing; the medical practitioner examines the patient for signs of illness, and treatment is directed at the amelioration or control of the condition. In the language pathology context, a patient-centred model of intervention entails working with patients to maximize their communicative abilities. Usually this occurs in a one-to-one situation, with patients receiving individual consultation, assessment and treatment sessions, although group therapy is also possible. Within these situations, the content of the therapy may be very different. It may be directed at reducing the degree of impairment (in the WHO sense of this term, p. 234) of linguistic or related cognitive skills – for example, developing their phonological knowledge, improving their grammatical ability, or facilitating their memory or ability to pay selective attention. Alternatively, treatment may try to minimize the level of communicative disability by enabling the patient to develop compensatory behaviours which circumvent the underlying impairments. For example, a patient with a disorder of comprehension might ask speakers to repeat a misunderstood message, or to slow down their speech rate, or to chunk the message into more easily understood components. Included within disability-type approaches are the many systems of augmentative communication or communication aids. For a very large number of children and adults, the normal use of spoken language is out of the question, because of the gross nature of their physical or intellectual disability. Signing and other forms of supplementary communication have long been in use (p. 215), as have simple mechanical devices used for pointing at letters, words, or symbols on a chart. But this is only the tip of a vast iceberg of innovation involving new technology, which affects the lives of many speech-handicapped people, such as those suffering from cerebral palsy, other types of dysarthria, and learning disabilities. The growth in computer technology has led to the production of portable and increasingly affordable systems, such as speech synthesizers for use in supplementing the communicative ability of patients.[9] The final component of treatment

---

[9]Several introductions to this field are now available: J. F. Curtis, *An Introduction to Microcomputers in Speech, Language and Hearing* (Boston, College-Hill Press, 1987); S. von Tetzchner and M. H. Jensen (eds), *Augmentative and Alternative Communication: European Perspectives* (London, Whurr, 1996). On the nature of alternative and augmentative communication, see R. L. Schiefelbusch (ed.), *Nonspeech, Language and Communication: Analysis and Intervention* (Baltimore, University Park Press, 1980); C. Kiernan, B. Reid, and L. Jones, *Signs and Symbols: Use of Non-vocal Communication Systems* (London, Heinemann, 1982).

might address issues linked to a handicap (again, in the narrow sense of the WHO definition). Instead of treatment focused directly on language, management might be of the counselling or psychotherapeutic type, to help patients cope with the anxiety and frustration of their communicative disability, and also with the attitudes of able-bodied society towards them.

Within patient-centred approaches, therefore, there are a number of fundamentally different modes of treatment, but the type of intervention which is most common in the language pathology clinic is that aimed at improving the patient's impaired linguistic or language-related cognitive skills. Let us take an example of how this type of therapy might work. The first stage in any treatment process is to evaluate assessment results and identify therapeutic targets and possible routes which it would be fruitful to follow. To illustrate this process, let us take the example of a 3-year-old boy whose assessment of spoken language indicates that he appears to have difficulties in grammatical development. His utterances usually consist of single-element structures, when we would expect to hear two- and three-element structures at least at this age. More detailed analysis of grammar and vocabulary indicates that his utterances consist predominantly of nouns (e.g. *dog, socks, cup*), adjectives (e.g. *dirty, broken*) and a small number of adverbs and prepositions (e.g. *up, now*), but very few verbs. The clinician adopts two strategies: the first is to encourage the child to link together two items from his existing vocabulary (e.g. *dirty socks, cup broken*); the second is to develop his verb vocabulary, with a hypothesis that once he has access to a larger number of verbs, it will be possible to develop a wider range of sentence structures (e.g. Subject–Verb, Verb–Object, Verb–Adverbial). In pursuit of the first goal, the clinician reviews the vocabulary already available to the patient, and sets up contexts in which the existing vocabulary can be used in two-element combinations, for example playing at dressing dolls with dirty and clean sets of clothes. This gives the child's interlocutor the opportunity to present him with examples of two-element combinations (e.g. *dirty vest, clean dress*), such examples being referred to as *models*, and the interlocutor's behaviour as *modelling* utterances to the child. The importance of this procedure cannot be over-estimated in intervention with developmental disorders. It is based on the notion that children are active in learning language; for them, language is a puzzle which they are endeavouring to solve. In order to solve the puzzle, children need language input or data from which they can attempt to recognize units and structures. Initial guesses about the way language works are compared with new material (i.e. the child verifies hypotheses against further data) and are tested through their use in the child's own language repertoire. Providing children with clear and unambiguous models ensures that the data they use in cracking the language code will be of good quality and will facilitate correct hypothesis formation. In the present case, after initial modelling, the patient is gradually encouraged and given the opportunity to produce the two-element utterances himself; for example, a situation might be engineered in which he sorts articles of clothing into two piles for the laundry, and reports on his activities to an adult. The patient's attempts at the two-element utterances are encouraged, and supported by further models from the clinician or parent.

The second therapeutic goal – that of developing the patient's verb vocabulary – could be tackled in a variety of ways. One method might be to use picture-books or cards depicting various actions. The therapist would label them or model the relevant verb to the patient, and then ask him to repeat the verbs back, encouraging and reinforcing successful attempts. A second strategy might be to play games involving a large number of actions, for example playing with pots and pans, using such actions as cook, stir, pour, wash and dry. The situation provides the opportunity for the patient to hear a large number of verb examples, with the meaning of each verb being demonstrated by the clinician, and the child performing the corresponding action with the pots and pans. Ultimately roles are switched and, instead of the clinician providing a commentary to the play, the child is encouraged to direct and recount activities. These two therapeutic strategies are rather different: the first is more familiar as a formal teaching situation; the second is embedded within play. For this reason, the second strategy might be the preferred one to adopt, particularly if the patient is a young child or an individual with learning disabilities. Because the second talk is placed within a context which is familiar in the world outside the clinic, behaviours which are taught in this setting are more likely to generalize to other situations.

The patient-centred model of treatment represents the popular conception of how language pathologists work with patients – that is, working in a one-to-one situation, developing new linguistic and communicative behaviours. But it is an expensive mode of service delivery. One-to-one teaching means that the clinician is unable to see very many patients in a working day, and that patients are treated for only a short time. This is a serious difficulty. Communicative behaviour is immensely complex, and disorders of communication require detailed and thus time-consuming assessment in order to identify deficits and plan a remedial course. Some patients have severe linguistic and intellectual deficits which entail that learning will not take place easily or quickly. Such individuals need intervention programmes which develop and stimulate new behaviours on a round-the-clock basis, rather than for an isolated hour or so once in the week. In such situations, other models of service delivery, such as carer- and context-centred treatment, are needed to supplement a patient-centred model. It should be emphasized that the latter two models do not exclude or neglect the patient, even though they are not 'patient-centred'. In all three models, patients and their communicative strengths and weaknesses are at the core, and all three aim to improve communicative functioning. They differ in the immediate target of the intervention, but the ultimate target is always the communicatively-disordered patient.

Carer-centred (or interlocutor-centred) and context-centred treatment are similar in many ways, as both highlight the role of the patient's usual interlocutors. Contexts or environments are inanimate, and can be modified only through the actions of families or other carers. As the intervention is directed at the patient's usual carers and their everyday environment, it is less likely to meet the problems of poor generalization of behaviours taught in a clinical context. Both models are particularly relevant to clinical intervention with patients who have profound linguistic and cognitive disabilities, and also to clinical situations where a therapist is faced with too many patients and too little time. Carer and environmental intervention may also be essential in cases of developmental language disorders where the pathology has been partly attributed to environmental factors. The first therapeutic strategy may well be to modify the environment and the language of the carers so that the patient receives appropriate language input – that is, input which is in tune with the patient's language processing abilities and which is neither too complex nor too simple.

In situations where the patient suffers from a profound linguistic or cognitive disability, for example dementia, learning difficulties or severe aphasia, carer-centred intervention aims to develop new communicative behaviours in the individuals with whom the patient usually interacts, in order to facilitate the exchange of messages between them. These may be behaviours which will facilitate patients' understanding of the carers' language, or patients' ability to convey their needs to the carers. Patients with a language comprehension disorder may begin to understand better if certain parameters of the message are modified. Patients with difficulties in attending to messages may have fewer problems if the message is accompanied by 'alerting signals', which indicate to patients that they must try to attend selectively to the linguistic message which is about to be sent to them. Examples of alerting signals are simple verbal commands such as *'listen'*, or non-verbal signals such as taking patients' hands or encouraging them to look at the speaker whilst they are spoken to. The message itself may be modified in a number of ways; for example, 'topic-fronting' can be used, particularly with patients with short attention or memory spans. Topic-fronting puts salient information right at the beginning of the utterance, so that if the patient manages only to receive and decode the first fragment of the message, that fragment will be highly informative. Thus, *what are you doing this weekend?* might be modified to *this weekend, what are you doing?*

Other elements of utterance form might also be altered; for example, interlocutors might avoid sentence structures which the patient has been shown to have difficulties understanding. Sentences in the passive voice and sentences containing subordinate clauses within the main clause are structures which many linguistically-disordered patients have difficulties in understanding. Various phonological variables can be modified: words which convey important information can be heavily stressed, or the tempo of speech can be altered. Many patients with comprehension disorders understand more when they are given more time to process an utterance; thus, simply by slowing the rate of speech there may be a positive effect on performance. In addition to manipulating linguistic variables, non-verbal information can be altered. Use of touch whilst talking may assist the patient with a severe input disorder to keep attention on the message. Pointing to the referent of part of a message may establish what the communication concerns – for example, holding a cup while asking patients if they would like a drink. All these examples show ways in which the interlocutor can behave in order to give language-disordered patients inputs that they are more likely to process successfully. Interlocutors can also alter their behaviour in order to assist patients' ability to express their needs. Instead of asking what are known as *open questions* (i.e. questions which can be answered by a wide range of responses), the patient can be presented with alternatives (e.g. *do you want tea or coffee?*), or a single choice, to which they can respond *yes* or *no*.

The third model of service delivery – context-centred intervention – involves a careful assessment of the patient's communicative environment, and the identification of factors which facilitate and (in the case of developmental language disorders) encourage language learning or those which are inhibitory. The types of intervention that may occur include the control of potentially distracting noise, the reduction of which permits patients to concentrate on, and listen to, speech. This is a particularly significant factor for the hearing-impaired and those with attention disorders. Also, environments have to be created in which there is something to communicate about. This is true particularly of institutional settings which are dominated by a high degree of routine. In such contexts, the linguistically-disabled patient may be relieved of the need to communicate because wants and desires are routinely met by the staff of the institution. This may seem to be a positive thing, but the needs which are met are identified by the institution and not by the patient. Therapists working in institutional settings sometimes 'sabotage' routines in order to create a context for communication. One clinician working in a school for children with learning disabilities reported the remarkable effect on her patients' communication when a student clinician inadvertently served up cheese-cake upside-down during lunch-time!

Whichever model of intervention is used – and often they are used in combination – there are common features. Intervention is based upon the careful assessment of the nature of a problem, and upon the observation of how carers and context operate to encourage or discourage effective communication. Just as a teaching programme is based upon a detailed assessment of a patient's linguistic and cognitive competencies, so also programmes aimed at modifying carer behaviour and contexts are based upon an analysis of which variables, when modified, will effect communication. Therefore, before suggesting that carers do modify aspects of their behaviour – for example, the type of vocabulary and sentence structures, or the rate of speaking – the clinician needs to ascertain that these modifications are likely to be effective and to have a positive effect on the patient's communication. A second common factor between all types of intervention also links to assessment. Throughout the intervention process, the clinician is re-assessing the patient's linguistic performance, and judging whether significant changes are occurring. Where changes in a positive direction are identified, it can be assumed that the hypothesis which motivated treatment was correct and that an appropriate therapeutic strategy has been identified and followed. Where change does not occur, the clinician is forced to re-assess both the original hypothesis and the therapeutic approach.

We began this book with a discussion of the effects of linguistic disability on all aspects of the life of an individual – personal, social, educational and occupational. In subsequent chapters, we have tried to show that language pathology is a coherent field of intellectual enquiry, and tracked the medical and behavioural science influences upon it. In a review of the range of linguistic disability that may occur, we have stressed the still urgent need for research into many disabilities. In this, our final chapter, we have moved to the more practical concerns of the assessment and treatment of disability, and the need for further research has again emerged. We do not apologize for this concluding emphasis. Only from such research will come greater knowledge of language pathologies and new and better ways of dealing with them, so that ultimately all patients will benefit.

Revision Questions

1. What are patient-centred, carer-centred and context-centred intervention? Give an example of a therapeutic strategy directed at each one.
2. How are the terms 'impairment', 'disability' and 'handicap' different? Apply these terms to a person with a limp, a child with a specific language disorder, and an adult with a stutter. Which components of their difficulties would be 'impairments', 'disabilities' and 'handicaps'?

Tutorial Activities

1. Apply a preventive approach to disability to the frail elderly population. Try to visit, or recall a visit, to a residential home for the elderly. Consider how the day-room or lounge of the residential home was organized. Consider the following:

(a) How was the furniture arranged?

(b) Was there any distracting background noise in the environment?

(c) Could residents make easy eye contact with other residents and how far away were they from other focuses of interest such as a television screen?

Research the effects of ageing on visual and auditory acuity, and cognitive abilities such as attention. Relate your research to your observations of the environment of the residential home. Are there any recommendations you could make to modify the environment in order to prevent communicative and other difficulties developing?

2. Reflect on your own experiences of being tested or assessed. What factors may result in your performance on the test not being typical of your actual level of competence?

Further Reading

Patient Accounts

Bauby, J. D. (1997) *The Diving Bell and the Butterfly* (London, Fourth Estate)

Copeland, J. (1973) *For the Love of Ann* (London, Arrow Books)

Griffiths, V. E. (1970) *A Stroke in the Family* (Harmondsworth, Penguin)

Hampshire, S. (1981) *Susan's Story* (London, Sidgewick & Jackson)

Parr, S., Byng, S. and Gilpin, S. (1997) *Talking About Aphasia* (Milton Keynes, Open University Press)

Schaller, S. (1991) *A Man Without Words* (University of California, Summit)

West, P. (1972) *Words for a Deaf Daughter* (Harmondsworth, Penguin)

Biological and Medical Background

Bowsher, D. (1988) *Introduction to the Anatomy and Physiology of the Nervous System* (Oxford, Blackwell, 5th edn)

Espir, M. L. E. and Rose, F. C. (1983) *The Basic Neurology of Speech and Language* (Oxford, Blackwell, 3rd edn)

Greenfield, S. (1997) *The Human Brain: A Guided Tour* (London, Weidenfeld & Nicolson)

Martini, F. (1995) *Fundamentals of Anatomy and Physiology* (Englewood Cliffs, NJ, Prentice-Hall, 3rd edn)

Springer, S. and Deutsch, G. (1993) *Left Brain, Right Brain* (New York, W. H. Freeman, 4th edn)

Psychology Background

Aitchison, J. (1992) *The Articulate Mammal: An Introduction to Psycholinguistics* (London, Routledge, 3rd edn)

Aitchison, J. (1994) *Words in the Mind: An Introduction to the Mental Lexicon* (Oxford, Blackwell, 2nd edn)

Berk, L. (1997) *Child Development* (London, Allyn & Bacon, 4th edn)

Ellis, A. and Young, A. (1996) *Human Cognitive Neuropsychology* (Hove, Psychology Press)

Eysenck, M. W. and Keane, M. T. (1995) *Cognitive Psychology* (Hove, Erlbaum, 3rd edn)

Gleitman, H. (1995) *Psychology* (New York, W. W. Norton, 4th edn)

Harley, T. A. (1995) *The Psychology of Language: From Data to Theory* (Hove, Erlbaum)

Kolb, B. and Whishaw, I. (1996) *Fundamentals of Human Neuropsychology* (New York, Freeman)

Pinker, S. (1997) *How the Mind Works* (Harmondsworth, Allen Lane)

Taylor, I. and Taylor, M. M. (1990) *Psycholinguistics: Learning and Using Language* (Englewood Cliffs, NJ, Prentice-Hall)

Language and Linguistics Background

Clarke, J. and Yallop, C. (1995) *An Introduction to Phonetics and Phonology* (Oxford, Blackwell, 2nd edn)

Crystal, D. (1996) *Rediscover Grammar* (London, Longman, 2nd edn)

Crystal, D. (1997) *The Cambridge Encyclopaedia of Language* (Cambridge, Cambridge University Press, 2nd edn)

Denes, P. B. and Pinson, E. N. (1993) *The Speech Chain: The Physics and Biology of Spoken Language* (New York, W. H. Freeman, 2nd edn)

Dunbar, R. (1996) *Grooming, Gossip and the Evolution of Language* (London, Faber & Faber)

Flecher, P. and MacWhinney, B. (eds) (1995) *The Handbook of Child Language* (Oxford, Blackwell)

Greenbaum, S. and Quirk, R. (1990) *A Student's Grammar of the English Language* (London, Longman)

Hardcastle, W. and Laver, J. (eds) (1997) *The Handbook of Phonetic Theory* (London, Blackwell)

Holmes, J. (1992) *An Introduction to Sociolinguistics* (London, Longman)

Pinker, S. (1994) *The Language Instinct* (New York, Morrow)

Yule, G. (1996) *Pragmatics* (Oxford, Oxford University Press)

Language Pathology

Beech, J. R., Harding, L. and Hilton-Jones, D. (eds) (1993) *Assessment in Speech and Language Therapy* (London, Routledge)

Bishop, D. and Mogford, K. (eds) (1993) *Language Development in Exceptional Circumstances* (Hove, Psychology Press)

Caplan, D. (1992) *Language: Structure, Processing and Disorders* (Cambridge, Mass., MIT Press)

Grunwell, P. (ed.) (1990) *Developmental Speech Disorders* (Edinburgh, Churchill Livingstone)

Fletcher, P. and Hall D, (eds) (1992) *Specific Speech and Language Disorders in Children* (London, Whurr)

Howard, D. and Hatfield, F. M. (1987) *Aphasia Therapy: Historical and Contemporary Issues* (Hove, Erlbaum)

Hulme, C. and Snowling, M. (eds) (1997) *Dyslexia: Biology, Cognition and Intervention* (London, Whurr)

Lesser, R. and Milroy, L. (1993) *Linguistics and Aphasia* (London, Longman)

Yule, W. and Rutter, M. (eds) (1987) *Language Development and Disorders* (London, MacKeith Press)

Author Index

Subject Index